THEOLOGY AS
HISTORY AND HERMENEUTICS

A Post-Critical Conversation with Contemporary Theology

Laurence W. Wood

EMETH PRESS
www.emethpress.com

Theology As History and Hermeneutics
A Post-Critical Conversation with Contemporary Theology

Library of Congress Cataloging-in-Publication Data

Theology as history and hermeneutics : a post-critical conversation with contemporary theology / Laurence W. Wood.
    p. cm. --
Includes bibliographical references (p.   ) index.
ISBN 0-9755435-5-5 (alk. paper)
1. Postmodern theology, 2. Hermeneutics --Religious aspects --Christianity
BT83.597 .W66 2005
230/.046 22

                            2004093652

Contents

Preface vii

1. The Modern Concept of Self-Revelation 1
   The Rise of Modern Thought 1
   The Modern Idea of Revelation as Self-Revelation 5
   Jesus Christ as the Only Revelation 6
   The Different Meanings of the Word of God 7
   The Bible as a Witness to Revelation 9
   A Critique of Barth's Concept of Self-Revelation 13
   Self-Revelation as Indirect rather than Direct 14
   Story or History? 19
   Summary.. 21

2. The Modern Historical-Critical Method and Biblical Inspiration...27
   Fundamentalism and Biblical Literalism 27
   American Evangelicalism and Biblical Inspiration 29
   Pannenberg and Post-Critical Evangelicalism 30
   Historical Events and the Word of God 32
   Form Criticism and the Doctrine of Biblical Inspiration 36
   N. T. Wright and the Historical Critical Method 45
   The Internal Witness of the Holy Spirit...................... 54

3. A Post-Critical Hermeneutic of the Self—
   A Relational Ontology 61
   John Macmurray: "The Failure of Modern Philosophy" 61
   Paul Ricoeur: A Narrative-Based Ontology 64
   Toward a Relational Ontology 69
   Jean-Paul Sartre: Human Nature or Human Condition?...... 72

4. A Post-Critical Concept of Truth 77
The Rise of Postmodern Science 77
Richard Rorty: A Critique of Modernism 78
Polanyi: A Post-Critical Philosophy 81
Jean-Francois Lyotard: A Critique of Metanarrative 85

5. Pannenberg's Theology of Universal History 91
Reality as History 93
Theology and the Historical Method 96
Pannenberg's Theology of the Resurrection 98
The Historical-Critical Method and Jesus' Resurrection 99

6. Critical and Post-Critical Hermeneutics 105
Pre-Critical Hermeneutics 105
Schleiermacher—The Psychologizing of Hermeneutics
        and Authorial Intent 108
Dilthey: The Critique of Historical Reason 110
Bultmann: The Pre-Understanding of Human Existence . . .113
The New Hermeneutic of Gerhard Ebeling
        and Ernst Fuch 116
Pannenberg and the Integration of History and
        Hermeneutics 119

**7. Paul Ricoeur: Phenomenological Hermeneutics And Postmodern
    Deconstructionism** 129
"To Believe Again" 130
Hermeneutic Phenomenology 131
Biblical Language as Poetic 134
Testifying Truth 136
A Hermeneutic of Revelation 137
The Autonomous Text, not Autonomous Reason 138
A Reader-Response Theory of Interpretation
        and the Deconstructionism of Derrida 140
Transcending Postmodernism 143
Theology as a Growing Tradition .145

8. Postliberal Hermeneutics and Narrative Theology 153
Theology as Realistic Narrative 153
The Cultural-Linguistic Method 155
Stanley Hauerwas and Narrative Theology 158

**9. Postmodern Hermeneutics, Ideological Criticism, and
   Liberation Theologies**..173
   Latin American Liberation Theology 174
   Black Liberation Hermeneutics 180
   Feminist Liberation Theology 184

10. Moltmann's Concept of The Trinitarian History of God 197
   Moltmann's Multidimensional Model of Experience 200
   The Perichoretic Unity of the Trinity 203
   The Modern Concept of Person 205
   Trinitarianism as Panentheism 209
   The Panentheism of American Process Thought 213
   The History of God 216
   The Postmodern Relevance of Moltmann's Doctrine
      of the Trinity 220

11. A Hermeneutical Validation of Faith............................225
   Canon and Criterion 225
   Scripture As Canon or Criterion? 228
   The Impasse between Canon and Criterion 235
   William Abraham or Kierkegaard? 235
   Heinz W. Cassirer—A Personal Testimony 238

Bibliography 243

Index 253

About the Author 261

Preface

This book is a post-critical evangelical conversation with modern and postmodern thought about the idea of history and hermeneutics. Modern thought, as used here, does not mean the idea of being up-to-date or something new. It refers to the rejection of traditionalism and authoritarianism of the premodern world in favor of autonomous reason. Modern thought began around 1600. René Descartes formally developed its basic features in 1637 in his extended essay, *Discourse on Method*. His basic premise was that knowledge is founded upon universal, autonomous, and rational principles of critical thought. This premise is also known as modern foundationalism.

Post-foundationalism and post-modernism are terms used to describe those who have lost confidence in the modern premise that critical reason is able to give a universal account of the way the world really is. A term related to post-foundationalism and post-modernism is post-critical. I mean by post-critical evangelicalism an adherence to the Trinitarian faith of the Church without modern foundationalism and without the notion of irrefutable orthodoxy. Post-critical evangelical theology agrees with much of the recent thinking across the university curriculum, which has adopted a post-critical, post-foundationalist concept of truth. Some forms of post-modernism tend toward irrationalism and appear to be like recalcitrant children of modernism because they are more intent on deconstructing the idea of autonomous, critical reason than in reconstructing a more modest claim to knowledge. The choice of the term post-critical is preferred over postmodern because the latter term is often associated with a reactionary stance. Post-critical is a term used to indicate an appreciation for the emphasis upon the need for critical thinking, but post-critical thinking is more modest in its claims about what it knows and recognizes that all knowing entails personal and subjective aspects. The modern idea of objectivist thinking which claims to have irrefutable truth independent of subjective and personal experience appears to be impossible.

Modern objectivism, based largely on Kant's critical philosophy, skims the surface of reality without adequately exploring the depth of meaning that arises out of one's particular historical situation and cultural tradition. Modern thought once gloried in its critical methodology as the hallmark of enlightened thinking, but it is now being criticized on the grounds that it was not sufficiently critical of its own assumptions and was thus a victim of absolutizing its own culturally conditioned values. Post-critical is a term, first used by Michael Polanyi, to suggest the need to move beyond the "critical philosophy" of Kant without abandoning the importance of criticism. To be post-critical is to value the importance of a synthesis of history and reason, which were inadequately linked in the fact-value dichotomy of Kant's critical philosophy. To be post-critical is to value the importance of a synthesis between subjective and objective dimensions of reality without falling into Romantic subjectivism and Nietzschean nihilism, on the one hand, or into the dualism of fact and value in Enlightenment thought, on the other hand.

Traditional American evangelical theology has often been unwittingly linked with a modernist view of rationality. In *The Remaking of the Modern Mind* (1946), Carl F. H. Henry criticized fundamentalism because it too narrowly restricted itself socially and culturally. He called for fundamentalism to be open to the intellectual currents of the day and to engage in dialog with serious contemporary issues.[1] However, the rise of the new evangelicalism out of fundamentalism in the middle of the 20th century assumed that the mind could develop an irrefutable knowledge of Christian doctrine, based on the foundational principles of a rational hermeneutics. In an article entitled, "The Conservative Option," Harold O. J. Brown said evangelical theology distinctly believes in "propositional revelation, and absolutes in the realm of knowledge."[2] Carl Henry argued for "rational truths" as opposed to "paradoxes."[3] He argued for intellectual objectivism as opposed to symbolic and analogical thinking.[4] He believed "only the literal knowledge and service of the Living God will counteract the erosive threat of secular" thought.[5]

Equipped with this method of rational objectivism, evangelical theology has often employed a confrontational style of apologetics with its opponents on the basis of dogmatic intellectualism, whereas post-critical evangelicalism prefers a friendly and dialogical conversation with other points of view, realizing that there is no absolute and irrefutable theology. Instead of talking about "heresies," post-critical evangelicalism prefers to speak of more or less adequate and inadequate understandings of doctrine. Instead of verbal inspiration, the inerrancy of Scriptures, and propositional revelation as the rational criteria of divine truth, post-critical evangelicalism emphasizes that the biblical texts are the inspired and reliable testimony to the *saving* history of God. Not doctrinaire truth and rational criteria, but testifying truth and historical narrative represent the essential format of the Bible. The methodological priority of historical narrative over doctrinal abstractions was well expressed by B. B. Warfield (1851-1921) when he said the truth of revelation is not dependent upon any theory of inspiration, but upon the narrative of history.[6] However, Warfield for all practical purposes set this insight aside in favor of a rationalistic defense of Reformed orthodoxy.

I will propose in this work that theology is being faithful to itself, not when it seeks merely to accommodate itself to the spirit of the times, but when it responsibly connects the message of the gospel to the present age. This means theology is dialogical because there is a dialectical relationship between faith and culture. Aspects of the modern world and the postmodern world are indebted to theology, but theology is also indebted to the insights of culture. The principle of critical thought, as the distinctive feature of the Enlightenment, was one of the mature results of Christian faith itself, but modernist theology often faltered in using critical thought because of its dualistic epistemology. A post-critical evangelical theology is not interested in reversing the gains of modern critical thought, but it seeks to move beyond the excessive claims of rationality to a more modest assessment of the nature of truth. It particularly rejects the comprehensive dualism of modern thought, which made the idea of revelation unintelligible.

Post-critical evangelical theology appreciates the postmodern critique of modern criticism. It appreciates the emphasis upon historical particularity and cultural conditioning for understanding the meaning of human life as opposed to the modernist notion of universal rational criteria. In fact, it can be argued that postmodern thought is indebted to the Christian tradition at this point because theology has always seen its identity in terms of history. The Scriptures highlight that the identity of Israel was shaped in the events of its history, especially the central events of the exodus and the conquest, and that Christian identity is based on the central events of Easter and Pentecost.

This work will examine the different approaches used in recent theology, and it will explore in particular the postmodern influence. Postmodernism is generally considered to be as revolutionary and decisive as the shift from the premodern to the modern era.[7] While there is no specific date for the daybreak of this new era, the fall of the Berlin Wall in 1989 may be considered a symbolic event as marking the end of the modern period. The collapse of Marxism and its philosophical objectivism symbolized the collapse of modernism in its most extreme form.

Postmodernism rejects the comprehensive dualism of modern thought between subjectivism and objectivism.[8] It rejects the modern claim that truth can be universally established through the creative powers and decisions of the rational will. It emphasizes a *feeling* of unity in life and the importance of inclusive relationships. It celebrates the idea of pluralism and rejects the idea of a single, universal truth. The premodern world assumed the *intellectual* nature of reality and the objectivity of truth as-it-really-is. Hence the creeds and teachings of the Church took precedence over individual conscience and personal beliefs because these doctrines represented the objective revelation of God and were infallibly preserved in the ecclesiastical tradition. The modern world assumed the *volitional* nature of reality and the subjectivity of truth as-it-appears. Hence its focus was on ethics as an expression of the universal laws of the moral imperative. The postmodern world gives priority to a sense of *personal feeling,* which gives synthesis and meaning to the fullness of life.

Postmodernism recognizes the need to transcend the radical subject-object dualism of the modern world in terms of a more inclusive synthesis. Richard J. Bernstein has shown that this dichotomy created "an uneasiness that has spread throughout intellectual and cultural life" and "affects almost every discipline and every aspect of our lives."[9] As a means of resolving this uneasiness, Bernstein shows that the postmodern trend is "a movement beyond objectivism and subjectivism."[10]

One of the important concepts in the postmodern, Internet age is the word, connected. "Feeling connected" has also become a popular postmodern term to express a sense of being a vital part of one's world. Although postmodernism emphasizes "being connected," it often obscures the connecting poles of subject and object and veers toward monism or nihilism. In order to distinguish their position from relativism and nihilism, some theologians speak of a *reconstructive* postmodern theology,[11] but I prefer to speak of transcending modernism as well as transcending postmodernism. Constructive aspects of the premodern, modern, and postmodern contributions to theology need to be appreciated. Specifically, the *intellectual* insights of the Early Church Fathers and the creeds of the premodern world, the modern emphasis upon the decision-making activity of the *will* to affirm and to appropriate truth critically and creatively, and the postmodern feeling of synthesis and inclusiveness contribute significantly each in their own way to the task of theology.

The larger purpose of this work is to integrate theology with history and hermeneutics, and it will do so primarily in dialog with multiple attempts in contemporary theology to transcend the comprehensive dualism of modern thought. The systematic theology of Wolfhart Pannenberg will serve as a special guide in this task. Pannenberg was one of the first theologians to offer a serious critique of modern theology and its comprehensive dualism. Process theologian John B. Cobb, Professor of Theology Emeritus at the Claremont School of Theology, Claremont, California, has said: "It is doubtful that there is another thinker alive today who is as comprehensive in the command of wideranging disciplines as Wolfhart Pannenberg." Cobb thinks Whitehead was the greatest philosopher who ever lived, and "on the process side, only Whitehead himself can compare with Pannenberg." Cobb further comments: "The single most sustained and thoroughgoing embodiment of this theological response to the decay of modernity is that of Pannenberg. Pannenberg has rethought the relation of Christianity and the Enlightenment profoundly and brilliantly."[12]

Paul Ricoeur's phenomenological hermeneutics will also serve as a guide for integrating history and hermeneutics, particularly in reference to the difference between the Jesus of history and the Christ of faith. The premodern world emphasized ontology (being), as reflected in the Apostles' Creed with its cognitive affirmation of what Christians objectively believe about God; the modern world shifted from ontology to epistemology (a consciousness of being), as reflected in the philosophy of Descartes who equated truth with rational certainty; the postmodern world now turns away from epistemology and universal rational criteria to hermeneutics (language).[13] However, Ricoeur incorporated the legitimate concerns of epistemology into an expanded definition of hermeneutics, showing that access to reality is the function of semantics. Ricoeur integrates history and hermeneutics by showing that the poetic function of language is to preserve the original unity of event and meaning. Hence he speaks of the textuality of reality that overcomes subjectivism and objectivism. Post-critical evangelicalism is sympathetic to this postmodern turn toward hermeneutics.

The contributions of Jürgen Moltmann will also be noted. His writings have in large part been responsible for the focus on the doctrine of the Trinity in contemporary theology. His suggestions for addressing social and political issues have been creative and constructive, reflecting some of the central concerns of postmodernism. His writings have been particularly well received in America. One of his many books earned him the 2000 Louisville Grawemeyer Award in Religion, presented by Louisville Presbyterian Theological Seminary and the University of Louisville.

Prominent in the background of contemporary theology are the writings of Karl Barth. One of his distinctive contributions was to modify the traditional concept of revelation as *self*-revelation. It will be seen in this work that contemporary theology largely assumes this modern notion of revelation as self-disclosure. However, a post-critical evangelical critique will insist on the need to include the witness of salvation history and the reader's existential engagement in the biblical narrative as part of the meaning of God's self-revelation.

Finally, a post-critical evangelical theology is genuinely evangelical. Its main purpose is to preserve and to expand upon the interpretation of the Trinitarian faith of the Church as formulated by the Early Church Fathers, particularly the Cappadocian Fathers. Hence the last chapter of this work focuses on the canonical heritage of the Church.

I would like particularly to thank the following students for their much appreciated assistance: Bethann Ayers, David Brubaker, and Beverly McFadden.

Notes

1. Carl F. H. Henry, *The Remaking of the Modern Mind* (Grand Rapids: Wm. B. Eerdmans Publishing Company, 1946).

2.. Harold O. J. Brown, "The Conservative Option," *Tensions in Contemporary Theology*, ed. Stanley N. Gundry and Alan F. Johnson (Grand Rapids: Baker Book House, 1976), p. 441.

3. Carl F. H. Henry, "The Nature of God," *Christian Faith and Modern Theology*, ed. Carl F. H. Henry (New York: Channel Press ,1964), p. 86.

4. Ibid., p. 85.

5. Ibid., p. 93.

6. .B. B. Warfield, *The Inspiration and Authority of the Bible*, ed. Samuel G. Craig (Philadelphia: The Presbyterian and Reformed Publishing Company, 1948), p. 121.

7. Cf. *Postmodern Theology*, ed. Frederic B. Burnham (New York: Harper & Row, Publishers, 1989; *The Truth about The Truth*, ed. Walter Truett Anderson (New York: G. P. Putnam's Sons, 1995); Albert Borgmann, *Crossing the*

Postmodern Divide (Chicago: University of Chicago Press, 1992).

8. Richard Rorty, *Philosophy and the Mirror of Nature* (Princeton: Princeton University Press, 1979), pp. 17ff.

9. Richard J. Bernstein, *Beyond Objectivism and Subjectivism: Science, Hermeneutics, and Praxis* (Oxford, England: Basil Blackwell Publisher, Ltd., 1983), p. 1.

10. Ibid., p. xiv.

11. David Griffin, "Series Introduction," to Jerry Gill, *The Tacit Mode, Michael Polanyi's Postmodern Philosophy* (Albany: State University of New York Press, 2000, p. xi.

12. *The Theology of Wolfhart Pannenberg,* ed. Carl E. Braaten and Philip Clayton (Minneapolis: Augsburg Publishing House, 1988), pp. 55, 58.

13. Cf. Jürgen Habermas, *Postmetaphysical Thinking,* trans. William Mark Hohengarten (Cambridge, MA: The MIT Press, 1992), p. 12.

1

The Modern Concept of Self-Revelation

The Rise of Modern Thought

René Descartes (1595 – 1650) is known as the father of modern thought because he tried to secure a basis for absolute knowledge of God, the self, and the world on the basis of reason alone.[1] This is why his philosophy is known as rationalism. As a young man, he received a Roman Catholic education and said he always appreciated the theology of the Church. In spite of this, he was threatened with an enormous feeling of doubt about God.[2] The premodern world relied upon religious authority. The source of knowledge was the Bible and church creeds, which had the guarantee of the Church that its teachings and interpretations of these sources possessed divine authority. This ecclesiastical assurance did not resolve Descartes' doubts, and so he sought to establish a rational foundation for belief in God that was independent of revelation.[3]

His fundamental premise was that one could reason one's way through the morass of confusion and doubt into the light of absolute certainty and irrefutable knowledge.

This premise presupposed that there was an unbridgeable cleavage between the subjective and objective poles of reality. Simply relying upon the five senses leads one to an uncertain knowledge of what is true about anything. The sun in the sky or our physical bodies is only a probable conclusion of our five sense perceptions. Is there anything one can know absolutely for sure? The premodern world answered that one could know the existence of the ultimate realities of the self, the world, and God based on divine revelation correlated with natural theology. Descartes was not content with this authoritarian approach to truth. He would be satisfied with nothing less than unquestioned certainty based on a rational consideration of things. The kind of certainty that Descartes required was the axiomatic certainty of geometry. Unless philosophy could attain this level of absolute knowledge, doubt would subvert human happiness. If there was a real world beyond our five senses, its truth must thus be determined by logic. This had bad implications for the idea of biblical revelation that was based on the historical acts of God in the world and which depended upon eyewitnesses for its verification. Yet according to Descartes' method of rationalism, the five senses are not the best way to learn about God, for irrefutable knowledge comes only from inborn ideas, which are axiomatically known by reason.

The divorce between the facts of history and the ideas of reason, popularly referred to as a fact-value dichotomy, became the hallmark of modern thought. Ephraim Lessing (1729-1781), a German dramatist and literary critic with a strong interest in religious philosophy, formulated the classical problem of faith and history as implied in the dualistic epistemology of modern thought: "Accidental truths of history can never become the proof of necessary truths of reason."[4] He argued that the resurrection of Jesus is not an adequate basis for belief in divine revelation because it is at best only a probable event as compared with the eternal truths of reason, which offers absolute certainty about the ideas of God, the self, and the world to those who can think logically. At most, he believed the Bible offers myths and legends to help the common people to lead pious lives, but philosophy is the best alternative to think about God through rational reflection.

The philosophy of Immanuel Kant (1724-1804) was the highpoint of Enlightenment thought.[5] He emphasized that a critique of reason will show that the ideas of God, the self, and the world can be inferred on practical grounds with logical rigor. He did not share Descartes' view that the idea of God could be absolutely proven, but he did believe that universal principles of morality could be irrefutably proven. There principles are derived out of what he called "the imperative of morality."[6] His dualistic view of the world into phenomena (things as they appear) and noumena (things as they really are) led him to a skeptical conclusion about knowing the world beyond our five senses. Truth is always a synthesis of applying the universal concepts of our understanding with the phenomena of human experience. There is no knowledge of things that transcend our finite world. Hence God and transcendent realities are impossible to know, except as mere logical, abstract inferences based on the practical use of reason.[7] The theological implication of this dualism between phenomena and noumena is that God cannot be revealed in history because history is the realm of finite happenings in the phenomenal world, which is governed by "the universal natural law" of cause and effect.[8] Unlike Descartes' rationalism, Kant believed that truth is a rational interpretation of our sense experiences, not a mere reflection on innate ideas that are given independently of the empirical world. What we know comes to us through the five senses, and yet sense experience fails to tell us anything concretely about the world beyond. We infer there is a world beyond us, but we are barred from entering into it because we are confined to a world of human experience. This means there can be no special divine revelation in history. In an essay, "What Is Enlightenment?" Kant defined autonomous reason as the only method for knowing. He defined the age of Enlightenment as being released from one's self-inflicted tutelage. If one will simply have courage to use one's own reason instead of taking cues from others, one will discover the universal principles and moral values that underlie the meaning of the world.[9]

Christian scholarship was profoundly transformed by the rise of critical thought, especially as it was formalized in Kant's critical philosophy. The only certainties that remained were the scientific facts of the world such as discovered in Newtonian physics and universal moral principles established by rational reflection. Faith based on the events of history was seen as too insecure for thoughtful people. How can faith and one's eternal happiness be made dependent upon the shaky foundation of historical knowledge, since all history is governed by probability? How can one go from the probabilities of history to the certainty of faith? How can the resurrection of Jesus be defended rationally in the light of its historical uncertainty? Reason seemed far superior to a historical faith in making knowledge claims about God, the self, and the world, and the consequence was that the Trinitarian theology of the historic faith of the Church was set aside in favor of a reconstructed history of Jesus based on the rationalistic principles of Enlightenment thought.

The basic premise of this new Kantian-based theology, which is classically called modernism or liberalism, was that Jesus is not a divine person, but another human being with a high degree of God-consciousness who is a model of faith for those who seek to follow in his steps. The classical novel that represents this liberal reinterpretation of Jesus as an example of morality is Charles Sheldon's book, *In His Steps*, which continues to be published although it was first written in 1897.[10] Liberal theology believed the life of Jesus was contained in the gospels, but the gospels must be re-interpreted non-miraculously and as containing a moral lesson.

Ernst Troeltsch (1865-1923) developed the three classical principles

of historical criticism, which he believed must be used in biblical interpretation. These were the principles of criticism, analogy, and correla-
tion. These principles meant the biblical text must be subjected to the
same critical assessment as any other historical document, the alleged
events of the past must be judged on the analogy of what we know
today as normal human experience, and the past must be seen as form-
ing a nexus of events linked together by cause and effect.[11] The idea of
an absolutely unique occurrence, such as the incarnation of God in Jesus
of Nazareth, was ruled out from the beginning with these principles
serving as the governing points of biblical interpretation.[12] Troeltsch
believed the traditional view of Jesus Christ as the absolute center of
human history is impossible to retain in the light of the rise of modern
historical criticism.[13]

Not everyone in the latter part of the 19th century and the early part
of the 20th century accepted liberal theology, although they were few in
number. Martin Kähler (1835–1912), a German Protestant theologian,
wrote a penetrating critique of the attempts of scholars to rewrite the
life of Jesus based on modern historical critical presuppositions in his
book, *The So-Called Historical Jesus and the Historic, Biblical Christ*. His
argument centered on the insight that the gospels were not written as
mere historical documents intending to give a literal biographical
account of the life of Jesus. They were primarily confessions of faith and
secondarily historical reports. Kähler made a distinction between the
"historical" (*historisch*) and the "historic" (*geschichtlich*), to indicate that the
history of Jesus is not scientific history (*Historie*) but meaningful and
interpreted history (*Geschichte*).[14] The gospels have a theological intention: "To awaken faith in Jesus through a clear proclamation of his saving activity."[15] He rejected the rationalistic presuppositions of critical history, which believed it could explain Jesus by using historical-critical principles for interpreting the New Testament. Kähler's emphasis was that
faith is a gift of God, not the product of historical criticism or rational
reflection. He believed that to interpret Jesus strictly in moral terms as a
witness of faith instead of the object of faith is a superficial conclusion
based on erroneous theological notions.[16]

The most significant critique of liberal theology came from the pen
of Karl Barth (1886-1968). Although his father was a Swiss reformed
New Testament scholar who rejected liberalism, Karl Barth accepted this
new theology during his student days. Barth was influenced by the two
foremost liberal theologians of the day—Adolf Harnack and Wilhelm
Hermann, who taught at the Universities of Marburg and Berlin. His

espousal of liberal theology did not last for long, however. Shortly after he became a pastor, he realized that liberal theology did not preach very well and he was shocked to find out just how far removed it was from a realistic reading of the Bible.[17]

Barth was to become the most significant theologian of the 20th century, and his critique of liberal theology was the most incisive of any theologian. However, Barth did not simply repudiate his liberal training. Nor did he ignore Enlightenment thought. His theology was a serious attempt to rehabilitate Reformed theology as a constructive response to modern thought. One of Barth's main concerns was to show how faith does not need to feel threatened by the modern, rational demand for absolute certainty in the realm of historical truth. He began his theology with "the doctrine of the Word of God," not with a general understanding of history.[18] There is no need for extended critical and scholarly remarks and discussion about the Word of God as an intellectual preparation for doing theology other than the Word of God.[19] The certainty about God's existence is not based on critical scholarship, but one comes to know God by the free action of God alone through the proclamation of the gospel, Barth insisted.

The Modern Idea of Revelation as Self-Revelation

The most constructive and penetrating response to the rise of the modern historical consciousness was thus Barth's neo-orthodox theology, although it was to undergo important modifications by some of his students. His intent was to protect revelation so that it would not be put at the mercy of the critical historian. As opposed to the direct link between the scriptures and revelation in premodern, pre-critical orthodoxy, Barth redefined revelation in modern terms as God's *self*-revelation. Instead of revelation as the objective facts of salvation history, revelation is equated with the subjectivity and actuality of God's very selfhood. God's self-revelation is God's Word as distinct from the words of the Bible. God's Word is the presence of God's very self as revealed in human consciousness through the Bible.[20] The words of the Bible convey information about God and are a witness to God's self-disclosure, but the Word of God is God's very self, not the Bible.[21]

The certainty of divine revelation depends upon God's self-attestation and not upon the probabilities of historical research and rational demonstrations because the content of revelation is not something about God contained in the Bible, but God's very selfhood. This subjective idea of *self*-revelation finds its most immediate source in German idealism, especially in the Hegelian concept of the Spirit, which reveals itself to itself through human consciousness (i.e., the Spirit, or Idea, comes to the full awareness of its essence through the human spirit.).[22] Hegel calls this fully developed consciousness of the Idea, the Absolute Idea, or the Notion. [23]

This connection between Hegel and the neo-orthodox view of revelation shows that Barth was a "modern" theologian, although he offered a serious critique of it. This can be seen in Barth's qualified appreciation for the concept of self-revelation developed by Philipp Marheineke (1780-1846), a professor of theology at Berlin and the leader of the right-wing, conservative Hegelians. Marheineke defined revelation: "In the human spirit God is manifest to Himself not through it but through Himself, and in that way is manifest to the human spirit also."[24]

Jesus Christ as the Only Revelation

In defining revelation as *self*-revelation, one can understand why Barth said that there is only one revelation—the person of Jesus Christ.[25] If revelation means "*self*-revelation," i.e., what God reveals is God's *self*, then Barth properly drew the logical deduction that only in one event can God be revealed, namely, in the Christ event. If God should be revealed elsewhere, then it would be obvious that God's very selfhood in Jesus had not been really revealed. The idea of several revelations would be a logical inconsistency. When one thus speaks of *revelations*, one is not employing the use of this word in Barth's strict sense.[26]

For Barth, the subject of revelation and the object of revelation are one essence, i.e., subject and object are identical. Barth thus emphasized the unity of God with Jesus, for if God is revealed in Jesus, then Jesus must be God. Barth asked: "But who can reveal God but God Himself?" Thus, he argued that if Jesus reveals God, then "he must himself be God."[27] In this way, Barth said that the *revealer*, the *means* of revelation, and *what is revealed* are the same. [28] This is a Trinitarian concept of revelation. The Father reveals the Son through the Holy Spirit. Revelation is thus a direct knowledge of God in Jesus Christ and it can only be known through the Holy Spirit; it specifically cannot be comprehended on the basis of one's intellectual achievement. Because God reveals God's self in the human spirit, God is "His own double in His Revelation."[29]

The Different Meanings of the Word of God

A significant factor to be considered in defining revelation is whether or not it can be exegetically supported in Scripture. To be sure, there is no formal concept of revelation in the Bible,[30] just as there is no formal concept of history, ethics, ecclesiology, eschatology, etc. Rather, the scriptures *talk* history and revelation, but do not *talk about* them, e.g., John's gospel says, "the Word became flesh" (which is *talking* history), but it does not formally reflect on this event in the sense of a philosophical abstraction (which would be to *talk about* history). However, when a concept is used for purposes of systematic theology, it is expected to be consistent with the biblical witness.

Wolfhart Pannenberg, Emeritus Professor of Systematic Theology at the Faculty of Protestant Theology, Munich, has shown that the concept of revelation did not have a formal meaning with the early Greek Fathers as it was later developed in the Middle Ages in Europe, followed by the Protestant reformers, Protestant scholasticism, and modern theology. Rather, revelation was linked to Jesus Christ. To be sure, the patristic period understood the scriptures to be inspired of God, but it was Origen who formally used the term revelation in reference to biblical inspiration, although he did not limit revelation to biblical inspiration.[31] The idea of revelation as referring primarily to biblical inspiration arose in the Middle Ages.[32] The 16th century Protestant reformers also continued the link between biblical inspiration and revelation, although they did not limit the concept of the Word of God to the Bible. The concept of the "Word of God" was prominent in Luther's theology, and he spoke of the Bible as the Word of God, although he also used the concept of the Word of God with six different meanings, including references to Christ as the visible Word.[33] However, Melanchthon and Protestant scholasticism more intentionally developed a link between biblical inspiration and revelation (=the Word of God) much as had Thomas Aquinas in the Middle Ages.[34]

If Melanchthon and Protestant scholasticism on the European Continent defined the Bible as an authoritative book of doctrines, the English reformers were more interested in incorporating the Bible into its liturgy and worship than in intellectualizing it in formal doctrines. Paul Tillich said no other Protestant denomination has given so much attention to doctrine as the Lutheran Church. He says the Reformed tradition gave greater emphasis to an ethical interpretation of the Bible, while the Anglican tradition was more interested in liturgy and worship.[35]

In the eighteenth century, John Wesley was a reformer within the Church of England, but he did not disagree with the English Reformers on theological method. He also did not write a formal textbook on systematic theology; rather, he bequeathed to his followers a model of *Standard Sermons* which were intended to serve as the basis of what Methodists were supposed to believe and preach, following the example of the English reformers (particularly Thomas Cranmer) who produced the *Edwardian Homilies* which served as a basis of what members of the Church of England were supposed to believe. Wesley used the concept of the Word of God interchangeably with scriptures, but he did not intellectualize it into a code phrase for doctrines. Rather, the Word of God was primarily a personal address to believers enabling them to trust in Christ as distinct from merely an assent of the will to believe in orthodox doctrines, which Wesley noted that even the devil believed.[36]

Twentieth century theologian H. Orton Wiley described the concept of the Word of God in the Wesleyan tradition as having various meanings. He illustrated this in reference to concentric circles. At the center of revelation is the Eternal Word. Surrounding this center is the first circle, which represents the Word incarnate who is the most Personal Word of God. The second circle represents the Bible as the written Word of God. In this way, the Bible is the Word of God and also the record of the Word incarnate. The outer circle is the revelation of God in nature. The Bible is part of nature and the created universe and yet it is God's personal Word.[37]

Wiley also argued that the "Bible contains and is the Word of God"[38] in the sense that it is a report of "the revelation of God in history,"[39] particularly as "Christ was Himself the full and perfect revelation of the Father."[40] Because the testimony of Jesus is the "last word of all objective revelation," the scriptures "become the Word of God objectified."[41] Significantly enough, Wiley presented the Wesleyan view of the Word of God in direct contrast to the right-wing Hegelian theologian, Dorner, who made the divine inspiration of the Bible itself the basis of faith. Wiley argued instead that the scriptures are the basis of faith because they are the inspired record and witness of God's saving acts in history.[42]

The over-intellectualization of the Bible as the revealed Word of God in Protestant Orthodoxy led to a crisis of the "Scripture principle" during the Enlightenment as historical criticism challenged the idea of the verbal inspiration of the Bible.[43] Since the Bible was no longer perceived to be the inerrant Word of God, other methods were employed to explain the faith of the Church. One method was the nineteenth century quest for the historical Jesus, which was an attempt to get behind the biblical texts to the real facts themselves through the new rationalist method of historical criticism. Supposedly these facts would show that Jesus was only a human person with superior moral qualities. Schweitzer's *Quest of the Historical Jesus* was the classic summary of this failed attempt.[44]

Another response to the crisis of the Scripture principle was "the kerygmatic theology" of Karl Barth and Rudolf Bultmann, which dominated the twentieth century. It highlighted the character of the Bible as "word" as opposed to historical events. *Kerygma* is the Greek word for proclamation. A primary motivation for the emergence of kerygmatic theology was to circumvent the problem of critical history for faith. If historical criticism had made the link between revelation and the Bible untenable, kergymatic theology called for a "peaceful co-existence" between revelation and history by separating word and event.

In contrast to Barth's statement that "God's Word is God Himself in His Revelation,"[45] Pannenberg has shown that the basic idea of revelation is connected with God's action in the economy of salvation. To be sure, revelation is a call to personal participation in the life of the divine Trinity, but the revelation of God is primarily linked to the history of salvation. For example, the biblical phrase, "the Word of God," is equated with the apostolic kerygma, thus indicating that revelation as the Word of God is linked to tradition (1 Thess. 2:13; 1 Peter 1:25, Romans 10:8), not to God's selfhood. Also, the appearances of Jahweh in the earliest Israelite traditions are not the unveiling of the essence of God, but the imparting of certain information and thus may be called manifestations of God, but not a direct self-revelation. For example, in Exodus 3, God appears to Moses to inform him that he is to lead His people out of Egyptian bondage, but God's selfhood is only indirectly revealed to Moses.

The Bible as a Witness to Revelation

This brings us back to Barth who more than anyone else introduced the modern concept of the Word of God into theology. He wanted to come to terms with the crisis of the Scripture principle in the Enlightenment when the idea of verbal inspiration came under attack. In a sense, Barth's new definition of revelation as the self-revealing Word of God was an attempt to do "damage control" in the light of the application of historical criticism to the Bible. If the Word of God is not the Bible, then historical criticism cannot invalidate it. This is because the Word of God is revelation, and revelation is God's very self. The Bible is thus not the Word of God, but it is a witness to revelation and becomes in a dialectic sense the Word of God only in the moment of divine encounter. This implied that critical history was irrelevant in theology since God's Word is known through the Bible as a witness and not as a history book.

Although Bultmann's theology represented the most consistent form of kergymatic theology (=theology of the Word) with his denial of a real history of salvation, it was Barth who made the theology of the Word of God the primary motif in the twentieth century.[46] Because "God's Word is God's Son" rather than the Bible, it is impossible to control and systematize the Word of God in the sense in which high Lutheran Orthodoxy sought to do in the 17th century, which viewed the Holy Scriptures as a set of propositions to be systematically fixed like a body of laws.[47] On the other hand, Barth stated that God's very self is made known in human language, which contain propositions asserted by prophets and apostles and which are proclaimed in the Church. These propositions of Scripture *become God's Word*.[48] Barth thus differentiated between the form and the content of the Word of God. The content is God's self. The form is the language of the Bible. The form becomes the content in an indirect and dialectical identity when God so chooses to be revealed through the form.[49] Thus, *Paulus dixit* and *Deus dixit* are indirectly united in the moment of revelation. The fact that the words of the Bible and the Word of God come together only as an indirect identity is to point out that the identity is an *assumed* identity, which is brought about by the choice of God and thus is not an intrinsic identity.[50] The idea of the Bible *becoming* the Word of God in the moment of self-revelation is thus untouched and unharmed by the results of historical criticism.

Barth recognized that the preaching of the apostles is often equated with the Word of God.[51] For example, Barth showed this to be true of Paul, who writes: "Christ is speaking in me" (2 Cor. 13:3). However, the propositional truth of Holy Scripture is not revelation, but only attests revelation and becomes revelation when God freely chooses it to be revelation. If one should equate the words of the Bible as being inherently the Word of God (as the post-Reformation Orthodoxy did), Barth believed this would reduce the Living God to a dead book.[52]

If the words of the Bible become the Word of God only through God's initiative, is there any necessity for critically ascertaining their authenticity and historical reliability? Further, if Jesus Christ is the objective reality of revelation, does this necessitate the use of the historical-critical method for ascertaining who he really was? Barth's answer was a decisive NO. Rather, God's selfhood is revealed whenever God so chooses and in no way is it determined by human initiative. One might ask, why put such heavy emphasis upon the Bible as a necessary medium through which God is revealed? Could God not be revealed through some other form than the scriptures? Barth made it unmistakably clear that Scripture is linked to the Word of God because it is linked to "the original Word of God" in Jesus.[53] The theological uniqueness of Holy Scripture rests in the fact that the prophets and the apostles were witnesses of the one revelation which took place in Jesus Christ, who is the objective fact of revelation, i.e., he is very God and very man.[54] The prophets witnessed to Jesus Christ in "expectation," while the apostles witnessed in "recollection."[55]

Because of their unique position in relation to Jesus Christ, their witness is essential. Scripture in its witness to the original revelation in Jesus Christ is the Word of God when God so chooses it to become the divine Word. Barth illustrated this unity of form (Scripture) and content (revelation) in connection with the Incarnation of Jesus who is both God and man.[56] Even as in the Incarnation, God is free to be revealed in Jesus Christ, even so God is free to be revealed in Holy Scripture. In revealing God's self in Jesus, Jesus himself was identical with God. This unity of Jesus with God is an assumed identity, i.e., the man Jesus was not inherently God, but God willed and created this unity, thus effecting an indirect identity. Likewise, the Holy Scriptures becomes the revelation of God when God so creates and wills this indirect identity. To be sure, there are inherent differences between the incarnate Word and the Word of God in Holy Scripture. That Jesus became the Word of God in his humanity needs no repetition or confirmation, for he is the eternal presence of God.

On the other hand, the scriptures as the witness to the revelation of God in Jesus are signs through which Jesus is revealed. These signs must ever and again become the Word of God to us. This means the Church stands in constant need of the ministry of the Holy Spirit to enable the witness of the Bible to become the Word of God.[57] Barth further drew the distinction between a "verbal inspiration" and "verbal inspiredness." By the former he meant that God verbally spoke through the prophets and apostles by means of the inspiration of the Holy Spirit. By verbal inspiredness, Barth meant the attempt to freeze up the Word of God into the words of the Bible, thus bringing God under human control by reducing God to the level of a mere book.[58] To be sure, the words of the Bible contain propositions, but these propositions are not in themselves revelation, though they can become revelation when God so chooses. Because of this dialectical relationship between the Word of God and Holy Scripture, Barth will frequently refer to the scriptures as the Word of God.[59]

However, if one should merely equate the words of the Bible with the Word of God, i.e., if the words of the Bible in themselves are defined as revelation, then this is to speak of verbal inspiredness. Barth does not see the Reformers saying anything materially different from what he says in this regard.[60] Rather, the shift from the perspective of "inspiration" to "inspiredness" occurred in high Lutheran Orthodoxy about 1700.[61] The freezing up of the Word of God into the words of the Bible in effect reduced saving faith to mere history and based upon itself rather than upon the mystery of Christ and the Holy Spirit. The Bible became a "paper Pope" and, unlike the living Roman Pope who could interpret his own propositions, it depended solely upon the manipulation of "human power" and critical scholarship to be interpreted.[62] This reduction of the Word of God to the words of the Bible was followed by the Enlightenment, which treated the Bible solely as a historical book..[63]

Barth pointed out that the aim of the post-Reformation interpretation of Holy Scripture in affirming its inerrancy and infallibility even to the minutest details was an attempt to set forth the Bible as book of axioms which measured up to the same level of formal truth as philosophy and mathematics.[64] However, if high Lutheran Orthodoxy attempted to guarantee the Bible to be the Word of God by means of its rigid doctrine of "inspiredness," Barth on the other hand completely eliminates the necessity of any natural proof of the Word of God in Holy Scripture. To be sure, he has only one intention—to let the Bible speak on its own terms. Only in this way can the Word of God be found in Holy Scripture. But in no sense can one "find" any natural evidence of the Word of God in Scripture.[65]

This rejection of any natural proof for revelation necessarily follows from Barth's concept of *self*-revelation. If revelation is the direct self-disclosure of God, then obviously it is in no way dependent upon humans. Revelation is totally a matter of faith. It is a miracle.[66] It cannot be proven, only believed.[67] For this reason, Barth is willing to concede that the Bible as the words of humans is fallible, errant, and even contradictory, although this in no way affects the faith of believers in the Bible as the medium of God's revelation.[68] Barth maintains that historical investigation into the Bible in no way damages the concept of God's *self*-revelation through the Bible because revelation in no way depends upon the results of historical research.

A Critique of Barth's Concept of Self-Revelation

Bultmann proposed a question to Barth asking him what was his principle of selection for interpreting the Bible for "modern" people. Bultmann acknowledged that his existentialist interpretation was an attempt to see if the mythical picture of the world had a valid meaning for today, but he criticized Barth's hermeneutic on the grounds that it lacked a consistent methodology, complaining that Barth's theology was a series of arbitrary statements without any principle of selection.[69]

Bultmann's question misses the point of Barth's doctrine of Holy Scripture. Barth believes the proof of Holy Scripture lies in God's self-authentication of it. That the canon is Holy Scripture is the result of the Church confirming and establishing that which was already formed and given. The Church did not arbitrarily compose the canon, but the canon was formed because it imposed itself upon the Church.[70] Likewise today, Scripture as the Word of God needs no external authority for its support. This means the believer does not need to try to select certain portions of the Bible from other portions as more reliable or that one needs to distinguish between what is fallible and what is infallible—as if we could determine for ourselves what is the genuine Word of God for today.[71] The believer is not concerned with any "principle of selection." The question of the Bible as the Word of God is not a historical but a theological question. The only question is whether or not God so chooses to be revealed through the biblical "form."

If Barth asserts that revelation became historical in Jesus Christ and if the apostles are given a unique position in the Church because they were eye-and-ear witnesses of God's revelation in time,[72] then does it not follow that faith should be able to stand the test of critical rationality and historical examination? If this revelation did occur in time-space with human witnesses, must not the biblical texts then be treated as historical "sources" as well kerygma? Paul Althaus has argued that while the gospels are not intended to be merely objective and factual presentations but testimonies of faith, the gospels are *also* narratives and sources. He argued that the historical question of the gospel is not only theologically legitimate, but the New Testament itself invites historical inquiry.[73]

To be sure, Barth's emphasis upon the priority of faith over critical rationality is well taken, i.e., faith is a way of knowing as well as trust. But what one believes should not have to be sheltered from critical investigation. In defending the resurrection kerygma before King Agrippa, Paul appeals to the possibility of its public investigation. Paul says: "This was not done in a corner" (Acts 26:26). Paul makes it clear that the Word of God does not consist of gnostic secrets, but is open to all who can see, and if the gospel is veiled, it is because "the god of this world has blinded the minds of the unbelievers" (2 Cor. 4:2-4).[74]

Pannenberg has offered a sustained criticism of Barth's theology of the Word of God, arguing instead that the content of the Word of God in the Bible does not refer primarily to God's very *self* but to *events* and communication of *information*.[75] Pannenberg further believes that the Word of God in the Bible does not mean the direct self-disclosure of God.[76] In other words, Pannenberg objects to Barth's modernist concept of the Word of God on exegetical grounds. To be sure, Pannenberg recognizes that the point of biblical revelation is that God might be known, and so he does not consider it theologically wrong to define revelation as self-disclosure, but rather such a definition needs to be more carefully nuanced.[77] Considering the centrality of Barth's definition of the Word of God as the self-revelation of God, Pannenberg notes that the biblical support is "surprisingly thin."[78] In fact, he shows that the first time that the definition of revelation as *self*-revelation occurred was in German idealism.[79]

Just because German Idealism was the immediate source for the modernist concept of self-revelation is not in itself a reason to reject it *in toto*, especially if it is adequately nuanced to do justice to the biblical history of salvation, which is what Pannenberg attempted to do. Although Pannenberg had particular appreciation for the religious philosophy of Hegel, he saw the need for it to undergo an important correction before it could be theological serviceable,[80] and hence he did not consider his theology a kind of "theological Hegelianism."[81] In fact, Pannenberg offered a new definition of revelation that preserved and yet went beyond Barth's theology of the Word of God[82] by developing the idea of an *indirect* self-revelation.[83]

Self-Revelation as Indirect rather than Direct

Crucial to Pannenberg's revised concept of revelation is the distinction between *direct* and *indirect* self-revelation. Pannenberg clarifies this distinction in connection with the difference between direct and indirect communication. Direct communication means an exact identity between the content to be communicated and what is actually communicated.[84] In Barth's theology, there is no difference between the Word of God and God's self, for what is revealed is the revealer—thus a direct self-revelation of God. An indirect communication means that what is communicated is not identical with what was intended to be communicated. In an indirect communication there is a break between the sender and the receiver. What is intended to be communicated is considered from another perspective. [85]

Indirect or direct communication can be received immediately or mediated by a messenger. What is important is not the *act* of communicating, but the *content* that is actually communicated. Does this content reflect directly or indirectly what was intended in the communication? In theology, direct communication has God as its content in a mystical sense or similar to the epiphanies in the Old Testament, such as God's revelation to Moses in the burning bush.[86]

On the other hand, an indirect communication does not have God as its content in a direct way.[87] Though God is the originator of the revelatory events, nevertheless, God's essence is only known indirectly, i.e., by reflecting on the event, which God originated. Pannenberg believes that it is a fundamental idea of the New Testament that God's indirect self-revelation has progressively unfolded in the world, beginning with Abraham, and that it will be consummated in a complete direct self-revelation only at the end-time. Pannenberg develops this idea into a theology of universal history. God who was revealed to Abraham and throughout the history of salvation culminating in Jesus is the Lord of the universe and all history and that God's self-revelation took place in the real events of the world. This means *events* are basic to the idea of revelation, while the word of God is the interpretation of these events.

Pannenberg acknowledges that this idea of universal history goes back to German idealism, especially to Hegel, even as Barth's idea of self-revelation had it roots there. For Pannenberg, this recognition does not invalidate its use in systematic theology.[88] Rather, what is significant is whether or not the idea of universal history can properly articulate the idea of God's self-revelation. More specifically, is the idea of an indirect self-revelation of God in terms of a universal history implicit in Scripture?

A theology of universal history includes both word and event. This can be seen in the exodus event. Before the exodus, Jahweh tells Moses what is going to happen so that after the event the people will look upon it as the confirmation of the prophetic word. "And Israel saw the great work which the Lord did against the Egyptians, and the people feared the Lord; and they believed in the Lord and in his servant Moses" (Exodus 14:31). In Elijah's contest with the prophets of Baal on Mount Carmel, it was God's action in consuming Elijah's sacrifice with fire that proved Jahweh's divinity. "And when all the people saw it, they fell on their faces; and they said, 'The Lord, he is God; the Lord, he is God'"(1 Kings 18:39). Jethro (Exodus 18:11) and Naaman (2 Kings 5:15) likewise both acknowledged the sovereignty and deity of Jahweh on the basis of what happened.[89] The basis for Israel's belief in the divinity of God is thus found in the testimony of their history. They did not arrive at this fundamental conviction through philosophical speculation, but rather, it is derived from their experiences of history.[90]

Likewise in the New Testament the decisive factor of revelation is its historical character. For example, the mere claims of Jesus to authority in themselves did not verify his unity with God. Rather, the function of the miracle stories was to demonstrate this unity. In reply to the question, "Are you the one who was to come, or shall we look for another?" the proof that was offered is that the events of Jesus' life show him to be the fulfillment of history: "The blind receive their sight and the lame walk, lepers are cleansed and the deaf hear, and the dead are raised up, and the poor have the good news preached to them." [91] Jesus' miraculous deeds were seen as the eschatological fulfillment of the Old Testament expectation concerning the coming of the Messiah.

What is being argued here is that revelation is not a direct self-revelation, but is indirect in the sense that God is known on the basis of his historical acts, which means that God's self is not to be directly identified with what is actually revealed. To be sure, the purpose of God's revelation is *self*-revelation, but in so doing God actually communicates content other than God's pure presence. It is by reflecting on this "other content" that indirectly reveals who God is. This indirect self-revelation of God is progressively expanded in the course of historical development until it reached its proleptic culmination in the Christ event. "Proleptic" means the self-revelation of God has reached its climax in the course of the historical process and will not be overtaken by any other event until the eschaton at which time the *direct* self-revelation of God will occur. In other words, "prolepsis" is the provisional fulfillment of what is to come.

Revelation, as Pannenberg describes it, is related to "chain of tradition" that begins with the foundational events of the Old Testament and extends through the apocalyptic literature to the preaching of Jesus and the first community of believers, including Paul.[92] This chain of tradition has its goal in the resurrection of Jesus from the dead, which is the self-vindication of the God of Israel to be the God of all men. Jesus' substantial unity with God is believed to be true from the perspective of the resurrection event.

This emphasis upon the continuity of historical events reaching back into the earliest beginnings of Israel's history stands in conscious opposition to those scholars who seek to construct Christology on the pre-Easter Jesus without reference to his resurrection. Jesus' claim to divine authority can only rightly be understood in the light of Israel's historical development and the divine confirmation of Jesus' unity with God by his resurrection. Paul pointed out this continuous chain of tradition in which the revelation of God reaches its climax in Jesus of Nazareth. He spoke of (1) the historical continuity between Israel and Jesus, (2) his resurrection as confirmation of his deity, and (3) the universal goal of history in bringing salvation to all nations.

> Paul, a servant of Jesus Christ, called to be an apostle, set apart for the gospel of God which he promised beforehand through his prophets in the holy scriptures, the gospel concerning his Son, who was descended from David according to the flesh and designated the Son of God in power according to the Spirit of holiness by his resurrection from the dead, Jesus Christ our Lord, through whom we have received grace and apostleship to bring about the obedience of faith for the sake of his name among all the nations, including yourselves who are called to belong to Jesus Christ (Romans 1:1-6).

It is not just single historical occurrences that completely reveal the essence of God, but rather, it is a complex of events, which points to the revelation of God, culminating in Jesus Christ. "But when the time had fully come, God sent forth his Son, born of woman, born under the law, to redeem those who were under the law, so that we might receive adoption as sons" (Galatians 4:4-5).

This understanding of revelation as being the result of a complex of events is expressed by the Deuteronomist: "And because he loved your fathers and chose their descendants after them, and brought you out of Egypt with his own presence, by his great power, driving out before you nations greater and mightier than yourselves, to bring you in, to give you their land for an inheritances, as at this day; *know therefore this day*, and lay it to your heart, *that the Lord is God in heaven above and on the earth beneath; there is no other*" (Deuteronomy 4:37-39). That God's plan for Israel had been revealed to their "fathers," and the fact that they now were to live in the promised land constituted for them the revelation of God: "Know therefore this day...that the Lord is God." Thus, the purpose of history was to make Jahweh known to the people of Israel.[93]

The self-vindication of the deity of Jahweh was considered to be complete after the occupation of the promised land,[94] but the events of the fall of Judah and the exile brought about a revision in Israel's understanding of revelation. Revelation was now moved to a future expectation. While the exile itself came as the result of disobedience on the part of Israel, the present tribulation was only transitory, for in the end of their distress would come the salvation of Jahweh. The apocalyptic expectation of the prophets was a new understanding of revelation in connection with the exodus and conquest.[95] This is especially seen in Ezekiel and Isaiah who take up the theme of the Exodus and the occupation of the promised land as they describe the future action of God in restoring the fortunes of Israel. [96] Isaiah speaks of the future deliverance of Israel as being a new Exodus, which then will be followed with a new Covenant (Isaiah 54).[97]

What the prophets' expectation conceived as decisive is the future revelation of God. It will be the inauguration of a new aeon, which will also reveal the meaning of the present. History thus progresses toward this end according to the plan of God. Though the belief that God is the initiator of events is not uniquely a biblical teaching, the idea that God is revealed through historical events is a characteristic feature of revelation. Unlike the powers of the gods of the nations which ceases at the frontiers of their country, Yahweh initiated universal history and influences the destinies of Israel and Israel's neighbors (Amos 3:6, Isa. 47:7); Lam. 3:37). There is no place for polytheism or dualism in Israel's faith. Yahweh directs and controls the destinies of all people, not in the sense of a marionette, but leaves them with finite freedom of choice.[98]

The ultimate purpose of God's historical activity is to make God known to all peoples (Isaiah 43:9-10), to all "flesh" (Isaiah 49:26). "I gird you [Israel]...that men may know...that there is none besides me" (Isaiah 45:5-6). "And the glory of the Lord shall be revealed, and all flesh shall see it together" (Isaiah 40:5).[99] What is especially emphasized in the prophetic expectation is the extending of *Heilsgeschichte* into universal history. It is at the end of the present aeon that the essence of God shall be revealed, for then God shall come to inaugurate a kingship on earth so that it can be said that "the earth shall be full of the knowledge of the Lord as the waters cover the sea" (Isaiah 11:9; Hab. 2:14). This eschatological inauguration of the kingdom of God on earth would make it possible to say history is identical with the full knowledge of God. The end of history, rather than the ongoing course of history, is one with the essence of God. However, the course of history is also related to the end of history and hence the course of history also reveals indirectly the essence of God, although its perfection comes at the end. [100]

The significance of the resurrection of Jesus can be seen in the fact that the eschatological expectation of God's coming Kingdom of earth has already been pre-actualized in Jesus of Nazareth. Eschatology includes an "already" and "not-yet."[101] In the kerygma of Jesus is proclaimed the "already" of the Kingdom of God. The central proclamation of Jesus' kerygma was the imminent Kingdom of God: "But seek first his kingdom and his righteousness, and all these things shall be yours as well" (Matthew 6:33). Thus, the eschatological message of God's imminent reign formed the encompassing thrust of Jesus' preaching. Whatever attitude one took toward his message and his claim to divine authority would ultimately determine one's destiny. But, this "already" of the Kingdom of God stands in tension with the "not yet" aspect. The apocalyptic expectation had pointed to the earthly rule of the Kingdom of God, but such a political development did not happen. For this reason, Pannenberg points out if the resurrection of Jesus had not happened, then his message would have been a "fanatical audacity."[102] It was, in fact, because of his resurrection that Jesus' message concerning the expectation of the near end was vindicated, for this end was proleptically fulfilled in his own person. The "not yet" of the kingdom of God still remains to be fulfilled in the eschaton, when "the kingdom of the world has become the kingdom of our Lord and of his Christ, and he shall reign for ever and ever" (Revelation 11:15).

Story or History?

That the scriptures conceive of God as having acted concretely in history is generally recognized. That this historical activity is the central focus of Christian faith has in more recent times appeared to be problematic. One of the most visible critics of the concept of "revelation in history" is James Barr, Distinguished Professor of Hebrew Bible, Emeritus, Vanderbilt University. Barr agrees that the idea of God being revealed in world events is indeed a biblical notion, but he emphasizes that the idea of God communicating verbally is also a prominent feature of the Bible. More specifically, he does not define biblical "events" as history because the Bible does not distinguish between myth and history and hence all events in the Bible are placed on the same level of reality.[103]

More problematic is Barr's contention that there is no corresponding term for history in the scriptures. Barr recommends that "story" is a better term than "history."[104] Pannenberg disputes Barr's claim that there is no implied word for history in the Bible.[105] To be sure, the Bible does not speak of critical history in a modern sense of the term and it does not limit the meaning of history to human action. Israel, for example, considered history to be based in divine action. In Joshua 24:31, the elders were chosen because they were men who "had known all the work which the Lord did for Israel." The foundational events of revelation in the Old Testament were the Exodus and Conquest of Israel. These were considered to be events of real history. They were more than just a narrative or a story, but real history. Some have suggested that the word "metahistory" be used to distinguish the events of the Bible from the modern notion of history, but Pannenberg believes this has only limited value because the word implies that the events of the Bible are something other than real history.[106] More recently, the term "narrative" is the word of choice as opposed to "history" because it is not burdened down with the modern notion of positivism, and it is able to avoid the question of historical realism.[107]

The more substantive issue that Barr raises is that the Old Testament includes events, which the critical scholar today would consider mythical or legendary. Pannenberg agrees with this observation, and in fact Pannenberg will often use the word, story, for those parts, which he considers unhistorical. However, he disagrees that "story" should be substituted for history as the decisive mode of God's self-revelation. He contends that it contradicts the intent of the biblical message to make the realism of the history of salvation a "story" by turning what is narrated into a secondary matter.

Pannenberg agrees with the conclusions of modern historical criticism that many of the details are more like story than real history, but he believes that historical criticism can be used to show that it is unnecessary to discard the central events of salvation history as if the texts were merely literature, while the events which they record are merely a secondary concern.[108] Pannenberg has unnecessarily yielded too much at this point by conceding that the "resurrection stories" in the four gospels are largely legendary. N. T. Wright offers a more balanced view of the authenticity of the gospel history. Wright shows that these resurrection stories cannot be simply dismissed as legends, which his hypothesis/verification methodology is intended to point out.[109] Nevertheless,

Pannenberg shows that it is excessive skepticism to reject the resurrection as mere story–whatever judgment one makes about the gospel accounts. Pannenberg also points out that calling the biblical events a story instead of history may avoid the problem of historical criticism, but this approach can only do so at the expense of truth, emptying faith of its substance.[110] Pannenberg strenuously argues that theology must retain its emphasis upon the factuality of the historical action of God and hence cannot give up the concept of history.[111]

Summary

In summary: (1) The concept of revelation has been defined as the self-disclosure of God, i.e., the knowledge of God has its origin in God's self-disclosure. (2) Revelation as history is an indirect disclosure of God, i.e., the content of revelation in history does not directly coincide with the essence of God. The Revealer and what is revealed do not have an exact correspondence. Rather, the content of revelation tells us something *about* God, and only indirectly *who* God is. (3) There are as many revelations of God as there are divine events. (4) *Heilsgeschichte* takes on a universal character, for all history is seen to be moving toward the eschaton at which time the full direct revelation of God shall be visible. (5) Insofar as Jesus' substantial unity with God can be seen on the basis of Jesus' claim to divine authority and his resurrection from the dead, he is the pre-actualization of the eschatological future. Thus, those who respond to his message and abandon their own self-sufficiency in favor of his lordship have a share in the coming kingdom of God in the present. (6) The eschaton has been anticipated in Jesus' person because Jesus is God, and hence he possesses absolute significance for all humankind. This means no further revelation can overtake the Christ event so long as history is moving toward the eschaton. This suggests that all history is to be judged in the light of the Christ event. (7) It is the end of history that can be said to be one with the essence of God, i.e., God will be fully known in a direct self-disclosure in the eschaton. This points out that the course of history constitutes an indirect self-revelation, while the end of history is a direct self-revelation. (8) The revelation of God is real history, not a mere story and not mere narrative.

Notes

1. Rene Descartes, "Discourse on Method," *Essential Works of Descartes*, trans. Lowell Blair with an intro. By Daniel J. Bronstein (New York: Bantam Books,

1966), pp. 4-6.

2. Ibid.

3. Ibid.

4. *Lessing's Theological Writings,* translated with an introductory essay by Henry Chadwick (London: Adam and Charles Black, 1956), p. 53.

5. Ernst Cassirer, *Kant's Life and Thought,* trans. James Haden (New Haven: Yale University Press, 1981), pp. 83, 227.

6. Kant, *The Fundamental Principles of the Metaphysic of Ethics,* trans. Otto Manthey-Zorn (New York: D. Appleton-Century Co, 1938), p. 33.

7. *Critique of Pure Reason,* trans. Normal Kemp Smith (London: Macmillan and Co., Ltd. 1929). Cf. Ernst Cassirer, *Kant's Life and Thought,* pp. 139-217.

8. Kant, "Idea of a Universal History from a Cosmopolitan Point of View," *Theories of History,* ed. Patrick Gardiner (New York: The Free Press, 1959), p. 22

9. Kant, "What is Enlightenment?" *The Enlightenment, A Comprehensive Anthology,* ed. Peter Gay (New York: Simon and Schuster, 1973), pp. 384-389.

10. Cf. Timothy Miller, *Following In His Steps* (Knoxville, Tenn: the University of Tennessee Press, 1987), p. xiii.

11. Ernst Troeltsch, "Historische und dogmatische Methode in der Theologie," *Gesammelte Schriften* (Tübingen: J. C. B. Mohr, 1913), 2:731-738; Troeltsch, "Historiography," *Encyclopedia of Religion and Ethics,* ed. James Hastings (1914), 6:718.

12. *Die Bedeutung der Geschichtlichkeit Jesu für den Glauben* (Tübingen: J.C.B. Mohr, 1911), pp. 1, 15.

13. Ibid., p.1

14. Cf. Carl E. Braaten, "Martin Kähler on The Historic Biblical Christ," *The Historical Jesus And The Kergymatic Christ,* ed. Carl E. Braaten and Roy A. Harrisville (New York: Abingdon Press, 1964), p 80.

15. Martin Kähler, *The So-called Historical Jesus and the Historic, Biblical Christ,* trans. with an introduction by Carl Braaten (Philadelphia: Fortress Press, 1964), p. 127.

16. Cf. Carl E. Braaten, "Martin Kähler on The Historic Biblical Christ," *The Historical Jesus And The Kergymatic Christ,* pp. 79-105.

17. Cf. James Smart, *The Divided Mind of Modern Theology,* (Philadelphia: The Westminster Press, 1967).

18. Karl Barth, *Church Dogmatics,* trans. G. T. Thomson (Edinburgh: T & T. Clark, 1963), 1.1.168.

19. *Church Dogmatics,* 1.1.26-47.

20. Ibid.,1:339.

21. Ibid.

22. Cf. Wolfhart Pannenberg, "Introduction," *Revelation as History,* ed. W. Pannenberg, trans. David Granskou and Edward Quinn (London: Sheed and Ward, 1969), pp. 4-5. W. Pannenberg, *Jesus—God and Man,* trans. Lewis L. Wilkins and Duane A. Priebe (Philadelphia: The Westminster Press, 1968), p. 127.

23. Hegel, *Science of Logic*, trans. W. H. Johnston and L. G. Struthers, with an introductory preface by Vicount Haldane (London: George Allen and Urwin Ltd., 1929), 1: 62.

24. *Grundlehren der Dogmatik als Wissenschaft*, 1827, Paragraph 115, cited by Barth, *Church Dogmatics*, I, 1, 280. Cf. Pannenberg, "Introduction," *Revelation as History*, p. 5.

25. Barth, *Church Dogmatics*, 1.2.489.

26. Pannenberg, "Introduction," *Revelation as History*, p. 6; *Jesus—God and Man*, p. 129.

27. Barth, *Church Dogmatics*, 1.1.465.

28. Ibid., p. 340.

29. Ibid., p. 363.

30. Cf. John McIntyre, *The Christian Doctrine of History* (Edinburgh: Oliver and Boyd, 1957), p. 2. F. Gerald Downing, *Has Christianity a Revelation?* (London: SCM Press, Ltd., 1964), pp. 238-239.

31. Wolfhart Pannenberg, *Systematic Theology*, trans. Geoffrey W. Bromiley (Grand Rapids: Wm. B. Eerdmans, 1988), 1.217-218. Cited hereafter *ST*.

32. ST, 1:217.

33. Paul Tillich, *A History of Christian Thought*, ed. Carl Braaten (New York: Harper, 1972), pp. 243, 250-251.

34. ST, 1:217, 219.

35. Tillich, *A History of Christian Thought*, p. 304.

36. Wesley, *Sermons*, ed. Albert C. Outler (Nashville: Abingdon Press, 1991), "Salvation by Faith," 1:120ff. He referred to the Bible as "infallibly true." Wesley, *Sermons*, ed. Albert C. Outler, "The Means of Grace," 1:388. However, this should not be confused with the 20th century debate over inerrancy. Wesley's confidence in the scriptures was that they are sufficient and reliable. He did not engage in the newly emerging discipline of historical criticism in his day, and in this sense, his hermeneutic was pre-critical. Yet Wesley allowed that the Bible may contain incidental errors. For example, in reference to the genealogy of Jesus in Matthew and Luke, Wesley allowed the gospel writers took "these genealogies, as they stood in those public...records" and they did not attempt to "correct the mistakes" which they may have contained because the point of these "accounts sufficiently answer the end for which they are recited. They unquestionably prove the grand point in view, that Jesus was of the family from which the promised Seed was to come." Wesley, *Explanatory Notes upon the New Testament* (London: Epworth Press, 1958), p. 15. For Wesley, the scriptures are the source of doctrine and "sufficiently" contain the facts of revelation. The truth of the Bible corresponds what it intends to say about the history of salvation, not about incidental details. Wesley wrote in his journal (August 24, 1776) that "if there be any mistakes in the Bible, there may as well be a thousand. If there is one falsehood in that Book, it did not come from the God of truth." Cf. E. H. Sugden, *Wesley's Standard Sermons* (London: Epworth Press, 1961), 1:250n. However, this statement has to be seen in the light of Wesley's other statements,

as, for example, his comments about the genealogies of Jesus in the Gospels where he noted that they might not be entirely accurate. Such an "absolute" statement represents the pastoral concern of an evangelist to show that the scriptures are reliable rather than being a precise, scholarly, critical judgment.

37. H. Orton Wiley, *Christian Theology* (Kansas City, MO: Beacon Hill Press, 1964), 1:139. Wiley affirms that the scriptures are reliable in their overall intent, but he does not affirm their verbal inerrancy. Cf. J. Kenneth Grider, "Wesleyanism and the Inerrancy Issue", *The Wesleyan Theological Journal* 19.2 (Fall 1984): 58.

38. Wiley, *Christian Theology*, p. 137.

39. Ibid., pp. 133ff.

40. Ibid., p. 137.

41. Ibid.

42. Ibid.

43. Pannenberg, "The Crisis of the Scripture Principle," *Basic Questions in Theology*, trans. George H. Kehm (London: SCM Press, 1970) 1:1-14; Pannenberg, *ST*, 1:219ff.

44. *The Quest of the Historical Jesus* (New York: The Macmillan Company, 1954).

45. *Church Dogmatics*, 1.1.339.

46. Pannenberg, "Kerygma and History," *Basic Questions in Theology*, 1:83.

47. *Church Dogmatics*, 1.1.156.

48. Ibid.

49. Ibid.,1.2.499.

50. Ibid.

51. Ibid., p. 491.

52. Ibid., p. 522.

53. Ibid., p. 501.

54. Ibid., p. 490.

55. Ibid., pp. 487ff.

56. Ibid., pp. 499ff.

57. Ibid., p. 513.

58. Ibid., p. 518.

59. Ibid., pp. 473-537.

60. Ibid., p. 521.

61. Ibid., p. 522.

62. Ibid., p. 525.

63. Ibid., p. 523.

64. Ibid., p. 525.

65 Ibid., 1.1.465.

66. Ibid., 1.2.502.

67. Ibid., p. 484.

68. Ibid., p. 464.

69. Rudolf Bultmann. *Essays, Philosophical and Theological,* translated by James

C. G. Greig (London: SCM Press, Ltd., 1955), p. 261.

70. *Church Dogmatics*, 1.2.473.

71. Ibid., 1.2.531. Herein lies the significance of Tillich's statement that Bultmann saved the question of history for theology. Over against Barth who rejected the significance of historical-critical studies for faith, Bultmann rightly re-instated the problem of historical understanding for faith. Whatever opinion one may have concerning Bultmann's existentialist exegesis, it must be admitted that he has shown that one must at least come to terms with the problem of historical understanding. Cf. R. Gregory Smith, *Secular Christianity* (New York: Harper and Row Publishers, 1966), pp. 80-81.

72. *Church Dogmatics.*, 1.2.505.

73. Paul Althaus, *The So-called Kerygma and the Historical Jesus*, trans. David Cairns (Edinburgh: Oliver and Boyd, 1959), p. 25. The necessary change of emphasis today from "kerygma" to the "historical" is illustrated in Althaus' title, *The So-called Historical Jesus and the Kergymatic Christ.*

74. Pannenberg, "Dogmatic Theses on the Doctrine of Revelation," *Revelation As History*, p. 136.

75. Pannenberg, *ST*, 1:237.

76. Ibid. 1:240.

77. Ibid., 1:237; cf. ST, 1:243.

78. Ibid., 1:235.

79. Ibid., 1:222-223.

80. Ibid., 1:229.

81. Ibid., 1:228.

82. Ibid. 1:227.

83. Ibid., 1:243-257.

84. "Introduction," *Revelation as History*, p. 14.

85. Ibid., p. 14.

86. Ibid., p. 15.

87. Ibid., p. 15.

88. Ibid., p. 5.

89. Rolf Rendtorff, "The Concept of Revelation in Ancient Israel," *Revelation as History*, p. 42.

90. Ibid., p. 15.

91. U. Wilkens, "The Understanding of Revelation within the History of Primitive Christianity," *Revelation as History*, p. 77.

92. "Dogmatic Theses on the Doctrine of Revelation," *Revelation as History*, p. 131.

93. Edmond Jacob, *Theology of the Old Testament*, trans. Arthur W. Heathcote and Philip T. Allcock (New York: Harper and Row Publishers, 1958), p. 190.

94. Pannenberg, "Dogmatic Theses on the Doctrine of Revelation," *Revelation as History*, p. 132.

95. Jacob, p. 192.

96. Ibid., p. 193.

97. Ibid.

98. Ibid., pp. 188-189.

99. Rolf Rendtorff, "The Concept of Revelation in Ancient Israel," *Revelation as History*, pp. 45-46.

100. "Dogmatic Theses on the Doctrine of Revelation," *Revelation as History*, pp. 133-134.

101. Cf. Cullmann, *Salvation as History*, p. 202.

102. Pannenberg, "The Revelation of God in Jesus of Nazareth," *Theology As History*, ed. James M. Robinson and John B. Cobb, Jr. (New York: Harper and Row, 1967), p. 116.

103. James Barr, *Old and New in Interpretation, A Study of the Two Testaments* (London: SCM Press, LTD, 1966), 69, 81.

104. Barr, *Old and New in Interpretation*, p. 69.

105. Pannenberg, *ST*, 1:230-231.

106. Ibid., 1:230ff.

107. Postliberalism in particular prefers "narrative," as it will be discussed in chapter 19.

108. Pannenberg, *ST*, 1:231.

109. N. T. Wright, *The Resurrection of the Son of God* (Minneapolis: Fortress Press, 2003), pp. 401-682.

110. Pannenberg, *ST*, 1:232

111. Ibid., 1:232

2

The Modern Historical-Critical Method and Biblical Inspiration

Before the eighteenth century ecclesiastical writers were unaware of the critical historical problems of the biblical text. They simply affirmed the divine authority of Scripture and focused on the divine origin and content of the text. After the Enlightenment, the question arose if a serious theologian can believe that the Bible reports real history. Further, with the rise of historical criticism, can a serious theologian believe in the inspiration of Scripture? The relation between the historical method and biblical inspiration has created serious tensions and ongoing debates within the discipline of theology. This chapter will evaluate the contributions of Oscar Cullmann, Wolfhart Pannenberg, and N. T. Wright on this theme.

Fundamentalism and Biblical Literalism

Fundamentalism is a movement that was begun in the early 1920's in America in opposition to liberal theology. We noted earlier that liberal theology was an attempt to make the "inner life of the historical Jesus" the basis of doing theology. This new method of interpreting the Bible was supposedly a way around the crisis of the Scriptural principle by giving a moral re-interpretation of the life of Jesus. The inner life of Jesus was believed to be invulnerable to historical criticism because it did not appeal to historical miracles as a basis of faith. As already noted, the classic novel representing liberal theology was Charles Sheldon's *In His Steps*. Instead of miracles, such as Jesus' resurrection from the dead, serving as the basis of Christian faith, Sheldon presented the essence of Christian faith in terms of Jesus' example o f love for others. The one sure fact of history which liberal theology assumed was that the real Jesus of history lived a morally exemplary life. Jesus is not the object of faith, but the chief revealer of God's love.[1]

Fundamentalism emerged in opposition to a non-literal and non-miraculous interpretation of the life of Jesus. Fundamentalism is so called because some conservative apologists published a series of tracts called *The Fundamentals: A Testimony to the Truth* between 1910 and 1915. These tracts were mailed out to pastors, educators, missionaries, and lay people around the world, outlining five so-called "fundamentals" of the faith (including verbal inspiration of the Scriptures, the virgin birth, the substitutionary death of Jesus Christ, Jesus' bodily resurrection, and his imminent and visible second coming).[2] However, the primary concern was to defend a biblical concept of inspiration and authority.[3]

Stemming from these tracts, the word fundamentalism became the label for those who were considered theologically conservative. The conflict between liberalism and fundamentalism became severe. Edward E. Hindson points out modernists engaged in 'scientific' scholarship, which the fundamentalists repudiated as humanistic and man-made scholarship. The subsequent battle became a war of words.[4] The conflict turned bitter, and many of the fundamentalists withdrew from mainline denominations and started their own denominations, colleges, and seminaries.

The really distinguishing feature of fundamentalism was not the specific "fundamental" doctrines, which it espoused, but rather it was a movement that reacted to liberalism by adopting a method of interpreting the Bible in a literalistic way. The idea of biblical literalism was linked to a "domino" attitude—that if everything in the Bible were not literally true then everything in it would collapse.

Tillich defined fundamentalism as a primitivized form of classical Orthodoxy.[5] By classical Orthodoxy, Tillich meant the way in which the Reformation resulted in an ecclesiastical form of life and thought following the dynamic movement of the Reformation era. Classical orthodoxy was the systematic formulation and consolidation of the ideas of the Reformation.[6] Tillich saw fundamentalism as the product of a lay biblicism which failed to penetrate the biblical writings in a theologically significant way and thus made itself dependent upon traditional interpretations.[7] Its theology was consequently a superficially borrowed one.

Certainly many of its advocates were respected scholars, such as J. Gresham Machen,[8] a professor of New Testament at Princeton Theological Seminary and one of the founders of Westminster Theological Seminary, and B. B. Warfield,[9] a professor of systematic theology at Princeton Theological Seminary. In general, however, fundamentalism was a lay movement. As such, many of its adherents were not well trained in theology. As a lay movement, its advocates were typically literalistic in their view of things, but this is not surprising considering that the Enlightenment had bequeathed to modern culture the perspective of scientific literalism.[10] Fundamentalism was implicitly modernistic as theological liberalism was explicitly so with both movements assuming a picture theory of meaning. That is, both movements assumed that words must literally picture the nature of things if they report what is true about reality. Biblical literalism is the hallmark of fundamentalism and the bugbear of liberalism, and in both instances literalism is the legacy of Kantianism. One of the contributions of Pannenberg has been to challenge the Kantian positivistic assumption that words literally picture facts—as if there are pure facts that need no interpretation. In particular, Pannenberg has shown that the religious language is largely metaphorical.[11]

American Evangelicalism and Biblical Inspiration

It is customary today to use the label of fundamentalism in a pejorative way when one wants to condemn another's point of view as being too narrow. As a result, the term is no longer very useful. Few contemporary conservative scholars would use it as a term to describe their theological position. Carl F. H. Henry became a prominent spokesman for the inheritors of the fundamentalist movement and he preferred the term, neo-evangelicalism, to highlight a more progressive agenda of openness and dialog within the larger Christian community. Harold J. Ockenga first used the term, "neo-evangelicalism," in a convocation address at Fuller Theological Seminary in 1948.[12] "Evangelicalism" in America is now widely used to describe those who adhere to orthodox belief, but it is largely a movement within the conservative Reformed tradition with an emphasis upon the inspiration and authority of Scripture. The movement generally insists on biblical inerrancy and/or infallibility, but as Donald E. Bloesch, one if its leading proponents and professor of systematic theology at the University of Dubuque Theological Seminary, puts it, "these terms must be qualified" sufficiently in order not to imply an extreme literalism.[13]

However, evangelicalism is a term that has been used in different ways. Luther used it to describe his new movement, the "evangelical church"—which is still used to refer to the Lutheran Church in Germany. Those in the Wesleyan tradition, as well as in the Pentecostal tradition, are evangelical in the original sense in which it was used as a description of the Methodist revival. Its purpose was to revitalize the spiritual life of the Church. Evangelicals in the Wesleyan tradition are particularly interested in spiritual formation. They adhere to the historic Trinitarian faith of the Church, but are less interested than their evangelical Reformed counterparts in disputing contentious issues such as biblical inerrancy and millenarianism.

A more instructive term for categorizing the theology of many contemporary scholars is what I call "post-critical evangelical." Contemporary neo-evangelical theology relies on rational apologetics and propositional revelation with an attempt to prove the existence of God, the inspiration of the Bible, the historicity of the incarnation and resurrection of Jesus. In the 18th century, Wesley minimized the significance of rationality as a conclusive proof for Christian belief. He noted that the greatest proof of Christian faith was the life of believers who exemplify the redeeming grace of God in Jesus Christ, but he was critical of some forms of Pietism which retreated into pious subjectivity and showed disdain for the role of reason.[14] A post-critical evangelical theology agrees largely with the postmodern critique of irrefutable rationality. Post-critical evangelical theology assumes a more modest role of reason, affirming that life must be lived with rational probabilities rather than propositional certainties. Typical of the post-critical evangelicals is Stanley J. Grenz who shows that Luther's primary use of the term, evangelical, referred to the recovery of the gospel message, especially its emphasis on justification by faith.[15] Grenz identifies the pietist tradition as an important element in his understanding of evangelicalism as opposed to much of contemporary evangelicalism, which highlights in a one-sided way propositional doctrine and rigid orthodoxy as the key ingredients of salvation.[16]

Pannenberg and Post-Critical Evangelicalism

Pannenberg is often considered a crypto-fundamentalist largely because of his defense of the bodily resurrection of Jesus, but in actuality, Pannenberg's theology assumes a radical historical-critical method that is incompatible with a literalist reading of the Bible. His criticism of fundamentalism is that it involves itself in an unnecessary fear that God's revelation will be lost if we apply historical criticism to the Bible. At a conference at Asbury Theological Seminary in 1991, Pannenberg made this point in reply to a question about historical criticism: "That's my criticism of fundamentalism, of those who want to draw a fence around the Scriptures in order to defend them from the application of critical reflection. This is an indication of too little faith. Too little faith in God. If His revelation is true, He will take care of that Himself. Not we."[17]

If Pannenberg is not a crypto-fundamentalist, how should his theology be labeled? He is not a crypto-liberal because he affirms the realism of salvation history. He is not an existentialist theologian like Bultmann who identifies the "self" of *self*-revelation with the human self rather the "self" of a transcendent being.[18] He is not a neo-orthodox theologian because he sees historical events as the primary means of divine revelation instead of words. He is not a typical *Heilsgeschichte* theologian because the concept of salvation history has often been used to imply that the realism of God's acts in history is something other than real events in the world. The label, "new conservative"[19] does not fit Pannenberg either because he does not accept the doctrine of the virgin birth or the infallibility of the Scriptures. Pannenberg does not attempt to classify his own theology with any particular label, but it is clear that his real intent is to provide a post-critical version of the Trinitarian theology of the Cappadocian Fathers and their focus on the history of salvation.[20]

Post-critical evangelicals have generally welcomed Pannenberg's integration of critical history and faith along with his defense of Trinitarian orthodoxy.[21] So long as history was dominated by the historicist presupposition that irrefutable facts could be uncovered out of the dead remains of the past, faith and history were estranged from each other. Pannenberg has shown that critical history should have the more responsible task of providing provisional answers based on the logic of probability, not absolute certainties.

Pannenberg's strength is that he has consistently insisted on the centrality of history as the basis of faith, and certainly no systematic theologian has taken the biblical text more seriously than Pannenberg. Indeed it could be argued that he takes the biblical text more seriously than the "Word of God" theologians (like Bultmann and Barth) because he insists on the realism of salvation history. Evidence of his being serious about the Bible as the Word of God is seen in his reliance upon the Scriptures as the exegetical foundation of his thinking. His writings abound with biblical references and expositions. His classic treatise on Christology is an unrelenting, historical-critical analysis and exposition of the New Testament in dialog with contemporary New Testament scholarship.[22] If Bultmann criticized Barth because he had no "principle of selection," the same cannot be said about Pannenberg who insists on the theological relevance of historical criticism.

He rejects biblical authoritarianism and insists that the historical method is the basis for reading the Bible in a theological way. If the Biblical writers interpret events in the life of Jesus in a certain way, including the affirmation that Jesus was declared to be the Son of God by his resurrection from the dead (Roman 1:4), then the critical theologian today cannot set those claims aside as if they were obviously mythical; rather, the critical scholar must not allow one's own philosophical presuppositions to predetermine the outcome of critical research—if one is truly critical in the best sense of the term. It is required of the critical historian to look at the evidence and to see the reasons why the New Testament writers affirmed that Jesus was really raised from the dead. In this sense, Pannenberg affirms that the Bible contains the Word of God because it is a responsible report of what God has said and done regarding the foundational events of Christian faith.

Historical Events and the Word of God

Pannenberg points out that there are three principal meanings of the "Word of God" in Scripture.[23] First, there is the Word of God as promise. However, the prophetic word is not established as proof of God's divinity until its fulfillment in history has come about (I Kings 22:28; Deut. 18:9-22; Jer. 28:6-9). Second, there is the Word of God as forthtelling. As such, the function of the word is to proclaim God's Law and commandments. Third, the Word of God is designated as the apostolic kerygma in the New Testament, which is the primary meaning of the Word of God in the New Testament. Pannenberg says the message of the apostles was called the Word of God because it was based on the appearance of Jesus (Gal. 1:12, 15f). As the Word of God, the message of Jesus was not something initiated with human beings, but with God. The Word of God as apostolic proclamation was a report of the event of Jesus Christ in which God was revealed. This emphasis on historical event is expressed in such genitive constructions as "word of the cross," and "word of redemption." This report does not intend to be an objective and detached chronological "reporting" of things that happened, but rather they intend to be a "proclamation" of what happened.[24] Fact and interpretation are inextricably linked.

The kerygmatic proclamation entails the "universal notification" of God's act in Jesus; otherwise revelation would not result. Equally important is the realization that the kerygma does not "add" something to this revelation, but rather the kerygma is to be seen in the light of its historical content.[25] This means the kerygma as the Word of God has revelatory significance only to the extent that it points to a real person in history, Jesus. This further means the word has no autonomous status. The significance of the word lies in what it declares.

Pannenberg rejects the idea of modernist Christology which takes its starting point in contemporary Christian experience or in an uncritical acceptance of the kerygma of the primitive church. The validation of Christian faith is to be decided on the basis of its historical content, not on the mere proclamation of the kerygma. The content of faith relates to what Jesus was and then secondarily to what he is today for the believer. For Pannenberg, this means that Christology must depend on the historical method for critically reconstructing the events of Jesus' life. Christian doctrine is essentially a historical construct, based on the historical figure of Jesus Christ and on the critical evaluation of the testimony of the early Christian proclamation.[26] In particular, Pannenberg believes if we can trust the report of Jesus' resurrection as a reliable account of what really happened, then we are able to pray in sincerity to the exalted and living Lord.[27] He argues that theology can only show the truth claim of Christian faith as it goes back behind the kerygma to the events themselves. Pannenberg believes the kerygma invites this kind of critical examination because it is a report of events that are said to have happened. The New Testament must thus be taken as a historical source and not only as a preaching text.[28]

Because he believes the means of making certain the revelation of God in Jesus of Nazareth is through the historical method,[29] Pannenberg does not subscribe to an authoritarian concept of the "Word of God," which would have the effect of suppressing critical rationality and compelling belief. This is why he denies revelation is the product of verbal inspiration. Until the Enlightenment, the Bible had been more or less identified as the Word of God, which was conceived as supernaturally inspired. In neo-Orthodoxy and existentialist theology, revelation was no longer identified with the Bible, but with the Word of God as kerygmatic proclamation (Bultmann) or as Jesus Christ who is the source of the preached and the written word (Barth).[30] Pannenberg says the modern shift from the orthodox concept of revelation to neo-orthodoxy and existentialist theology left intact the idea of authoritarianism because the theology of the Word of God is not something that can be critically examined. However, for those who live after the Enlightenment, authoritarian claims are unacceptable and all truth claims must be subjected to critical rationality.[31] Pannenberg thus says he rejected authoritarian theologies in the interest of preserving the realism of salvation history.[32]

To be sure, Pannenberg admits that authoritarianism is a characteristic feature of both the Old and New Testaments, that the prophets conceived of their message as the authoritative Word of God and that the apostles (especially Paul) identified their message as the authoritative Word of God. Such authoritarianism is characteristic of episcopal and papal claims, as well as the Reformers' *sola scriptura*. However, Pannenberg sees the Enlightenment's demand for individual freedom over against all forms of authority the mature result of Christian faith itself.[33] He wants to separate the authentic biblical experiences of God (in the sense of being verifiable) from the authoritarian claims of the Bible itself. Pannenberg believes the Protestant Scripture principle has been dissolved. What is theologically normative is not the biblical texts themselves, but the historically verifiable events, which the texts report.[34]

Some have complained that Pannenberg is developing a works-righteousness theology with his idea that the theologian must be able to verify in principle the historical events of revelation. Pannenberg's reply is that the believer who tries to answer the feelings of doubt through the act of faith itself is already engaged in self-deceptive works-righteousness.[35] Pannenberg wants to guard theology against the charge of illusion in Feuerbach's or Freud's sense that the idea of God is merely a projection of human potential and desire.[36]

Pannenberg makes it quite clear that he is not intending to lessen the ministry of the Holy Spirit in the life of the believer. In reply to John Cobb's criticism,[37] Pannenberg denied that he intends to question the immediacy of God's actions in the life of believers.[38] His third volume of systematic theology is a carefully developed doctrine of the Holy Spirit in which he underscores the importance of "the immediacy of Individuals to Jesus Christ."[39] Cobb's criticism is prompted by Pannenberg's insistence that a direct self-*manifestation* of God[40] in the form of a verbal communication is not truly revelation for us, except as it can be "confirmed" to be true on the basis of its traditio-historical context.[41] What Pannenberg insists upon is the integration of word and event as constituting together the meaning of revelation.

Against the Word of God theology in Bultmann and Barth, Pannenberg shows that *events* are the primary focus of revelation, while *words* interpret, report, and empower their meaning to be appropriated in a personal way. He says historical events speak a language of their own—the language of facts.[42] These are not naked facts because these events can be properly interpreted only in the context of the tradition and history that produced them. However, one should not impose an interpretation on these facts that does not naturally arise.[43] Here Pannenberg is arguing that the revelation of God in the Scriptures does not need to be protected by any theory of inspiration, but its meaning and truth are self-evident to historical reasoning.

Does Pannenberg believe in biblical inspiration? The answer is no, if one is thinking of inspiration in the sense that the *interpretation* of the events in salvation history is externally tacked on by supernatural insight.[44] Nor does he believe in inspiration in the unique sense that the Holy Spirit guarantees the reliability of the record. Although he sees no need for a special theory of biblical inspiration, he affirms the importance of the Holy Spirit for accepting the knowledge of revelation. Pannenberg vigorously denied a criticism that he substituted the historical method for the inspiration of the Holy Spirit, calling it a crude caricature of his position and so obviously false that he should not even have to respond to it.[45]

In deflecting this criticism, he highlighted that personal faith is not at all dependent upon the results of biblical scholarship, but rather trust in the Jesus of the Scriptures is what assures one of salvation.[46] On the other hand, the purpose of biblical scholarship is to assure one about the logic of faith, and in this regard Pannenberg says that the discipline of theology always entails the historical method because the self-revelation of God has occurred in history.[47] He will not tolerate any divorce between theology and history or between faith and knowledge. Although scholarship may threaten faith with the loss of its basis in history, this is no reason to insulate oneself from critical thought. Even if there were a real contradiction between faith and knowledge, faith would not be served with a rejection of reason.[48] Further, knowledge is never simply a matter of an intellectualist proposition or rational insight, but rather knowledge involves the whole person—including one's response to the Word of God and personal trust in Christ. One truly knows God when intellectual understanding and personal trust are joined together.

More specifically, Pannenberg affirms that the Holy Spirit is inherent in the words of Scriptures and that faith in Christ is available to all who hear it regardless of their theological sophistication. He writes: "The word itself brings the Spirit with it."[49] This idea that the word itself is inherently Spirit-filled is typically Lutheran and not unique to Pannenberg's theology.[50]

Form Criticism and the Doctrine of Biblical Inspiration

If Barthian theology placed one-sided emphasis upon the "word" as the medium of revelation, Pannenberg moves in the other direction of not adequately affirming the Scriptures' self-understanding of being uniquely inspired of God. He also completely ignores Jesus' view of scriptural inspiration. Belief in the inspiration of Scripture is a basic assumption of the Bible, as stated in 2 Timothy 3:16: "All scripture is inspired by God." Phrases like "It is written" (Matt. 26:24), Scripture says" (John 19:24), and "God says" (Matt. 15:4) are used interchangeably in Scripture.

The fundamental meaning of inspiration is that revelation has been reliably interpreted and preserved in the biblical texts.[51] This does not entail the idea of *verbal* inspiration as if the very words of the Bible were dictated by the Holy Spirit bypassing the personal characteristics and foibles of the writers; rather, biblical inspiration is *dynamical* in the broader sense that the writers faithfully recorded and interpreted the events of revelation without setting aside their human frailties and characteristics.[52] Pannenberg believes the idea of biblical inspiration makes the historical method irrelevant, but this seems to be an overreaction to Barthianism. To be sure, Pannenberg also believes that God proactively preserves his revelation in the biblical witness,[53] but he does not link this providential oversight to the idea of biblical inspiration.

Oscar Cullmann (1902-1999) was an older contemporary of Pannenberg, and he was well known as the chief advocate of the theology of salvation history in his day. He was internationally respected as a New Testament scholar whose work in form criticism served as an alternative to Bultmann's form criticism. Pannenberg often cited from Cullmann's form critical studies, though he more often used the results of Bultmannian form criticism. If Pannenberg rejected the doctrine of biblical inspiration and if Barth suppressed the question of critical history, Cullmann integrated both of them

Form criticism, or form-historical method, emerged after Albert Schweitzer's *Quest of the Historical Jesus* in 1900 exposed the failure of various rationalist attempts to write a life of Jesus based on Enlightenment presuppositions. The basic idea of this quest was that the gospels were literary sources for writing the life of Jesus, but they needed to be stripped of their miraculous interpretations and reinterpreted in a naturalistic way. After the failure of this movement, younger scholars turned their attention to unwritten sources, which were believed to have been used to compose the gospels. These unwritten sources were believed to be fixed forms of orally transmitted traditions called pericopae. These oral traditions were shaped by and designed to meet the particular life situation and theological needs of the Christian community. Bultmann divided up these stylized forms into two broad categories— the sayings of Jesus and the narrative material (stories about Jesus). The sayings of Jesus include —(1) short pithy sayings or aphorisms and parables of Jesus, (2) conflict dialogs, and (3) apophthegm (a story used to illustrate a saying). (4) The narrative material includes historical stories and legends.[54]

These oral traditions were significant because they provided short summaries in which the life of Jesus was preserved in fixed form, memorized, and circulated among the Christian communities. The gospel writers were not so much authors as collectors of these oral traditions, putting them together in an organized fashion and using them as sources for writing the gospels. The term, form criticism, comes from a book written by Martin Dibelius in 1919, *Die Formgeschichte des Evangeliums* that means "the form history of the gospels." Dibelius was a pioneer of form criticism.[55]

The rise of form-critical analysis of the New Testament halted the attempt to write a life of Jesus because it was believed that no judgment could be made about the historical factuality of these short summaries. Hence the early form critics remained neutral on the question of critical history.[56] However, Bultmann's influential book, *History of the Synoptic Tradition* (1921), introduced a very negative view about the reliability of these forms. Instead of reporting history, these oral traditions were a way of doing theology in story form (myth). Bultmann also introduced the criterion of dissimilarity for determining which of the forms represented Jesus' teachings. That is, if a saying is different from the gospel writer's own style and ideas, and if the saying is unique within its Hellenistic background, then it can be concluded that it is authentic saying of Jesus.[57] Using this criterion, Bultmann believed there were only forty sayings that were authentic.[58]

Cullmann often pointed out that Bultmann's skeptical results were not due to form criticism, but rather to the Heideggerian existentialist presuppositions, which he superimposed on his analysis of the biblical text.[59] To be sure, Cullmann is keenly aware of the difficulty of distinguishing in the kerygma between what the apostles received from Jesus himself and the new interpretation that they placed upon his life in the light of his resurrection. It is generally recognized among form critics that the gospels are not intended to be like a modern biography, as though they were giving us an in-depth view of Jesus as he appeared to his contemporaries. In other words, the idea of a red-lettered New Testament, highlighting the very words of Jesus is a misunderstanding of the nature of the gospel texts. Rather the kerygma is confessional in nature; its intent is to show that Jesus is the Son of God. The gospel traditions were recognized as confessions of faith, which were developed out of the needs of the communities of faith (*Sitz im Leben*).

Does this mean that Bultmann is right to have a skeptical attitude about the possibility of knowing who Jesus really was and what he thought of himself? Cullmann believes that an analysis of these oral traditions has enabled the New Testament scholar today to get back to the real historical Jesus with some degree of success so that they can determine with adequate probability what Jesus taught and believed about himself. That is, using the criteria of form-critical analysis, the biblical scholar is now able to identify when the Gospel writers record their own view and when they report the words of Jesus himself.[60]

Of course, the modern distinction between interpretation and event was not a matter of critical concern to the early Church. While they were very much interested to know the truth about Jesus, it never occurred to them to make a sharp distinction between the Jesus of history and the Christ of faith. Bultmann drove a wedge between the historical Jesus and "faith in Christ." He believed the Christ of faith was a creation of the Christian community, which used Hellenistic ideas to interpret Jesus Christ.[61] Cullmann's constructive work in form criticism, on the other hand, was an impressive refutation of Bultmann's excessive historical skepticism, which was steeped in existentialist presuppositions. Cullmann insisted that the Old Testament and the Jewish social setting was the basis for interpreting the historical Jesus rather than the heavy influence of Hellenistic culture.[62] Furthermore, he insisted that the oral traditions, which formed the basis of the gospels, were not secondary accretions created simply by the needs of the various Christian communities. To be sure, the Church put words in the mouth of the historical Jesus. However, it used genuine sayings of Jesus for this purpose, and these additions were consistent with its own tendencies.[63] Cullmann argued that the early Church reinterpreted the traditions about Jesus based on Jesus' resurrection, which provided a new perspective through which the historical Jesus could be more properly viewed, but they did not superimpose an interpretation upon the traditions that was not inherent in them.

Based on the studies of H. Riesenfeld, *The Gospel Tradition and its Beginnings. A Study in the Limits of Formgeschicthe* (1957) and B. Gerhardsson, *Memory and Manuscript, Oral Tradition and Written Transmission in Rabbinic Judaism and Early Christianity* (1961), Cullmann noted that in the rabbinic schools in Jesus' day the very words of rabbis would be carefully learned by their pupils in fixed oral forms. Similarly, the disciples preserved the words of Jesus.[64] Cullmann complained that Bultmann's form-critical method was arbitrary because it assumed these traditions were merely formed by various early Christian communities ("community formations") based on their religious prejudices rather than being real history.[65] Instead of a break between the Jesus of history and the Christ of faith, Cullmann argued that the Christ of faith is the historical Jesus who died and rose again.

Cullmann was not a systematic theologian, but as a biblical scholar he intentionally avoided philosophical and systematic theological categories. He believed the Early Church Fathers were doing something improper when they sought to integrate Greek philosophy with the apostolic faith. This is because Cullmann believed the Church Fathers subordinated the saving history of Jesus to the question about "natures."[66] Cullmann insisted that the doctrine of Christ is about events and not about philosophically abstract concepts like "natures."[67] He rejected speculations about substance and natures because the method of philosophy contradicts the method of salvation history.[68] Cullmann says the New Testament is not directly concerned with Jesus' nature, but with his function.[69] He was also mildly critical of Pannenberg for relying on philosophy, but otherwise Cullmann respected him for his advocacy of the history of revelation.[70]

Cullmann particularly disagreed with the way that Bultmann's form criticism is tied to the philosophy of existence. Bultmann's concept of self-understanding as the essence of faith is forced upon the New Testament kerygma as a substitute for salvation history. Cullmann pleaded for fairness and openness in the form-critical analysis of the biblical traditions as opposed to Bultmann's presupposition that no one living in the modern age could possibly believe in miracles; hence, Bultmann argues the oral traditions could not possibly reveal who the real Jesus is because they are bound up with miraculous events.

Cullmann did not agree with Bultmann's belief that the various oral forms in the early Christian tradition functioned as "independent monographs." Rather they were linked together through their relation to salvation history, which served as a kind of thread holding all the distinct parts together as a larger whole.[71] He also contended that the life of Jesus was based on Jesus' own self-consciousness and in the faith that Jesus' inspired among his followers.[72]

Cullmann's critique of systematic theology reflected his concern that philosophical presuppositions were often used to distort the message of the New Testament, as in Bultmann's form critical analysis. He also wanted to highlight the importance of "functional" language in explaining what Jesus thought of himself. He believed that an appreciation of the relational language of the New Testament avoids the implications of a metaphysical way of speaking of Jesus, which has clouded our perception to see the real historical Jesus for who he was. As opposed to the categories of systematic theology, Cullmann analyzed the titles in the New Testament to describe Jesus' relationship to God, such as "Son of God," "Son of Man," "Messiah," etc. To what extent were these titles superimposed upon Jesus by the faith of the primitive church rather than being titles, which Jesus explicitly embraced? Cullmann argued that the messianic implication of these titles was derived from Jesus himself.[73]

One of the premises of Bultmann's form criticism is that these oral traditions excluded the possibility of eyewitness testimony. He calls the Easter event the product of "devout imagination."[74] Cullmann disputed this assumption by arguing that there were those present in the early Christian community who knew Jesus personally (including the apostles) and who could have corrected oral confessions if they contained wrong information.[75]

Cullmann also showed that these confessions contained references to a chain of traditions in which revelatory events are to be interpreted. This chain begins with the traditions of Abraham, Moses, and the prophets and continues on with the New Testament traditions. Each new tradition in this link is assimilated into the earlier tradition in such a way that the flow of events cast light back upon previous events, as the old is interpreted anew.[76] In this way, the history of salvation from the Old Testament to the New Testament is continuous flow of interpretations until the goal of saving history reached its goal in Jesus' resurrection.

The significance of understanding this chain of traditions is that earlier traditions can be more properly understood from the standpoint of their future developments.[77] Hence Cullmann argued that the real person of Jesus could not be understood until *after* the resurrection of Jesus. This does not mean that the disciples placed a different interpretation on the life of Jesus than Jesus had himself; rather that the life and words of Jesus were more fully appreciated and understood. Cullmann thus argued Bultmann failed to see that the events in the life of Jesus and their interpretation formed part of the proclamation of Jesus and that the disciples were able to see their true meaning for the first time after Jesus' resurrection.

The Johannine concept that the Holy Spirit would inspire the disciples to remember the teachings of Jesus as he had promised "is a particularly apt expression"[78] for explaining how this process came about. On the basis of himself being inspired by the Paraclete, the fourth evangelist was convinced that his Christological interpretation of the words that he attributed to Jesus brought out "in their full richness and ultimate refinement" the things that Jesus had taught the disciples.[79]

What about the claims of Jesus in John's gospel that "I and the Father are one" (John 10:3)? Is this a claim that the historical Jesus explicitly made? Or is this claim only attributed to Jesus by John? Both questions reflect a misunderstanding. Cullmann maintained that a form-critical analysis of John's gospel shows that this claim is based on Jesus' self-understanding as the Son of God even though the pericope itself is more explicit than what Jesus may have literally said.[80] John was not interested in reproducing the Jesus whom he knew before the resurrection, but rather he intended to interpret the historical Jesus as seen from the perspective of the resurrection.

Cullmann defined this reinterpretation of the life of Jesus a "Christological epistemology." It was an epistemology of the Holy Spirit reminding the evangelist of the teaching of Jesus so that he was able to interpret the life of Jesus properly. The resurrection of Jesus from the dead showed him to be the Son of God (Romans 1:4) and it refocused the earlier events of his life so that they were seen from the perspective of Easter. This is the central interpretative event, which put everything in the chain of traditions into proper perspective, from Abraham to Jesus.[81]

Cullmann also shows that it was the disciples themselves who linked the earthly Jesus to the risen Lord. The uniqueness of their situation is that they were eyewitnesses who linked the teachings of the historical Jesus and the new events surrounding his resurrection. In this way, the disciples were witnesses of the incarnate Jesus and the exalted Christ, and significantly they proclaimed the exalted Lord as continuing the work of the incarnate Lord.[82] Cullmann makes the point that the traditions about Jesus that were shaped by the early Christian communities were based on the apostolic kerygma.

Pannenberg also argues that the form-critical method has shown that

Jesus' self-consciousness included knowledge that he was one with God, not in the metaphysical sense of being the second Person of the Trinity, but rather "Jesus knew himself functionally...to be one with God himself."[83] Pannenberg further notes that "if the pre-Easter Jesus had not been related at all to his unity with God in his self-consciousness, then ...he would not be one with himself and *to that extent* not one with God."[84] Pannenberg acknowledges the difficulty of determining the self-consciousness of Jesus by means of the form-critical method, but, he says: "If Jesus is essentially one with God as person and thus in the whole of his concrete human life—even though this unity was ultimately decided and came finally to light only in the resurrection—this cannot take place entirely outside Jesus' pre-Easter life and consciousness. If this were the case, one could not properly speak of a unity of his whole existence with God."[85] Pannenberg further notes, in a significant way, that a person "normally has some sort of knowledge about what constitutes his being a self."[86] Otherwise, one "lives in self-contradiction because it is essentially constitutive for the self that it have consciousness of itself."[87] Of course, human beings do live in self-contradiction according the doctrine of original sin. Some live in self-contradiction because of mental illness, but Jesus is proclaimed as both sinless and the norm of human life. Pannenberg thus reasons that to think of Jesus, as living in contradiction to his true essence during his earthly existence, would be deny that he was truly God.[88]

In the light of Jesus' unique understanding of himself as one with God as his Father, Pannenberg believes the resurrection confirms his self-understanding and demonstrates that Jesus really is God. The further significance of the resurrection is that it shows that Jesus was with God from eternity.[89] Although the historical Jesus was self-aware of his unity with God, the full implications of his claim did not come into full view until after the resurrection.[90]

In contrast to Pannenberg, Cullmann noted that Jesus had promised that the Holy Spirit would come upon the disciples after his death/resurrection and that the Holy Spirit would enable them to be faithful interpreters of who he is. Cullmann shows that the primary idea in John's Gospel is that the meaning of Jesus' life made its full impact upon the disciples only after his death. This is spoken of in terms of a "remembering" because of the Paraclete who was promised to lead them "in the truth."[91] In this way, Cullmann believed it is appropriate to say the words and deeds of Jesus are based on "the exalted Lord himself."[92]

This means "the *full* revelation" of the significance of Jesus' life was first known to the early Church in the light of Easter.[93] The form-critical method shows the disciples transmitted the preaching of Jesus and at the same time interpreted it anew in the light of his resurrection.[94] Consequently, Cullmann believed the disciples' recollection of Jesus' life and preaching as being made possible through the Spirit is a particularly good Johannine expression.[95] For Jesus authorized and approved in advance of his death the New Testament kerygma, and John believed his own gospel writing was fulfilling this prediction.

Pannenberg rejected the significance of this Johannine concept of biblical inspiration, and I think inconsistently so. If Pannenberg believes that the historical method demonstrates with a high degree of probability that Jesus was raised from the dead, thus confirming his claim to be one with God, in like manner, does not the resurrection also give us reason to believe Jesus' statement that his disciples would be his faithful interpreters after the Holy Spirit came upon them. In this sense, Cullmann has demonstrated that belief in biblical inspiration is reasonably based and consistent with historical criticism. Cullmann believed it is responsible to believe that the gospels give a substantially reliable portrayal of the life of Jesus, including the report of Jesus' virgin birth.

In his treatise on systematic theology, Pannenberg has offered a helpful guide in understanding the history of the development of the doctrine of inspiration and the role it has played in the life of the Church.[96] He shows that the rise of historical criticism created seemingly insoluble problems for the Protestant doctrine of biblical inspiration (the Scripture principle) in view of new scientific and historical evidence that emerged during the period of the Enlightenment.[97] He points out that subsequent attempts of "accommodation" with historical criticism have become "increasingly hollow,"[98] including Barth's notion of the self-authenticating Word of God in Scripture. He says that the intent of the doctrine of biblical inspiration was to offer an advanced guarantee to the reader of the Bible that its teachings are true. However, Pannenberg concludes that systematic theology does not need this guarantee.[99]

Not only does Pannenberg believe the importance and relevance of the doctrine of biblical inspiration have been greatly exaggerated, more importantly, he believes it serves as a liability to faith when used to suppress an open, honest, and critical inquiry into the nature of the Bible. Whatever the collapse of the doctrine of biblical inspiration might mean for the Church, there is one thing that Pannenberg is certain of—this collapse did not mean the collapse of the truth of Christian doctrine.[100]

It can be argued that Pannenberg's systematic theology is the most convincing treatment and defense of Christian doctrine since the Enlightenment. He has shown that the Trinitarian faith is well based in the apostolic tradition, and he does so without appealing to authoritarian sources or ideas that would preclude an honest, critical investigation into the truth claims of the Bible.

Pannenberg is also right to show that the problems raised by historical criticism concerning the irreconcilable phenomena in Scripture cannot be set aside. However, a more serious problem emerges regarding those events in Scripture, which are not available for critical assessment by the historical method. To discount these events as mere story or legend, as Pannenberg does, leads to an impoverished understanding of the history of salvation.

Even though many things reported as events in the Bible do not fall under the category of being historically verifiable, Cullmann said that it is consistent with the historical method to include them as real events. Because these *historically uncontrollable events* are often so intertwined with *historically controllable events,* it is impossible at times to differentiate the controllable from the uncontrollable events. Cullmann chooses to speak of events, such as, the creation, fall of Adam, the second coming of Jesus, etc., as "historical myths," i.e., events which are divine events though *real* events which do not come under what is *historically controllable.* These occurrences, which are historically uncontrollable events, nevertheless "really *happen"* and are not simply metaphysical or nontemporal.[101] What Cullmann calls *historically uncontrollable events* are what Pannenberg calls *story* or *legend.* Cullmann referred to them as "historicized myths" because they are actual events though they are not historically controllable and thus they are not mere stories or legends.

Because events play such a prominent role in the biblical revelation, this makes historical-critical research necessary, and Cullmann believed that it is incumbent upon the scholar to be intellectually honest. Cullmann noted that just as eye witnessing was the basis of the apostolic faith, so historical-critical research precedes the faith of the exegete today.[102] Cullmann pointed out that what does fall under the category of being historically controllable indirectly confirms those parts, such as the creation, the eschaton, etc., which are not under historical control. Especially the witness of the prophets and the apostles are the key to faith in that they stand in close proximity to revelatory events. Cullmann maintained that the apostles' eyewitness testimony is more important than the other biblical witnesses because their witness contained the decisive events associated with Jesus Christ. In this way their witness indirectly guarantees the revelations of all the previous witnesses.[103]

Cullmann illustrated the distinction between the historically controllable and the historically uncontrollable elements of the biblical witness in reference to Jesus' resurrection. In itself, the resurrection is not capable of direct historical control, although it is connected to facts which are at least capable of proof within the historical framework—the resurrection appearances and the empty tomb.[104] On the basis of the apostle's testimony, one can affirm the bodily resurrection of Jesus from the dead, while acknowledging such an affirmation is not subject to a direct historical demonstration, though nevertheless it is a valid historical statement.

What Cullmann has argued is that the knowledge upon which faith has its point of departure does not altogether qualify as historically controllable knowledge. This is not to bring in the Holy Spirit as a stop-gap for ignorance, but it is a fundamental recognition of the cognitive aspect of faith, i.e., the inspiration of the Holy Spirit. To be sure, if one only relies upon the inspiration and testimony of the Holy Spirit without a corresponding emphasis upon a critical historical understanding, then Pannenberg is justified in saying that such a faith may possibly be self-deluded.

It is also important to see that faith in Christ involves faith in the *witness* of the prophets and the apostles. Faith in Christ entails an acceptance of the credibility of the witnesses of divine revelation, who themselves stand in a relationship to the witness of their predecessors, which culminates in the final witness of the apostles to Jesus Christ. This chain of witnesses to divine revelation, which culminates in the witness of the apostles, is the basis for Cullmann's belief that the apostles' witness guarantees in an indirect manner the revelations of all the previous witnesses."[105] Without historical criticism, this faith in the witness of the apostles would be a blind faith in authority, and yet historical criticism is inadequate without the divine inspiration of the Scriptures. Cullmann as a form-critical scholar demonstrates that the idea of biblical inspiration should not be viewed as being in competition with the historical critical method.

N. T. Wright and the Historical Critical Method

In recent years, a third quest for the historical Jesus has been inaugurated. The first quest for the historical Jesus was based on the liberal assumption that Jesus was a teacher of universal principles and values.

The emergence of form criticism assumed the quest for the historical Jesus was not possible given the kind of confessional material in the gospels, and with Bultmann the form critical method became associated with outright skepticism about the historical Jesus. The second quest was begun in 1953 by Bultmann's former students who believed it was important to show that Jesus as a teacher embodied the values which he proclaimed so that he could be seen as a model of faith. [106] This new quest was more or less stagnant until it was renewed with the "Jesus Seminar," formed by a group of North American scholars in 1985. They discussed each of the sayings of Jesus and then voted on whether or not they were authentic.[107] Cullmann had mentioned such a practice among Continental European scholars, noting that at least English scholars had not "made use of this cheap argument."[108] Now American scholars have followed up with their own measurement of authentic sayings by counting the verdicts for or against authentic sayings. This "Jesus Seminar" movement remains relatively negative about what could be really known about Jesus, depending heavily upon modernist presuppositions connected with Bultmannian form criticism.[109]

The third quest of the historical Jesus is composed of recent New Testament scholars who believe that through the use of the historical method a reliable picture of Jesus will emerge.[110] Participants in this quest range vary considerably in their theological and historical judgments, but they are generally optimistic about rediscovering who the pre-Easter Jesus really was. They are also less dependent upon Bultmannian form critical presuppositions. One of the distinguishing features of this group of scholars is their rejection of a modernist epistemology and its positivistic view of historical criticism in biblical studies.[111]

N. T. Wright is an Anglican bishop and a highly profiled British New Testament scholar who is a leader of this third quest. Wright's groundbreaking and remarkable scholarship as seen in his *Jesus and the Victory of God* has already occasioned a detailed response by the leading New Testament scholars in the English-speaking world.[112]

Bultmann believed the gospels were based on oral traditions, shaped by the early Church communities who were enmeshed in a Hellenistic culture. Thus the gospels do not give us a true account of Jesus as a Palestinian Jew, but rather they used Jesus as a basis for developing their own theological ideas that they shared with other Mediterranean cultures. Wright describes Bultmann's form critical method as creating a "deJudaized Jesus preaching a demythologized, 'vertical' eschatology."[113] Over against this, Wright believes the newer evidence emerging in New

Testament studies has shown that the earliest traditions of Jesus reflected in the gospels are written from the perspective of Second Temple Judaism.[114] More specifically, Wright insists that Jesus must be interpreted from the standpoint of Jewish eschatology and apocalypticism as these themes pertain to the kingdom of God.[115] He shows that Jesus words and actions are consistent with his Jewish context, and with the social-cultural world of Galilee.[116]

Wright also shows that the gospel traditions do not present a modern-style biography, but rather the Gospels are Jewish-style biographies and intend to show how the story of Israel was re-enacted in the single life of Jesus. So the Gospels tell the story of Jesus as though his life was the history of Israel in miniature.[117] Contrary to the assumption of Bultmannian form criticism, the theological intent of these Jewish-style biographies intend to give us a true picture of the real Jesus of history. Wright believes these "biographies" provide us with reliable records of the way Jesus perceived himself. He shows that an interest in "what actually happened" is not just a modern question.[118]

Unlike Bultmann who existentialized faith by divorcing it from the historical Jesus, Wright integrates faith and history, showing that theology is very much related to the work of the critical historian. It is not the case that the theologian has to rely upon a philosophy of existence, or any philosophy for that matter, in order to reconstruct the relevance of the past. If the historical critical method discovers that the life and words of Jesus break down all of our preconceptions of what constitutes reality, then a new metaphysic will be needed to replace them.[119] In other words, form critics generally superimpose their theological preconceptions upon the confessions of the early Church, thus compromising their task as critical historians. An example of this is Marcus J. Borg who is one of the "Jesus Seminar" participants. He argues against Wright's acceptance of miracles really happening in the life of Jesus on the grounds that Borg cannot accept as real history the report that Jesus was able to do things "without parallel anywhere else." He calls this attitude a "metahistorical" point of view.[120]

Long before the rise of the third quest, Pannenberg offered a probing critique of the historical method in an essay, "Redemptive Event and History" (1959).[121] He called for a readjustment of the principles of the historical method that had been classically articulated by Ernst Troeltsch. In particular, Pannenberg refuted the modernist concept of anthropocentrism, which excluded consideration of a transcendent reality acting in history.[122] Pannenberg's proposal for the integration of critical history and theology helped to prepare the way for the current optimism about rediscovering the historical Jesus. Although the contributions of Oscar Cullmann in emphasizing the realism of salvation history are significant, Pannenberg was the first theologian successfully to take on the Bultmannians and to challenge their basic existentialist assumptions, which distorted the historical-critical method and concealed the real Jesus of history. His work, *Jesus—God and Man* (1968), was a thorough investigation into the life of Jesus based on form critical studies, and he demonstrated that the real Jesus of history became the resurrected Lord. His work thus anticipated and cleared the way for the third quest.

Wright, in this respect, recognizes that Pannenberg is one who got it right about the importance of Jewish eschatology and apocalypticism for understanding the historical Jesus.[123] When Pannenberg first proposed this way of interpreting the historical Jesus, he was immediately criticized for it because the prevailing assumption of form criticism at that time was that apocalypticism was not truly Jewish.[124] The third quest of the historical Jesus has now made the Jewish concept of eschatology and apocalypticism the basis for getting back to the historical Jesus and to what he meant by the coming of the kingdom.[125]

Wright shows that the third quest for the historical Jesus, unlike Bultmannian form criticism, believes that a reliable history of Jesus can be written. First-century sources, including Josephus and the Qumran materials, along with recent studies of the history and literature of the period, provide historical evidence for what first-century Palestine was like.[126] The application of the social sciences to the historical method is beginning to influence scholars to interpret Jesus within the context of his own background as opposed to a modernist reinterpretation of Jesus based on the principle that the past must be viewed analogously to what is true about the present.[127] What emerges out of this material is that the traditions about Jesus reported in the gospels correspond closely with the Jewish milieu of the times. In other words, the gospels provide a realistic and faithful report of the life and words of Jesus.[128]

Wright's painstaking analysis of the gospel traditions from the standpoint of critical history leaves no stone unturned. His comprehensive knowledge of the scholarly literature on the quest for the historical Jesus is remarkable, and his analysis of this data is consistent with historical methodological principles. Marcus J. Borg, his strongest critic, considers Wright to be "brilliant" and "among the half dozen most brilliant people I have met in my life."[129] Their difference lies primarily in their assumptions about the historicity of the gospel traditions. Borg relies largely on the assumptions of Bultmannian form criticism,[130] which Wright believes is now being bypassed in the more recent work of New Testament scholars because it is too philosophically prejudicial in its presuppositions.[131] Borg, however, says that "mainline" New Testament scholars generally still hold to Bultmannian form criticism.[132]

Wright's method for reconstructing the history of Jesus is based on the principle of hypothesis-verification.[133] The critical historian develops a hypothetical reconstruction of Jesus' worldview, and then attempts to verify this hypothesis by examining the sayings and deeds of Jesus in the light of the worldviews of first-century Judaism and first-century Christianity. Using the principles of similarity and dissimilarity to discover what is unique about the life and teachings of Jesus over against first-century Judaism and first-century Christianity, the historian is able to make a responsible judgment about the historicity of the various traditions contained in the gospels.

Does the specter of historicism with its assumption of objectivism appear in this methodology? Wright rejects the idea of a positivistic view of history; he rejects the idea of "a provable series of events" and "mathematically certain data."[134] Rather, history is a "complexity of hypothetical reconstruction" and practical verifications.[135] He believes that faith has an interest in the outcome of critical history, but it cannot predetermine the actual results. He specifically rejects apologetics based on post-Enlightenment rationalism.[136] He does not presume that the historian can prove the idea of God,[137] and he rejects the notion of "detached objectivity."[138] At the same time, he rejects the notion that historical judgments fall into the category of subjectivism. Rather, he believes that the critical historian can reach reasonable and fair conclusions about the past.[139] To avoid the critical historical question is a form of docetism.[140]

Assuming this hypothesis-with-sufficient-verification methodology, Wright believed that Jesus intentionally subverted the prevailing worldview of his day by setting himself and his followers up as a counter-Temple movement.[141] This hypothesis is tested against the Jewish concept of the Temple and what the gospel narratives report about him. Judaism regarded the Temple as the primary symbol of Israel's identity. It was regarded as the dwelling-place of Israel's God and the political center of the kingdom.[142] It was the place of sacrifice where forgiveness of sins and cleansing from defilement were offered. The Temple was also the political center of the world for the Jews. Israel had been brought out of the land of Egypt and established as a kingdom in the land of Canaan. This country was a holy land because it was the place of God's abode, and the Temple built by Solomon became the specific location of God's habitation in the kingdom of Israel.

The second Temple was rebuilt by Herod the Great. The hope of Second-Temple Judaism was that the glory of the former Temple would be restored with the coming of the Messiah who would come in judgment against their enemies and bring them once again out of bondage, the kingdom would be reestablished, and Yahweh would return to Zion to occupy the Temple.

This eschatological-apocalyptic hope stood in stark contrast to the realities of Jesus' day. The leaders in charge of the Second Temple enjoyed autonomy and were the ruling class of Palestine with royal aspirations, but there were large segments of Jewish life that resented these Temple leaders. Among them were the Pharisees (and their rabbis) and the Essenes who offered an alternative to the religion of the Temple.[143] The Pharisees in Jesus' day were already beginning to develop a theology of the Torah as a substitute blessing for the Temple. The Essenes considered their own community as a substitute for the Temple. Wright shows that there was widespread resentment against the priests and religious leaders who controlled the Temple, and hence the Temple and its management were often criticized.[144]

Wright probes into the Jewish background to explore the significance of Jesus' protest against the Temple when he came to the Temple on his last trip to Jerusalem (Mt 21.12-17; Mark 11:1-25; Lk 19.45-48; Jn 2.13-22). His hypothesis-verification method confirms that Jesus considered himself to be in a long line of prophets like Isaiah, Jeremiah, Ezekiel, and Daniel who predicted the destruction of the Temple.[145] This method also confirms Jesus' vocation as a prophet announcing the God of the Jews would become the king as Israel returned from exile and Yahweh returned to Zion.[146] His actions portrayed himself as the true king, and he understood himself as "more than a prophet" as John the Baptist earlier declared.[147] His actions in the Temple were symbolic to show its imminent destruction. Jesus acted in accord with the eschatological expectation that the Temple would be destroyed and then rebuilt. However, he did not believe that it would be rebuilt with brick and mortar. Rather, his self-perception was that he was the new Temple.[148]

He further perceived his action in the Temple to be messianic, not in the sense that Jesus knew himself to be the incarnate second person of the Trinity, but in the sense that he was the long-awaited Messiah to lead the Jews out of exile into the kingdom that once had been theirs.[149] Jesus knew that he would die for the causes he advocated, but he believed his death would be the means of realizing the kingdom of God for Israel and the whole world.[150] Wright argues that the passion narratives cannot be simply dismissed as *vaticinia ex eventu*.[151] To be sure, the atonement theology of early Christianity is an advanced understanding of the passion of Jesus, but the basis for this theology is present in Jesus' own self-understanding.[152]

His attack on the Temple and offering himself as a counter-Temple alternative were the culmination of a number of issues that led to Jesus' death. Among these was his claim to be a prophet, which was alleged to be false because he was subverting the traditions of second Temple Judaism. It was feared by the authorities that his claim to be the Messiah could possibly lead to political insurrection, which was a constant threat. Finally, placing himself alongside the God of Israel was blasphemous.[153]

Wright offers a well-reasoned argument to show that Jesus' self-consciousness as portrayed in the gospel narratives is consistent with first-century Judaism. Significantly, Wright's comprehensive historical reconstruction of the life of Jesus leads to the conclusion that Jesus did not die a deluded soul, as Schweitzer had concluded, but rather his death was a prelude to something revolutionary in scope that would have lasting consequence in the history of humankind.[154]

This leads to the historical question, which the Bultmannian school believed was impossible to ask—what did Jesus think of himself in reference to God?[155] Wright believes the historical method provides an answer to this question. Jesus perceived himself as having a unique relation to God as his Father, and he assumed a role and vocation, which was possible only for the God of Israel to assume.[156] This included Jesus' belief that he was the eschatological fulfillment of the coming of God to his people in person and power to restore Israel and to return to Zion,[157] thus placing himself alongside God.[158]

Why did the early Christians begin to worship Jesus? It was because the early Christians believed that his pre-Easter mission was confirmed through his resurrection from the dead.[159] The bodily resurrection was uniquely a Jewish notion, based on Daniel 12:2-3,[160] and not based on Zoroastrianism.[161] The idea that the resurrection would occur in a single individual prior to a general resurrection arose only because Jesus was raised from the dead.[162] Yet the idea of the resurrection was not sufficient in itself to demonstrate that Jesus was God. Rather, the resurrection event and his life, deeds, and teaching together confirmed that he was the Son of God.[163] Wright argues that this worship of Jesus was not something begun with Hellenized Christianity as some form critics assert, but with "the very, very, early Jewish" Christians[164] because it was intimately bound up with the realization that he stood in close proximity to the one God of Israel.

The significance of Wright's third quest of the historical Jesus is that he shows the historical method and biblical inspiration are not necessarily antithetical. As Wright shows, faith should not avoid historical criticism.[165] There perhaps was a day when theology felt the need to protect itself from the onslaughts of historical criticism, but as Pannenberg, Cullmann, and now Wright have argued, this is no longer necessary. Faith and the historical method can form a responsible partnership.

This easing of tension has been enhanced by increased understanding of story telling as a form of reliable history in peasant communities in Middle-Eastern cultures. Because the telling and retelling of significant events give these peasant communities their sense of identity, preserving the accuracy of these oral traditions is important to them. This evidence contradicts a major premise of Bultmannian form criticism, which assumed that oral tradition was historically unreliable.

Earlier we noted that Cullmann appealed to the researches of Riesenfeld and Gerhardsson to show that the apostles guaranteed the accuracy of the life and words of Jesus similarly to the way that rabbinic schools passed on the teachings of their masters in fixed oral forms. Wright notes that contemporary research by Kenneth E. Bailey has shown that oral traditions in the Near East to this day are noted for their accuracy and reliability. As a result of his extensive research in several Middle-Eastern countries, Bailey has demonstrated that there are three kinds of oral traditions in this culture. One is *informal* and *uncontrolled,* as when a rumor of some atrocity spreads like wildfire. Another is *formal* and *controlled,* as when Muslims learn the entire Koran by memory. This formal and controlled oral tradition assumes a formal relationship between a teacher and students. There is also an *informal* and *controlled* oral tradition. There is no formal relationship between a teacher and pupils in an informal oral tradition. Any member of the peasant community can join in preserving this tradition so long as they are well-established members. The accuracy of the tradition is preserved because it is under the control of the larger community who would object to innovations that might be imported like smuggled goods.[166] Wright believes the *informal* and *controlled* oral tradition is representative of the traditions preserved in the gospels. There are variations and differences of minor detail in the informal but controlled oral traditions, but the core of the narrative remains intact.[167]

Bailey shows that the idea of eyewitnesses and ministers (*hyperetes,* Luke 4:20) is a possible indication of an informal but controlled tradition. *Hyperetes* is an official in the synagogue in charge of the scrolls, but the early Christian community did not have buildings and formal institutional structures like Judaism. Hence a *hyperetes* in the Christian community served as an approved witness of vital Christian traditions. In a peasant village community, several persons were responsible for telling its key stories; likewise within the Christian community. Paul speaks of having received traditions, which he passed on (1 Cor. 11:2, 23: 15:1-3). He was not himself an eyewitness of these early traditions, but he was part of an extended network of approved transmitters of the tradition.[168]

Bailey believes the early oral traditions of Jesus were written down in the Four Gospels because after the fall of Jerusalem in 70 A.D., the disintegration of the early Palestinian Christian communities made it impossible to maintain control over the oral traditions; hence the controlled oral tradition was preserved. Wright agrees with this observation, although he notes that another reason for the written Gospels was to help propagate Christianity.[169] Bailey believes that the apocryphal gospels, such as the *Gospel of Thomas,* developed out of the lack of control over the oral traditions that resulted from the social disintegration of Palestinian villages. This lack of control of the tradition thus permitted particular persons and groups to rewrite the gospel from the perspective of their gnostic ideology.[170]

This brings us to a final consideration of Wright's search for the historical Jesus. He uses the term, narrative, to describe the "storyline" of Israel in which Jesus is seen as bringing to a climax the history of Israel.[171] However, Wright is interested in establishing if these narratives constitute real history. Oftentimes the term narrative may be used without any reference to real history, and this is why in systematic theology the term, history, is preferred to specify the realism of the events. Cullmann's idea of salvation history captures the sense of both the narrative (interpretation) and history (events).

Wright uses the problematic term, "metanarrative," to describe the larger biblical history of salvation.[172] This term was originally used by Jean-Francois Lyotard to describe the foundationalist thinking of the Enlightenment because it assumed that is was possible to interpret the whole of reality through rational reflection using metahistorical principles.[173] However, the biblical history of salvation is not metahistory. Of course, Wright uses this term to mean that the biblical narratives are linked together by the larger, overarching "storyline" of salvation culminating in Jesus. However, "meta" could be misunderstood to mean something "beyond" history, and in light of the original use of this term to describe modernism, it might be better to avoid it. Christian theology is not based on metahistorical principles of foundationalism, but on the history of salvation.

The Internal Witness of the Holy Spirit

Pannenberg, Cullmann, and Wright show that the historical method is an indispensable aid to faith. The validation of Christian faith relies in part upon the apologetical task of theology to show that the biblical narratives are reliable, but this apologetic must be rigorously honest about the evidence. This critical knowledge, however, is not a substitute for faith, but it serves faith by removing the gnawing doubt that faith has no basis beyond itself.[174] Beyond this, the validation of Christian faith comes about through the internal confirmation of the Holy Spirit. This means that one's experience with the risen Christ confirms itself in "love, joy, peace, longsuffering, gentleness, goodness, faith, meekness, temperance" (Galatians 5:22-23). Paul speaks of the inner witness of the Spirit that we are children of God (Romans 8:15-16). This implies that faith in the sense of participating in the reality of the risen Lord through the inspiration of the Holy Spirit is a way of knowing, although not without at least assuming the validity of salvation history. Pannenberg points out that believers know the reality of the risen Lord because the Holy Spirit makes Jesus known as the fulfillment of the divine promises.[175]

Without this confirming presence of the Holy Spirit, the question of Kähler is all the more pertinent: "How can Jesus Christ be the authentic object of the faith of all Christians if the questions what and who he really was can be established only by ingenious investigation and if it is solely the scholarship of our time which proves itself equal to this task?"[1]

Notes

1. Cf. Timothy Miller, *Following In His Steps* (Knoxville: The University of Tennessee Press, 1987), p. xiii.

2. Edward E. Hindson, "The Historical Significance of *The Fundamentals*," *The Fundamentals for the Twenty-First Century*, ed. Mal Couch (Grand Rapids: Kregel Publications, 2000), pp. 15-27. Cf. Henry H. Knight III, *A Future for Truth, Evangelical Theology in the Postmodern World* (Nashville: Abingdon Press, 1997), pp. 17-35.

3. Edward E. Hindson, "The Historical Significance of *The Fundamentals*," *The*

Fundamentals for the Twenty-First Century, p. 21.

4. Ibid., p. 18.

5. Tillich, *A History of Christian Thought,* p. 276.

6. Ibid.

7. Ibid., p. 306.

8. J. Gresham Machen, *Christianity and Liberalism* (Grand Rapids: Wm. B. Eerdmans, 1923), is a well-argued discussion on the contrast between conservative Christianity and theological liberalism.

9. B. B. Warfield, *The Inspiration and Authority of the Bible,* ed. Samuel G. Craig (Philadelphia: The Presbyterian and Reformed Publishing Company, 1948), is a collection of articles written during his lifetime, but published posthumously in a single edition. It still constitutes a milestone on this theme. Warfield affirmed the inerrancy of Scripture, but he did so because he thought it was an implication of the biblical view of inspiration. However, he believed the truths of Christianity did *not* depend "upon any doctrine of inspiration whatever." Ibid. p. 121.

10. For a discussion of the fundamentalist tradition and its subsequent development into a highly significant theological movement known as evangelicalism, see Henry H. Knight III, *A Future of Truth* (Nashville: Abingdon Press, 1997), pp 17-35.

11. Pannenberg, *Jesus—God and Man,* pp. 74-88.

12. Cf. Harold J. Ockenga's preface to Harold Lindsell, *The Battle for the Bible* (Grand Rapids: Zondervan Publishing House, 1976), p. 11.

13. Donald G. Bloesch, "The Primacy of Scripture," *The Authoritative Word, Essays on the Nature of Scripture,* ed. Donald K. McKim (Grand Rapids: Wm. B. Eerdmans, 1983), p. 133.

14. Outler, *Sermons,* 2:466-467, "The Mystery of Iniquity." Cf. Wesley, "Advice to the Clergy," *The Works of John Wesley,* ed. Thomas Jackson (London: Wesleyan Conference Office, 1872), 6:359-60.

15. Stanley J. Grenz, "Concerns of a Pietist with a Ph. D.," *The Wesleyan Theological Journal* 37.2 (Fall, 2002): 60.

16. Ibid., pp. 64-71.

17. "Theta Phi Panel Discussion with Wolfhart Pannenberg," *The Asbury Theological Journal,* 46.2 (Fall 1991): 22

18. Cf. Moltmann, *Theology of Hope,* trans. James W. Leitch (New York: Harper & Row, 1965), p. 61.

19. Cf. William Hordern, *New Directions in Theology Today* (Philadelphia: Westminster Press, 1966), p. 77.

20. Cf. Pannenberg, *ST,* 1:280.

21. Cf. Stanley J. Grenz, *Theology for the Community of God* (Nashville: Broadman and Holman Publishers, 1994). x, 62.

22. Cf. Pannenberg, *Jesus—God and Man,* pp. 74-114.

23. "Dogmatic Theses on the Doctrine of Revelation," *Revelation as History,* pp. 152-155.

24. Ibid., p. 154.

25. Ibid., pp. 154-155. *Basic Questions in Theology*, 1:85.

26. Pannenberg, *ST*, 1:x.

27. *Jesus—God and Man*, p. 28.

28. Ibid., p. 25.

29. Ibid., p. 99; *Basic Questions in Theology*, 1:139, 160, 195-198.

30. Pannenberg, "Response to the Discussion," *Theology As History*, p. 226.

31. Ibid., pp. 226-227.

32. Ibid., p. 227.

33. Ibid., pp. 227-228.

34. Pannenberg, "La signification de l'eschatologie pour la comprehéhension de l'apostolicité et de la catholicité de l'église," *Istina*, XII (1969), 163. Cf. *Basic Questions in Theology*, 1: 4, 6, 7, 12; "Response to the Discussion," *Theology As History*, p. 228.

35. Ibid., p. 270.

36. Ibid., p. 239.

37. Cobb, "Past, Present, and Future," *Theology As History*, p. 209.

38. "Response to the Discussion," *Theology As History*, p. 238.

39. Pannenberg, *ST*, 3:122-135.

40. A direct self-*revelation* would be the full disclosure of God's essence, whereas a direct self-*manifestation* involves only the appearance of God without any reference to a disclosure of his essence. Cf. "Introduction," *Revelation as History*, p. 9.

41. "Response to the Discussion," *Theology As History*, p. 238.

42. "Dogmatic Theses on the Doctrine of Revelation," *Revelation As History*, pp. 152-153.

43. Ibid., pp. 137.

44. Pannenberg, "Response to the Discussion," *Theology As History*, p. 237.

45. Ibid., p. 268-269.

46. Ibid.

47. Ibid., p. 269.

48. Ibid., p. 274.

49. Ibid., p. 196; *ST*, 1:250

50. Pannenberg, *ST*, 1:250.

51. For a helpful discussion on the contemporary issues involved in the idea of biblical inspiration, cf. I. Howard Marshall, *Biblical Inspiration* (Grand Rapids: Wm. B. Eerdmans Publishing Co., 1982.

52. Cf. H. Orton Wiley, *Christian Theology*, 1.176.

53. "Theta Phi Panel Discussion with Wolfhart Pannenberg," *The Asbury Theological Journal*, 46.2 (Fall 1991): 22

54. Rudolf Bultmann, *The History of the Synoptic Tradition*, trans. John Marsh (Oxford: Blackwell, 1963), pp. vii-viii.

55. Ibid., p. 3.

56. Cf. Oscar Cullmann, *Salvation in History*, translated by Sidney G. Sowers

(London: SCM Press, Ltd., 1967), pp. 49-50.

57. Cullmann embraced this principle in his form-critical analysis of the Christological titles. *The Christology of the New Testament*, trans. Shirley C. Guthrie and Charles A. M. Hall (Philadelphia: Westminster Press, 1963), p. 7.

58. Cf. Donald Guthrie, *New Testament Introduction* (London: The Tyndale Press, 1970), p. 199.

59. Oscar Cullmann, *Salvation in History*, pp. 1, 49-50, 120, 170; *The Christology of the New Testament*, p. 7.

60. *The Christology of the New Testament*, p. 7.

61. Bultmann, *The History of the Synoptic Tradition*, p. 370.

62. *Salvation in History*, pp. 25ff., 84-135; *The Christology of the New Testament*, pp. 3-10.

63. *Salvation in History*, p. 189.

64. Ibid., pp. 111, 191.

65. Ibid., p. 191.

66. *The Christology of the New Testament*, p. 4.

67. Ibid., p. 9.

68. Ibid., pp. 306-307.

69. Ibid., p. 4.

70. *Salvation in History*, p. 58.

71. *The Christology of the New Testament*, p. 315; *Salvation in History*, p. 85.

72. *The Christology of the New Testament*, p. 317.

73. Ibid., p. 8.

74. *The History of the Synoptic Tradition*, p. 66

75. *Salvation in History*, pp. 98-99.

76. Ibid. p. 99.

77. Ibid., p. 99.

78. Ibid., p. 104.

79. *The Christology of the New Testament*, p. 286.

80. Ibid., p. 303.

81. *Salvation in History*, pp. 102-103.

82. Ibid., pp. 102-103.

83. *Jesus—God and Man*, p. 334.

84. Ibid., p. 326.

85. Ibid., pp. 325-326.

86. Ibid., p. 326.

87. Ibid., p. 326.

88. Ibid., p. 326.

89. Ibid., p. 153.

90. Ibid., p. 135.

91. *Salvation in History*, p. 103.

92. Ibid., p. 106.

93. Ibid., p. 103.

94. Ibid., p. 104.

95. Ibid., p. 104.

96. Pannenberg, *ST,* 1:26-48.

97. Pannenberg, *ST,* 1:46.

98. Ibid..

99. Ibid., 1:48.

100. Ibid.

101. *Salvation in History,* p. 143.

102. Ibid., p. 73.

103. Ibid., p. 296.

104. Ibid., p. 143.

105. Ibid., p. 296..

106. Gerhard Ebeling, *Word and Faith,* trans. R. G. Smith (London: Collins, 1961), p. 292. Cf. *The New Hermeneutic,* ed. James M. Robinson and John B. Cobb, Jr. (New York: Harper & Row, 1964).

107. *The Five Gospels, The Search For The Authentic Words of Jesus,* new translation and commentary by Robert W. Funk, Roy W. Hoover, and The Jesus Seminar (San Francisco, CA: HarperSanFrancisco, 1997), p. 35. Cf. N. T. Wright, *Jesus and the Victory of God* (Minneapolis: Fortress Press, 1996), pp. 28-82.

108. *Salvation in History,* p. 192n. 1.

109. *The Five Gospels, The Search For The Authentic Words of Jesus,* pp. 2-5. Cf. Wright, *Jesus and the Victory of God,* pp. 28-82.

110. Ibid., p. 84.

111. *The Resurrection of the Son of God,* p. 15.

112. *Jesus & The Restoration of Israel, A Critical Assessment of N. T. Wright's Jesus and The Victory of God,* ed. Carey C. Newman (Downers Grove, Illinois: InterVarsity Press, 1999), pp. 289-290.

113. Ibid., p. 79.

114. Ibid., pp. xviii, 5, 52, 81, 89, 100, 104, 131.

115. Ibid., p. 101, 104, 149.

116. Ibid. p. 149.

117. *The New Testament and the People of God,* pp. 401-402.

118. *The Resurrection of the Son of God,* p. 6.

119. *Jesus and the Victory of God,* p. 8. Cf. *The Resurrection of the Son of God,* pp. 714ff.

120. Marcus J. Borg, "An Appreciative Disagreement," *Jesus and the Restoration of Israel,* p. 232.

121. Wolfhart Pannenberg, *Basic Questions in Theology,* 1:15-80.

122. Ibid., 1:39ff.

123. *Jesus and the Victory of God,* p. 26.

124. Cf. Robert North, "Pannenberg's Historicizing Exegesis," *The Heythrop Journal,* 12.4 (October 1971), 393; H. D. Betz, "The Concept of Apocalyptic in the Theology of the Pannenberg Group," *Journal for Theology and the Church,* VI (1969), 192-207; William R. Murdock, "History and Revelation in Jewish Apocalypticism," *Interpretation,* XXI (1967), 167-187.

125. *Jesus and the Victory of God,* p. 84.

126. Ibid., p. 84-85.

127. Ibid., p. 53.

128. One of Wright's critics complained that he did not seem to reject "a single Synoptic pericope" as unhistorical. Borg, "An Appreciative Disagreement," *Jesus & the Restoration of Israel,* p. 231.

129. Ibid., p. 227.

130. Ibid., p. 331.

131. *Jesus and the Victory of God,* p. 87. Cf. N. T. Wright, *The Resurrection of the Son of God* (Minneapolis: Fortress Press, 2003), p. 596.

132. *Jesus & the Restoration of Israel,* p. 331.

133. *Jesus and the Victory of God,* p. 87.

134. Ibid., p. 8.

135. Ibid., p. 9.

136. *Jesus and The Restoration of Israel,* p. 251.

137. *The Resurrection of the Son of God,* p. 736.

138. Ibid., p. 29.

139. Ibid.

140. Ibid., p.23.

141. *Jesus and the Victory of God,* p. 108.

142. Ibid., p. 406.

143. Ibid., pp. 406-412.

144. Ibid., pp. 411-412.

145. Ibid., pp. 416.

146. Ibid., pp. 415, 612.

147. Ibid., p. 417.

148. Ibid., p. 426.

149. Ibid., pp. 427, 478.

150. Ibid., pp. 562, 609ff.

151. Ibid., pp. 574ff.

152. Ibid., p. 592.

153. Ibid., pp. 551-552.

154. Ibid., p. 612.

155. Ibid., pp. 612ff.

156. Ibid., p. 649.

157. Ibid. p. 615.

158. Ibid., pp. 649ff.

159. Ibid., pp. 110, 131, 659f.

160. *The Resurrection of the Son of God,* pp. 108-109.

161. Ibid., pp. 87, 125.

162. Ibid., pp. 24-25.

163. Ibid., pp. 244-245.

164. *Jesus and the Victory of God,* pp. 612ff.

165. Ibid., p. 662.

166. Ibid., p. 134.

167. Ibid., pp. 133ff.

168. Ibid., p. 135.

169. Ibid., p. 135n. 30.

170. Ibid., p. 136n. 33.

171. Ibid., p. 197.

172. Ibid., p. 206.

173. Jean-Francois Lyotard, *The Postmodern Condition: A Report on Knowledge,* trans. Geoff Bennington and Brian Massumi (Minneapolis: University of Minneapolis University, 1984), p. xxiv.

174. *Basic Questions in Theology,* p. 270.

175. *ST* 1:250.

176. Kähler, *The So-Called Historical Jesus and the Historic Biblical Christ,* p. 102.

3

A Post-Critical Hermeneutic of the Self— A Relational Ontology

We noted earlier that the idea of revelation as *self*-revelation was a modern notion. It was largely based on Barth's theology derived from Hegel's concept of God as Absolute Subject.

What about the human self? Modern philosophy first influenced modern theology to re-define God as a *revealing Subject* as a result of its definition of the human self as a *thinking subject*. So God as revealing Subject and the human self as thinking subject are corollary ideas. The idea of God as revealing Subject has more recently been rejected by a growing number of contemporary theologians in favor of understanding God in relational terms of Trinitarian Persons. Before we examine the Trinitarian understanding, we will show how the modern idea of *thinking subject* as the defining characteristic of human personhood has come under critical reexamination.

John Macmurray: "The Failure of Modern Philosophy"

John Macmurray (1891-1976), a Scot philosopher who taught at the Universities of Oxford, London, and Edinburgh, offered a penetrating critique of the modern concept of the self in the Gifford Lectures in 1953-1954, which were first published in two volumes, *The Self As Agent* and *Persons in Relation*. Although these volumes continue to be published and widely respected,[1] Macmurray is not as well-known among philosophers of the 20th Century as one might expect.[2] Yet, his writings continue to be the subject of doctoral theses and published writings even though they may not be as visible as other recent authors.[3]

As one of the most lucid critics of modern thought, he speaks forthrightly about "The Failure of Modern Philosophy."[4] This polemic against modernism was the main focus of his Gifford Lectures. In these lectures, Macmurray said the Cartesian concept of "I think" was a new beginning in philosophical reflection in the 17th century, which can be refuted only from a perspective on the outside of modernism and by beginning with a new starting point. It cannot be rehabilitated, but must be deconstructed by a new way of thinking.[5]

Macmurray attributed much of the religious and societal crisis in the world today as having been created by the modern dualism of pure subject over against the world as object.[6] He noted this dualism inevitably led to irreligion. This is because it begins with a criterion of truth that is rooted in a hermeneutic of doubt. Macmurray noted how unnatural the systematic method of doubt is, and the assumption that certainty arises out of doubt is faulty. The more doubt is exercised the greater skepticism is increased.[7] Macmurray went on to show that modern philosophy assumes that the method of doubt does not require a reason, although believing does.[8] The point that he was making is that belief and doubt are based on practical considerations, not theoretical.[9] He argued against the idea that one's practical reasons for believing can be reinforced by a systematic method of doubt, which supposedly will lead one to theoretical certainty. How can one doubt what one believes? How can theoretical doubt lead to certainty, except as an imaginary certainty and pretended knowledge?[10]

Macmurray, anticipating postmodern thought, has shown that the modern idea of objective truth existing independently of the knower is an illusion. He argued that it is meaningless to talk about truth unless it is a personal knowledge of the truth. Personal belief is an essential part of knowledge. Although one may have an entire system of logical propositions, this system in itself is not a body of knowledge—unless it is believed by someone.[11]

Knowledge is thus more than just a formal, abstract, thinking process. Knowledge is *personal*, and the personal is more than just the capacity to engage in theoretical thinking. The personal is the unity of the self in its multidimensional aspects, and the self includes more than just the mind. A person knows something, not just one's mind or feeling but one acts as a whole being.[12] Instead of the *self as subject*, Macmurray proposed that the *self as agent* is a more apt description.[13] As agent, oneself is defined in terms of "I do" instead of "I think." A person is one who acts with intention, and it is the person, not his consciousness, who knows. Consciousness as such is not knowledge, but rather persons acting in their whole being constitutes knowledge.[14] Acting therefore is the decisive component of personhood, while thinking is largely a formal and secondary function. When a person acts, their consciousness of seeing, hearing, remembering, and thinking is not something that is separated from, but is rather integrated into their bodily movement. Hence the body-mind dualism is a fiction.[15]

A further problem of the modern concept of the self is that it depersonalizes others by treating them as objects rather than persons. Macmurray contended that the unity of personal life can only be understood from within the standpoint of mutuality of personal relationships instead of an individual, isolated self.[16] Modern thought, however, exalts the individual self. Macmurray called this modern self "egocentricity" because the self exists in isolation from the real world of social participation because it withdraws into a secluded world of contemplation.[17] Modern philosophy is egocentric because it starts with the isolated, thinking self, not with God, the world, or the community.[18] To be sure, the capacity to think abstractly is an important function of the self, but this is a secondary and derivative function. As opposed to the idea of a self who is constituted by the capacity to be a thinking subject, Macmurray proposes the idea of the self whose personal existence is constituted by the capacity to participate in relationships with others. In this sense, the self is primarily defined, not as a knowing subject, but as an agent who acts holistically.[19]

To begin with the self as a thinking subject is to exclude knowledge of others, including knowledge of God. The self is locked into a prison house of subjectivity. Macmurray particularly described the inadequacy of Kant's philosophy because it made the "I think" the center of reality. All humans were defined as "I think" and the result was a radical individualism in which everyone is looked upon as a multiplicity of "I's." We can practically only address others as a "you," but the implications of Kant's subjectivism is that others must be seen as an "I," and hence there is no basis for a "you and I." As a result, Kant's philosophy has no place for the other as a "you" and no basis for personal community.[20]

Macmurray argued that knowledge is based on action, and action is motivated by the desire for "friendship."[21] This focus on others as persons is denied by the modern dualism of the self as subject and the world as object. Rather, the thinking self is a self-negation because it is isolated from dynamic relations with others and alienated from the divine Other. By withdrawing into its own thoughts it takes up the attitude of a spectator instead of being a participant in community with others.[22] The dualism of the theoretical (the spectator attitude) and the practical (the participant attitude) means a loss of the integrity of the self. One's personal values, motives, and choices are vital aspects of the meaning of persons,[23] but a focus on the abstract "I think" depersonalizes human life.

Macmurray argued the way to restart a more authentic philosophy of human life is to begin with the primacy of the practical as opposed to the primacy of the theoretical.[24] We should replace the "I think" with the "I do." The self is not primarily a thinker, but a doer. Positively, the self is an agent; negatively, the self is a thinker.[25]

In a dramatic reversal of modern philosophy, Macmurray argued that knowing is not the result of thinking, but thinking already presupposes knowledge. Knowledge of the world is a result of our action and participation in it. One does not gain knowledge by retreating into pure thought. Rather, we think about those things that we already know.[26]

The divorce between the theoretical and the practical has led to an intellectualistic and egocentric view of the self, resulting in an irreligious view of the world. Taking its cue from the ineradicable dualism of Descartes, the concept of the self in modern philosophy is thus plagued with the twin problems of the self as an abstract subject and egocentricity (individualism). Inevitably, the "I think" premise of modern philosophy led to atheism. On the other hand, the primacy of the practical leads one to think of the unity of the world and the underlying unifying intention of the world.[27] The modern conflict between religion and atheism is a conflict between whether the world entails intention or not.[28] If the concept of agency is a practical implication about our world, then belief in God is a responsible belief; for the concept of agency entails the notion of intention and purpose to life and openness to God and others. If the concept of the self as a thinking subject has priority, this tends towards egocentricity and paradoxically towards the negation of the self and atheism.

Paul Ricoeur: A Narrative-Based Ontology

Paul Ricoeur has given considerably attention to a postmodern reconfiguration of the self in his book, *Oneself As Another*. He begins with a rejection of the modern concept of the self as a thinking subject. He notes that the modern concept of the self begins with Descartes and was radicalized in Kant, Fichte, and Husserl, ranging from being the first truth of philosophy to being a vast illusion.[29] Ricoeur downgrades the belief that mere thinking is the primary activity of being human. Rather, his emphasis is upon "the primacy of reflective meditation."[30] That is, one reflects upon what constitutes ones true being rather than focusing upon "the immediate positing of the subject," as Descartes' *cogito* proposed. Descartes thus began with the thinking subject—the "I think"; therefore

I am"—but Ricoeur begins with an analysis of what "I am" through reflective meditation. Descartes assumed that mind, soul, intellect, or reason are interchangeable terms,[31] but Ricoeur points out that Descartes' concept of the thinking self is an abstract subject, which is not the same as the traditional view of the soul. Rather, Descartes superimposed his concept of the thinking subject upon the traditional meaning of the soul. Socrates was the first person to identify the soul with reason, but Descartes redefined reason as the mere thinking activity of a subject, thus reason was reduced to the bare act of thinking.[32] Here reason is without any content as such; it is simply the abstract capacity to think. To be sure, Descartes assumes a whole body of innate ideas which thinking can discover, but so far as the decisive meaning of the self is concerned, it is reduced to the sheer act of thinking which allegedly is able to rise above all doubts to a sure knowledge of the truth of everything that is real.

Ricoeur does not reject completely this modern concept of subjectivity; rather he reconstructs this view to make room for a larger understanding of the nature of the self in its historical development. He distinguishes between two aspects of personhood. There is the "I" and there is the "self." The "I" (*idem*) refers to the unchanging sameness of oneself, whereas the "self" (*ipse*) refers to what is "other" than the "I" which undergoes change.[33] In terms of the subject-object distinction, Ricoeur defines oneself as dialectically constituted by being a subject of one's reflection and by being an object of what is reflected upon.[34] Ricoeur sees his definition of oneself as a mediating position between the philosophy of "the thinking subject" (Descartes and Kant) on the one hand, and its "overthrow" on the other hand, particularly in the philosophy of Nietzsche.[35] He refers to his concept of personhood as a "hermeneutic of the self."[36]

Ricoeur criticizes Descartes' view as entailing the idea of a timeless, ahistorical, abstract identity that is different from identity gained through one's historically-based narrative.[37] Ricoeur's narrative concept of the self emphasizes the elements of sameness and otherness. Oneself is not an instantaneous given, but rather it is formed out of the concrete realities of society through the give-and-take of one's life narrative.

Ricoeur points out that Descartes' concept of the thinking subject as the foundation of all truth involves a serious dilemma. In his *Third Meditation* Descartes argues for the necessity of God as the foundation for whatever one knows with certainty, but then this undermines his previous argument that the thinking subject is the foundation of all knowledge. The dilemma is a vicious circle. The consequence was either to consider the thinking subject as a sterile idea from which nothing else could be determined, or else to make the idea of God the foundation of everything, thus eliminating the first foundation of truth in human subjectivity.

A third alternative is found in David Hume who was agnostic about the existence of a self. Hume asserts: "For my part, when I enter most intimately into what I call *myself,* I always stumble on some particular perception or other, of heat, or cold, light or shade, love or hatred, pain or pleasure. I can never catch *myself* at any time without a perception, and can never observe anything but the perception."[38] Ricoeur has pointed out the paradox of Hume's skepticism of the self. Hume was seeking what was impossible to find because the idea of an absolutely unchanging self does not exist, and yet Hume was presupposing the self that he was seeking to find.[39] Hume's analysis shows that at least *someone* was unable to find a self and this *someone* looks within oneself and finds nothing that can be called a self. Hume only allowed the immediate moments of sense perception to count as facts and since the self is not an empirical fact that can be literally seen, he doubted its existence. Hume's skepticism thus resulted in unsolvable conundrums such as denying the existence of the self while talking about himself.

Hume's philosophy served as incentive to Kant to develop a concept of the self that was consistent with reason. Prior to his encounter with Hume's skepticism, Kant had accepted the rationalist view of the thinking subject first proposed by Descartes.[40] Subsequently, he rejected Descartes' view that one can know the self simply through intuitive thinking, though he retained the concept of the autonomous self as the foundation of knowledge. However, this autonomous self is only a logical inference as a practical implication of reason, but what this self really is lies beyond the powers of human reason to know. Consequently, in Kant the self is a sterile, philosophical abstraction postulated as a transcendental idea and separated from any "autobiographical reference."[41] The person who speaks and acts is not the same as the autonomous self that serves as the transcendental unity of one's actions. The transcendental self is not the same as the actual self who speaks and is historically situated. Pannenberg has called Kant the real founder of modern subjectivity because of his concept of the rational autonomy of the self, whereas Descartes inconsistently made the self the foundation of knowledge while at the same time arguing that God's existence was also necessary as a guarantee for the reliability of our ideas. [42] Ricoeur notes that Kant paid a high price for his logic of the autonomous self—the loss of one's own sense of self who speaks and engages others in conversation and has a sense of personal moral responsibility.[43] The autonomous self has no history and no narrative to tell because it exists in isolation within itself. To be sure, Kant developed a systematic moral philosophy, but it was riddled with contradiction because of the divorce between the autonomous, transcendental self and the empirical self.

Ricoeur shows that the modern concept of the self was "shattered" by Nietzsche.[44] If Hume doubted the existence of the self because it was not an observable fact, Nietzsche doubted the existence of any facts at all. He believed the concept of nature was as much a myth as the concept of the self. In his *Course on Rhetoric*, Nietzsche argued that the idea of mechanistic causality in nature and the idea of a transcendental self were illusions created by a misunderstanding of the figurative meaning of language. Nietzsche intended to deconstruct the meaning of words by pointing out "the properly rhetorical functioning of the illusion" created by human language.[45] Truths are nothing but a host of metaphors and anthropomorphisms, including the notion of the self. Truths are nothing but illusions based on the embellishment of human relationships.[46]

If Descartes began with doubt as a method of reaching absolute certainty about the nature of the self, Nietzsche used doubt as a method of showing that there is no way to infer the existence of an enduring subject; only a multiplicity of selves.[47] To this extent, Nietzsche claims that there are no facts, only interpretations. This means that the idea of an outer world is just as illusionary as the idea of an inner world of self-certainty.[48] Both philosophical positivism and idealism are equal illusions resulting from a faulty methodology that confuses the figurative meaning of language with literalism. Nietzsche thus intended to deconstruct the meaning of language as traditionally understood. Only in this way did he believe that the full meaning of personal freedom could be actualized once it was liberated from the false illusions about a transcendental, immortal self.

It is not surprising that Nietzsche (who died in 1900) was the prophet of postmodernism with his announcement that a new age of human innocence was on the horizon. This new age would expose the modern myth about a centered self, and the result would be a new humanity liberated from the guilt-ridden, enslaving fear of the Judeo-Christian ethic and from the modernist concept of universal morality and truth.

Ricoeur agrees in principle with the deconstruction of the modern view of the self but not going so far as "the disintegration of the self pursued mercilessly by Nietzschean deconstruction."[49] Ricoeur proposes what he calls "a hermeneutics of the self." That is, the self is a dynamic of both sameness and difference, which is always being developed in the course of one's concrete, historical existence. The self is not primarily a thinking subject, but oneself is a concrete being who becomes aware of one's identity through reflective meditation. One becomes aware of one's sameness existing through time as one becomes aware of oneself as another. Oneself undergoes multiple developments so that oneself is always the same and yet is constantly changing into another. There is no core self that endures in a transcendental sense. This self is thus not an abstract thinking subject, but an agent of action who realizes itself through reflective meditation. It is not given immediately and instantaneously through sheer thinking, but through a long and tedious process of interpretation. Hence the concept of a hermeneutics of the self.[50] Ricoeur borrows a phrase from Alasdair McIntyre, *After Virtue*, "the narrative unity of life," to define the nature of the self.[51] Oneself is attained as one locates oneself in a narrative that gives meaning and purpose to one's existence.[52]

Ricoeur agrees with Nietzsche's view that language is primarily figurative as opposed to the literalism of the modern mindset. He moves however beyond the deconstruction of language to a renewed appreciation of poetics, symbolism, and metaphors as conveying a larger understanding of reality. Ricoeur thus argues that the concept of the self cannot be formulated directly through the literalism of intuitive thinking ("the philosophy of the cogito", as he called it),[53] but rather one must follow a more indirect route of reflecting on the activities of the self in its narrative and historic situation in order to identify the self. This "narrative conception of personal identity"[54] corresponds to Alasdair MacIntyre's concept of "the narrative unity of life"[55] This means the self cannot be defined in terms of an absolute identity isolated from others. We are involved with others from birth to death. The entanglement in the history of our parents, friends and work companions shapes who we are.[56]

In considering Ricoeur's narrative concept of the self, the question emerges: what is the mode of being that constitutes the self? Ricoeur does not avoid this question, recognizing ontological formulations are necessary. However, he believes the idea of selfhood must avoid abstract notions that give the appearance that the self is some kind of unchanging substance. This view was typical of the scholastic tradition with the Latin translation of *substantia*, which was carried forward into Kant's idea of the transcendental ego.[57] The ontological nature of the self is not a

Cartesian thinking subject. In contrast to a philosophy of the subject, Ricoeur proposes an ontology based on his hermeneutic of the self.[58] Ricoeur believes it is the nature of language to express being (ontology).[59] There is a degree of sameness in the self as there is a difference. Police courts prosecute people for something they did previously and it is considered to be a prosecution of the same self, yet this self is constantly changing, though not absolutely so. There is an identity of the self through time. This ontological nature of the self as other is not the ontology of Descartes or Kant; it is not the denial of the ontological nature of the self in Nietzsche; it is rather a combination of both ontological perspectives.

Does this ontology of the self entail the idea of the resurrection of the body and life after death? Clearly it does for Ricoeur, but he does not attempt to argue for this doctrine on philosophical grounds. He does not try to demonstrate it rationally, but rather in a Barthian sense his belief in the God of Jesus Christ is based on a response to a divine call.[60] Ricoeur insists that his proposal for a hermeneutics of the self is based on "autonomous, philosophical discourse," which stops short of discussing belief in the resurrection of the body. Ricoeur says that his reflections on the nature of the self are not an attempt to secretly insert his personal religious beliefs into his philosophy just as he has no intention of allowing his philosophy to secretly be seen as an expression of his faith.[61] At the same time, Ricoeur believes that his philosophical reflections on the nature of the self is enriched by biblical faith, and he believes it is important for philosophy to learn from the Christian idea of the self, but this is not to reintroduce a foundational premise, which he says "my hermeneutical philosophy never ceases to combat."[62] He rejects both a "cryptophilosophical" and a "cryptotheological" intention.[63] Ricoeur is a post-foundationalist. As a Christian, these beliefs, such as the resurrection, are based on the "call" of the gospel.

Toward A Relational Ontology

It is often assumed that the concept of ontology is to be contrasted with a relational view of things. Instead the contrast should be between a *substantialist* ontology and a *relational* ontology. As Paul Ricoeur has noted, the concept of being (substance) cannot be set aside in favor of a non-ontological way of viewing reality. For the concept of being is deeply embedded in our language as a primary means of expressing our experiences of reality. Variations of the verb to be ("is," "are," be") form almost every sentence we speak or write, and it would be reductionistic to think of being as simply serving a mere function of grammar without any onto-logical significance. Ricoeur's point is that since Martin Heidegger (the once Jesuit student who embraced atheism and became the leading existentialist philosopher in the 20th century at the University of Freiburg, Germany) opposed an "onto-theology" many theologians have concluded that theology must be non-ontological. Heidegger assumed that *Being* and God could not be equated since to speak of a personal God as Being would turn God into a *being*, and hence in Christian theology God is inconsistently defined as the highest being. Because Being is not one category among other categories, which describe particular beings, but rather Being stands above beings, Heidegger believed it was impossible to connect the Christian idea of God with "the metaphysic of being." So his question for Being was a philosophical quest, not a religious one. Heidegger believed "ontotheology" collapsed under the proclamation of Nietzsche that "God is dead." Instead, Christian faith must be "referred back to its Near Eastern place of origin and divested" of its marriage with Greek philosophy as performed by the Early Church Fathers.[64] Heidegger believed this means that Western culture is to be thoroughly secularized as its Judeo-Christian heritage is repudiated.[65] He further supposed that the task of Christian theology is to rethink the idea of God "after Nietzsche" in strictly Jewish thought forms without using the categories of Hellenism. However, Ricoeur notes that the idea of a Christian theology without ontology will result in post-Christian thinking tinged with neopaganism.[66]

Ricoeur sees this as a mistake for the future of theology as well as a mistaken interpretation of Christian theology in the past. He notes that Aristotle allowed that "being" could be said in many ways, and Ricoeur proposes that Hebrews thought of being in a new way.[67] He believes that theology and ontology are connected, but different from the way that Greek philosophy defined ontology. Ricoeur also points out that Heidegger overlooked the fact that premodern theology, as in Thomas Aquinas, did not simply equate God with Being as was done in "the latest scholastic version" and as it was also done with Descartes.[68] Thomas Aquinas defined God as the Act of Being who transcended beings and who thus cannot be defined as a being. The proper name for God is "He who is," and this means that God's essence and his existence coincide. Because of this, God cannot be literally defined because God is ineffable.[69]

Etienne Gilson[70] has argued that the Augustinian concept of God as Substance was replaced in Thomas Aquinas with the idea of God as the

Act of self-existence; God's essence is an act of Self-Existing. God is not simply equated with the Greek philosophy of being, but with the Act of self-existence. The history of salvation reflects the reality of God who is personal and who reveals God's self in the events of history. God is not lifeless abstract Being; God is not a being alongside other beings. God is ultimately Mystery who is revealed as personal and classically expressed in Exodus 3:15 as "I am who I am." But this "I am" of God is not to be fused with the concept of being in philosophy; rather we have a new way of understanding the nature of being: that God as the Act of being is One who self-exists.[71] This is a new way of speaking of being that Aristotle and Greek philosophy in general did not consider. Only in the biblical revelation did this new concept of being emerge. In this sense, biblical revelation implies a relational, historical ontology as opposed to the substantialist ontology of philosophy.

Ricoeur noted that theologian Jean-Luc Marion in his book, *God Without Being*, sought to redefine God in terms of love without ontology. Ricoeur observes that the idea of God in the "logic of superabundance of love" may appeal to those who like paradox and hyperbole, but it runs the risk of "reinforcing the current vogue of irrationalism."[72] He notes this disconnection of theology from philosophy is largely motivated by Heidegger's assumption that Nietzsche has shown that the God of metaphysics is "dead." This idea that "God is dead" assumed that Christian theology equated God with Being. Supposedly theology "after Nietzsche" must be radically different. This overlooks the fact that the God of modern philosophy is not the God of the premodern Christian world where it was recognized that God cannot be simply equated with the Aristotelian notion of being. The God of Moses who is revealed as "I am" cannot be made the equivalent of the God of Greek metaphysics. The ontological language of neo-Platonism used by the Early Church Fathers and of Medieval neo-Aristotelianism was adapted to say things about God that were never part of Greek philosophy. In this way, Christian theology *adapted*, but did not *adopt* Greek categories. Ricoeur observed that if theology pursues the path suggested by Marion, we run the risk of "disenculturing" and "marginalizing" ourselves. If we ignore the category of being used in our culture to express and to explain what we believe about God, we will be misunderstood at best, and not understood at all at worst.

Ricoeur believes that Christian theology must use the language of being (ontology) instead of merely the language of love. He believes this because the revelation of God as "I am Who I am" (Exodus 3:14) and the Hebraic *Shema*—"Hear, O Israel: YHWH our God is alone YHWH" (Dt 6:4)—are the presupposition for understanding that "God is love" (I John 4:8). The categories of being ("I am") and one (God alone is YWHW) cannot be simply dehellenized without remainder. Ricoeur maintains the "I am" (*'ehyeh*) of Exodus 3:14 cannot be cut off from the meaning of the verb "to be" in Greek *einai* (the Septuagint) and Latin *esse* (the Vulgate).[73] He particularly notes that the Greek translation of Exodus 3:14 as *ego eimi ho on* in the Septuagint was "a veritable event in thinking."[74] What Ricoeur maintains is that the Hebrew use of the verb introduced a new understanding of being.[75] Any attempt "to unknot" the connection between Being and God will not succeed;[76] for it has formed "the intellectual and spiritual identity of the Christian West."[77] At the same time, Ricoeur shows that the premodern philosophers opposed the abstract and essentialist concept of being because of Exodus 3:14.[78] In this sense, medieval theologians did not believe that the concept of God as being could be mastered through intellectual abstractions.[79]

The fact that the New Testament links Exodus 3:14 with the vocabulary of being shows that the translation of "I am who I am" served as point of connection between the cultures of Israel and Greece. For example, Ricoeur maintains that Revelation 1:4—"the one who is, and who was, and who is coming"—is a retranslation of Exodus 3:14. Likewise with the statement in the Gospel of John—"Before Abraham was, I am" (John 8:58). Ricoeur shows that in the New Testament the vocabulary of being was used in reference to God and Christ, and therefore the Christological use of the Greek verb to be (*einai*) and subsequently in Latin (*esse*) is found from the Early Church Fathers to the medieval theologians.[80]

Jean-Paul Sartre: Human Nature or Human Condition?

John McIntyre (b. 1916), Professor Emeritus of Divinity, Edinburgh University (Scotland), finds helpful insights in the existentialism of Jean-Paul Sartre, which can be used to correct the substantialism of Aristotle particularly as it relates to the understanding of Jesus' human nature. Sartre denied there is an underlying, universal essence of humanity, called human nature. He insisted that the existence of anything always precedes its essence. The condition of existing in the real world shapes individual persons to be who they are in their very essence. Sartre rejects the idea that individual people derive their being from some generalized notion of humanity. A universalized person is no person at all. An individual's nature is the consequence of one's own decisions made in the stress and strain of life.

Sartre thus disallowed the concept of a universal *human nature*, but he affirmed the universal *human situation*. By "situation," he meant the circumstances of one's actual existence of living and dying in a real world of people who strive alongside each other in the give-and-take of society. It is this universal human condition that shapes who we are. Sartre interpreted the categories of substance and nature in terms of human society, making them dynamic and concrete. The classical concept of *human nature* tended to be static and lifeless, as if there was some literal, universal entity or actual universal nature that was embedded in human life. As opposed to this abstract concept, Sartre defined the human situation or condition as universal.[81] McIntyre has observed: "What Sartre has succeeded in doing for the modern understanding of the universalism which must be a part of our interpretation of human nature is that he has transferred it from the realm of logical universals to that of human society, human beings in relation to one another, human beings in decision. There can be no going back from that secure position."[82]

McIntyre believes this shift away from the abstract concept of substance to an emphasis upon the concreteness of the human situation helps to clarify the meaning of the two-nature model of the Chalcedonian creed, which affirmed that Jesus Christ is fully human and fully divine but one person. One of the philosophical problems of this orthodox creed is that there can be no nature without a person who inhabits that nature. If Jesus has a human nature, then there should be a human person in whom the human nature resided. If Jesus also has a divine nature, there should be a divine person in whom the divine nature resided. This would mean, however, that Jesus is two persons. Yet it is clear the creed intends to say that Jesus is one Person, not two persons, who embodies a fully divine nature and fully human nature. If Jesus were two persons and two natures, then he would have been a split personality with no essential personal unity. Only if the two natures are inseparably connected in one Person can Jesus be the true incarnation of God. Considerable debate in the history of theology has occurred over the resolution of this dilemma ever since the 4th century.

McIntyre proposes a resolution to this problem by rethinking human nature in terms of human condition. Instead of thinking of the human nature of Jesus in terms of a bloodless, static, abstract and universal entity, it is better to think of the human situation, which Jesus as the Son of God shared with humanity. What we normally mean by the divine

Logos assuming human nature is that Jesus entered into our condition, with its sorrows, loneliness, broken relationships, injustices, political tragedies, and that he assumed the burden of our sins and died an unjust death. Through his sufferings we experience reconciliation to God. This redeployment of human nature in terms of the human situation highlights that actions, decisions, conversations, preaching, teaching, and death identify who Jesus was, not some abstract, universal essence.[83]

E. L. Mascall, a prominent defender of classical Christianity, believes too much has been made of the philosophical implications of the language of "substance" and "essence," which has been used to describe Jesus and his relationship to God and humanity. Whereas in philosophy, these words had more technical connotations, in Christian theology the words have more of a commonsense, relational meaning.[84] Likewise, R. G. Collingwood (1889–1943), who was Professor of Philosophy at Oxford University from the time of his graduation until his retirement in 1941, said the concept of substance in Christian theology was radically different from the original Greek philosophical meaning because it no longer meant an underlying unchanging core of being, but rather God as substance was defined as activity.[85] The fundamental belief of the early Greek Cappadocian Fathers was that God acted in history to reveal God's being in a Trinitarian manner. Though the Early Church Fathers and subsequent Medieval theology used the concept of substance, it was significantly transformed from a static, Greek substantialist ontology in the direction of a relational ontology.

Notes

1. John Macmurray, *Persons in Relation* (London: Faber, 1995), p. 61. John Macmurray, *The Self as Agent* (London: Faber, 1995).

2. Cf. Philip Conford, *The Personal World: John MacMurray on Self and Society* (Edinburgh: Floris Books, 1997).

3. Cf. David G. Creamer, *Guides for the Journey: John Macmurray, Bernard Lonergan, James Fowler* (University Press of America, 1997). John E. Costello, *John Macmurray: A Biography* (Edinburgh: Floris Books, 2002). by John E. Costello

4. Cf. "Handlists of Manuscript Collections" in the Edinburgh University Library. Cf. http://www.lib.ed.ac.uk/lib/about/pubs/lg51/guide/h35.shtml (19 April 2004).

5. *Self As Agent*, p. 75.

6. Ibid., p. 11,

7. Ibid., p. 76.

8. Ibid., p. 76.

9. Ibid., p. 76.

10. Ibid., p. 77.

11. Ibid., p. 78.

12. Ibid., p. 126.

13. Ibid., p. 38.

14. Ibid., p. 126.

15. Ibid., p. 118.

16. Ibid., p. 38.

17. Ibid., p. 11.

18. Ibid., p. 31.

19. Ibid., p. 11-12.

20. Ibid., pp. 71-72.

21. Ibid., p. 15.

22. *The Self As Agent,* p. 73.

23. Ibid., pp. 78-79.

24. Ibid., p. 84.

25. Ibid., p.. 90.

26. Ibid., p. 101.

27. Ibid., p. 221.

28. Ibid., p.. 222.

29. *Oneself As Another,* trans. Kathleen Blamey (Chicago: University of Chicago Press, 1992), pp. 4-5.

30. Ibid., p. 1.

31. Ibid., p. 7.

32. Ibid., p. 8.

33. Ibid., pp. 2-4.

34. Ibid., p. 3.

35. Ibid., p. 4.

36. Ibid., p. 4.

37. Ibid., p. 7.

38. Ibid., p. 128.

39 Ibid.

40. Ibid., p. 126.

41. Ibid., p. 11.

42. Wolfhart Pannenberg, *Metaphysics and The Idea of God,* trans. Philip Clayton (Grand Rapids: Wm. B. Eerdmans, 1990), p. 44

43. Ibid.

44. Ibid.

45. Ibid., p. 13.

46. Cf. the citation by Ricoeur, *Oneself As Another,* p. 13 from Nietzsche, "On Truth and Lies" in *Course on Rhetoric.* Cf. W. Kaufmann's translation, *The Portable Nietzsche* (New York: Viking Press, 1968 (1954), p. 46.

47. *Oneself As Another,* pp. 15-16.

48. Ibid., p. 15.

49. Ibid., p. 19.

50. Ibid., p. 17.

51. Cf. Alasdair MacIntyre, *After Virtue, A Study in Moral Theory* (Notre Dame, Indiana: University of Notre Dame Press, 1984).

52. Ibid., p. 114.

53. Ibid., p. 4

54. Ibid., p. 143.

55. Ibid., p. 158.

56. Ibid., p. 161.

57. Ibid., p. 305.

58. Ibid., p. 303.

59. Ibid., p. 301.

60. Ibid., pp. 23-24.

61. Ibid.

62. Ibid., p. 25.

63. Ibid., pp. 25ff.

64. Paul Ricoeur and André Lacocque. *Thinking Biblically: Exegetical and Hermeneutical Studies* (Chicago: University of Chicago Press, 1998), p. 357.

65. Ibid., p. 357.

66. Ibid., p. 357.

67. Ibid., p. 360.

68. Ibid., pp.348f.

69. Ibid., p. 356.

70. Etienne Gilson, *God and Philosophy* (New Haven: Yale University Press, 1941).

71. *Thinking Biblically*, p. 356.

72. Ibid., p. 359.

73. Ibid., p. 360.

74. Ibid., p. 331.

75. Ibid., p. 360.

76. Ibid., p. 331

77. Ibid., p. 331

78. Ibid., p. 335.

79. Ibid., p. 335

80. Ibid., pp. 339-340.

81. McIntyre, *The Shape of Christology* (Philadelphia: Westminster Press, 1966), p. 108.

82. Ibid.

83. Ibid., pp. 112-113.

84. Ibid., pp. 104, 333.

85. R. G. Collingwood, *The Idea of History* (New York: Oxford University Press, 1976), p. 47.

4

A Post-Critical Concept of Truth

The Rise of Postmodern Science

The pre-modern worldview was dominated by the philosophy of Aristotle on every subject from philosophy to science and religion.[1] Instead of relying on Aristotelian authority in science, the new method of modern science turned to empirical experimentation using mathematical and quantitative thinking in order to discover universal laws of nature. This new method of empiricism led to the idea of a mechanistic universe where everything was determined by an absolute law of natural causation, which allowed for no variations or supernatural interference.[2]

Postmodern science has now radically changed this belief in the idea of a mechanistic universe.[3] With the rise of special and general theories of relativity and quantum mechanics at the beginning of the twentieth century, nature is now seen as including decisively subjective and unpredictable elements. Instead of the modernist divorce between subject and object, there is an interaction between thought and experience, and this interaction is the basis for penetrating into the intelligible depths of nature. Postmodern science has demonstrated that the modern views of infinite time and absolute space, as well as the idea of atoms being the building blocks of the universe, are incorrect.[4] A radically new understanding of the world has opened up that has overthrown the so-called modern scientific worldview.

Quantum theory has demonstrated that there is a decisive element of uncertainty functioning at the subatomic particle level of reality.[5] For example, it is impossible to determine simultaneously both the position and the momentum of an electron as it rotates around the nucleus of an atom. What seems to happen is that the personal involvement of the physicist influences the behavior of these subatomic particles. What also seems to be happening is that subatomic particles are engaged in an interactive and relational play among themselves that cannot be fitted into the mechanistic view of modern science. Even more puzzling, electrons suddenly pop into existence out of nothing and then just as suddenly disappear.

This uncertainty principle has been the occasion for numerous debates and has led to a rethinking of the idea of objective rationality inherent in the universe. Whereas modern science based on Newtonian principles believed that things could be predicted with certainty, postmodern science has demonstrated that formal categories based on logical rules of thinking are not altogether applicable.[6] There seems to be a dynamic element of openness and freedom about physical nature that eludes the physicist's ability to control and to predict its behavior with rational clarity. This subjective, interactive, relational, and open-ended characteristic of physical nature has become a paradigm for the postmodern age. If the modern world was obsessed with the need for certainty in epistemology, religion, and science, the postmodern world celebrates the absence of certainty and embraces the ambiguities of the world in all things.

A significant influence contributing to the rise of postmodernism in America was a book by Thomas Kuhn, *The Structure of Scientific Revolutions* (1962).[7] Kuhn challenged the notion of "hard facts," contending that scientific knowledge is actually a social development in which competing interpretations (scientific paradigms) confront each other based on unstable evidence.[8] Kuhn's basic assumption was that the idea of objective truth and universal rationality do not exist. Rather, theories of science are developed through a series of paradigms that attempt to explain how things are. This work is widely considered to have been a milestone in contemporary philosophy, mapping out a new direction in thinking about the openness and subjectivity of truth.[9] As a result of this new environment of thinking, Richard Bernstein shows that "a new conversation is now emerging among philosophers—a conversation about human rationality—and as a result of this dialogue we are beginning to gain a new understanding of rationality that has important ramifications for both theoretical and practical life."[10]

Richard Rorty: A Critique of Modernism

A leading American spokesman for postmodernity is Richard Rorty, who was born in 1931 and has taught at the Universities of Princeton, Virginia, and Stanford.[11] He was trained as an analytic philosopher, the dominant philosophy in contemporary Anglo-American thought. Its primary feature is to clarify the meaning of words in order to evaluate the consistency of philosophical claims. With the publication of his book, *Philosophy and the Mirror of Nature*, he proposed that modern philosophy should be abandoned and considered analytic philosophy in particular as "one more variant of Kantian philosophy."[12] He believed the modernist self-understanding as the adjudicator of knowledge was based on the false assumption of a body-mind dualism and on the alleged task of the mind to represent faithfully the outside world of things. Modern philosophy imagined the mind to be like a mirror that reflects reality; thus the task of philosophy was to polish and inspect this mirror to insure that its pictures were accurately reflecting reality.[13] The mind allegedly has this ability to represent reality to itself because it possesses inherent foundational principles for knowing everything that can be known.

Rorty says that modern philosophy is an "escape from history." It is "an attempt to find nonhistorical conditions of any possible historical development."[14] Rorty notes that modern philosophy drew a radical distinction between the mind's perception of things and things themselves. This is a main point of difference between pre-modern and modern thought. For Descartes and Locke, reality is *represented* to the mind through ideas, as if the mind were an inner eye which surveys and reviews reality through the use of these ideas, whereas for premodern philosophy the mind is able to comprehend the essences of things directly.[15]

Another way of stating this difference is that the pre-modern age did not distinguish between "conscious states" and "the external world."[16] The concept that the mind is "a self-contained sphere of inquiry" over against the world it knows through representative ideas "originated in the seventeenth century."[17] Rorty has called for the "deconstruction" of this modern radicalization of the subject-object distinction and its representative theory of knowledge.[18] He proposes to put in its place a philosophy with "no inner mirror."[19] This philosophy recognizes that one's view of reality grows out a conversation with others in dealing with the practical affairs of everyday life instead of a philosophy that seeks to announce what is true, good, and beautiful based on an ahistorical point of view. It sees knowledge as conditioned by the historical contingencies of life.

In contrast to modern philosophy, historical contingency is viewed favorably as being the basis of one's life orientation instead of an ahistorical concept of universal, abstract principles, which transcend historical situations. In this sense, knowledge is historical and "a social phenomenon," not the result of a correspondence between "the knowing subject" and "reality."[20] As a post-modern philosopher, Rorty believes that "pictures rather than propositions, metaphors rather than statements . . . determine most of our philosophical convictions."[21] He is not denying the total relevance of the subject-object distinction or the practical notion that truth is a correspondence of things to reality (such as the statement, "The snow is white").[22] Rather, he is rejecting the mirror concept of the mind as if things in themselves are ontologically distinct from our perceptions of them. His is a neo-pragmatic philosophy stemming from the traditions of John Dewey and William James. It rejects the idea of truth as a correspondence between the mind and objects by believing that it can transcend the polarity of subject and object. Rather, this unity is achieved by a feeling of collegiality in an inclusive community that respects difference and cultural variations.

Rorty defends himself against those who charge him with relativism and irrationalism, arguing that these charges are the result of a "mindless defensive reflexes of the philosophical tradition" which is fixated on an epistemological dualism of subject and object.[23] Rorty replies: "Such charges have no weight."[24] Why? Because they are based on an outdated modernist dualism of knower and known. Rorty thus calls for "the demise of foundational epistemology"[25] because it falsely assumes "that to be rational, to be fully human, to do what we ought, we need to be able to find agreement with other human beings"[26] in the sense there are universal principles of rationality which underlie the foundation for all right thinking. Rorty proposes a "holistic, antifoundationalist, pragmatist" philosophy which puts an end to this kind of epistemology which has dominated the history of Western thought.[27]

In calling for "the demise of epistemology," Rorty is *not* calling for an alternative discipline of thought to replace it. More specifically, Rorty calls for *a new direction* that breaks with "the epistemologically centered philosophy" of the past.[28] He interprets this new direction as moving "from epistemology to hermeneutics," and he turns away from Anglo-American analytic philosophy to the European Continental trend in hermeneutics as represented in the philosophy of Hans Gadamer.[29] He notes that Gadamer's primary goal is "to get rid of the classic picture of man-as-essentially-knower-of-essences" in an attempt "to get rid of the distinction between fact and value."[30] Rorty sees hermeneutics as "an expression of hope that the cultural space left by the demise of episte-mology will not be filled."[31]

Hermeneutics rejects the idea that knowledge is an accurate repre-sentation of facts existing independently of the knower. Hermeneutics is edifying in the sense that it aims at "continuing a conversation rather than at discovering truth."[32] Hermeneutics assumes that we can know reality as we understand its parts, and we can only know its parts as we participate in it and share it with others. Interpretation is like coming to know someone rather than following a logical demonstration. It is like a conversation where we go back and forth trying to guess what is meant by statements until we feel we have adequately guessed and understood what is being said. Interpretation is consequently more a matter of understanding than formal epistemology.[33]

If epistemology is abandoned, then hermeneutics is what is left.[34] Rorty's proposals for a new direction in philosophy without epistemolo-gy is his way of getting "rid of the spirit-nature distinction, conceived as a division between human beings and other things."[35]

Polanyi: A Post-Critical Philosophy

Another influential thinker who challenged the prevailing modernist par-adigm of truth was Michael Polanyi (1891-1976), an internationally-known Hungarian physicist whom Thomas Torrance has called "one of the greatest scientist-philosophers of our age."[36] He received his doctor of philosophy degree from Budapest in 1917 and he moved to Berlin in 1920 where he became one of Germany's leading physical chemists. Because of the growing attacks on Jewish intellectuals, he moved to England in 1933 where he accepted a faculty position in physical chem-istry at Manchester University.[37] This transition from Germany to England also entailed a transition from an interest in physics to social thought. In 1948, he accepted a chair in social studies at Manchester University. After he retired from Manchester to accept a position of sen-ior research fellow at Merton College, Oxford, he wrote his main philo-sophical work, *Personal Knowledge* (1958). In this book, Polanyi devel-oped a post-critical epistemology that has had significant influence among Christian theologians.[38] Jerry Gill suggests this work may be the most important book written in the last four hundred years.[39]

Polanyi's main concern was to criticize the modernist view of scien-tific knowledge, which assumed that a knower could impersonally and from an emotionally detached point of view control and interpret reality explicitly and clearly. This mind-material dualism resulted in scientific materialism, while the mind was virtually sidelined as an uninvolved spectator. The dominant idea of scientific materialism is a mechanistic conception of the universe. Polanyi refers to this worldview as the "massive modern absurdity."[40] In contrast to this mind-material dualism, Polanyi believed that in "every act of knowing there enters a tacit and passionate contribution of the person knowing what is being known."[41] He thus defined knowing as embodied action, or "indwelling." [42] Knowing involves the personal involvement of the subject in the object itself. Polanyi writes: "The participation of the knower in shaping his knowledge, which had hitherto been tolerated only as a flaw—a shortcoming to be eliminated from perfect knowledge—is now recognized as the true guide and master of our cognitive process."[43] It is embodied experience, but knowing is a social event also in the sense that everything one claims to know can be publicly discussed. It is thus not subjective arbitrariness. It is this "intuitive" and personal grasp of things based on the real nature of things as it interacts with the mind that Polanyi found appealing in Einstein relativity theory.[44]

As opposed to the extreme dualism of Kant's critical philosophy, Polanyi emphasizes that knowing takes place in the context of a continuum.[45] First, there is one's *awareness* of things—ranging from *subsidiary* awareness to *focal* awareness. One is aware in a subsidiary way, for example, of the words in this sentence while being focused on the idea it presents. Immediately one's focal awareness can shift to the actual words of this sentence and then one becomes aware in a subsidiary way of the idea contained in this sentence. Second, there is a continuum of activity ranging from *bodily activity to conceptual activity*. In place of a body-mind dualism, there is reciprocity of bodily activity and thinking occurring simultaneously. Third, knowing is a continuum ranging from *tacit knowledge* to *explicit knowledge*. Subsidiary awareness, bodily activity, and tacit knowledge form one pole of the continuum, while focal awareness, conceptual activity, and explicit knowledge form the other pole. Jerry Gill, who is an analytical philosopher and specialist in the thought of Polanyi, has labeled this theory "the contextual and continua interpretation of cognitivity."[46]

The personal aspect of knowing is an ongoing process. People are always learning new things and linking them to previous knowledge. We shift from more or less tacit knowing to more or less explicit knowing every moment of our lives. It is the nature of personal knowledge to blend the old with the new and the well known with the unforeseen.

The critical philosophy of Kant assumed the priority of the explicit pole—that phenomena can be exhaustively interpreted with rational certainty, whereas the tacit pole was downgraded to a mere logical inference. Kant failed to see the interactivity of these two poles, believing that the mind could control the meaning of facts independent of personal feelings. For Polanyi, this is a myth of modernist epistemology. For what one feels emotionally, spiritually, and physically is a decisive component in the process of knowing, and it is this tacit (pre-verbal and personal) dimension that should be given priority over explicit knowing.[47] Polanyi writes: "Tacit knowing is in fact the dominant principle of all knowledge."[48]

Polanyi described his philosophy as "post-critical" many years before the term, postmodern, was introduced to the general public, and postmodernists such as Rorty included Polanyi among their number.[49] In his book, *Meaning*, Polanyi favorably discussed Thomas Kuhn's book, *The Structure of Scientific Revolutions*, which he said "brought further confirmation of my views in detail."[50] Polanyi's interpretation of Kuhn is probably wrong. While it may be true that Polanyi and Kuhn "both have stressed the personal contribution of the discoverer in discovery,"[51] Kuhn's postmodernism did not support Polanyi's view that truth is a grasp of the way things really are. While Kuhn allowed for the existence of the world beyond our senses, it is not clear that he allowed for an objective truth beyond one's own personal assessment. As Rorty argues in his book, *Contingency*, there is "a distinction between the claim that the world is out there and the claim that truth is out there."[52]

For Polanyi, the attainment of truth requires responsible, personal judgments, but truth is not the result of universal principles that can be used as algorithms.[53] He writes: "Nothing that is said, written or printed, can ever mean anything in itself: for it is only a *person* who utters something—or who listens to it or reads it—who can mean something *by* it. All these semantic functions are the tacit operations of a person."[54] Truth is a personal insight into the way things really are, whereas for Kuhn truth is a useful paradigm of the way things work until it no longer proves useful, and then new paradigms are constructed to replace the old ones. Likewise with Rorty, truth is not "out there" which can be learned through making responsible, personal judgments (as with Polanyi), but rather, truth is a pragmatic assessment of what is useful personally and socially. However, Polanyi agrees with the postmodern rejection of Kant's dualistic view of knowledge. He also agrees that knowing is a personal process that inevitably involves metaphorical language as opposed to rationally precise descriptions. He appreciated the social dimensions of truth and was a strong proponent of freedom of thought, yet he was a practicing Christian believer,[55] a faith that he had in common with his personal friend and literary executor, Thomas Torrance, Emeritus Professor of Christian Dogmatics of Edinburgh University.[56]

Much has been written on the religious implications of Polanyi's concept of tacit knowing.[57] The particularly attractive feature of his post-critical philosophy is his emphasis that all knowing involves an element of faith and trust. It is in the act of belief and trust that the scientist makes fundamental discoveries of the nature of things. Without the intuitive acts of knowing, the mind of the physicist could not penetrate into the intelligible functioning of nature. It is this concept of belief which the scientist assumes in scientific discoveries that is also relevant to the concept of belief which Christian faith assumes in its understanding of God's self-revelation in history. Belief, commitment, and personal trust are dispositional presuppositions for all knowing. Polanyi insists that the study of human experience in its various branches uses "essentially the same method."[58] Faith is not blind; rather it is the attitude of accepting that what one believes has been received from the inherent nature of reality itself. There is thus an overlapping disposition of faith between science and theology.[59]

Religious faith is more than a disposition. Polanyi believes that religious faith involves an element of commitment to God that has redeeming significance for the believer to understand what otherwise one cannot see. In articulating the religious implications of *Personal Knowledge*, Polanyi notes: "only a Christian who stands in the service of his faith can understand Christian theology and only he can enter into the religious meaning of the Bible."[60] This limitation is not a pietistic notion that assumes a radical distinction between reason and a heart-felt belief. The subjectivism of Pietism was itself a reaction to the modern elevation of reason over faith. Polanyi is not assuming a modern division of reason and faith, but he is arguing that all knowing involves the element of commitment, both in science and in Christian faith. So his emphasis that only believers can genuinely appreciate the meaning of the Bible is the outcome of his post-critical epistemology.

Wolfhart Pannenberg once said to me that he believed that the implications of Polanyi's epistemology were highly significant for Christian theology, particularly his views on tacit knowing. Pannenberg's unpublished dissertation on the doctrine of analogy was on the idea that language is inherently religious and that through a process of philosophical abstraction language came to be secularized.[61] Modern thought had trouble with the idea of metaphorical language, largely because of its concept of literalism and its view that truth is impersonal and controlled with absolute precision. Polanyi, along with postmodernists, has argued for a relational understanding of truth, emphasizing the personal and social dimensions of truth. Pannenberg's emphasis on the unity of reality and truth also places him among the post-critical epistemologists, but whether or not Pannenberg (or Polanyi) should be called a postmodernist depends on how broadly the term is used.

David Griffin, the editor of a series of books on postmodernism, has proposed that a distinction between *deconstructive* postmodernism and *reconstructive* postmodernism ought to be made. The former is concerned primarily with bringing the modern worldview and its concern for universal truth to an end. The latter is interested in preserving the valid issues of modern thought, but at the same time wanting to readjust its worldview to allow for a more holistic view of reality.[62] Griffin also points out the varied meanings of the term, postmodern, ranging from its use in artistic and literary circles to architecture, philosophy, and theology.[63] Given Griffin's definition, Polanyi could be considered as offering a reconstructive postmodern philosophy when he first introduced the term "post-critical" to describe his theology in 1958.[64]

Jean-Francois Lyotard: A Critique of Metanarrative

In 1979, the French philosopher, Jean-Francois Lyotard, introduced the term, "postmodern," to a broad range of scholars in his book, *The Postmodern Condition: A Report on Knowledge*, although the term was already being used to some extent on the American continent among sociologists and critics.[65] He is widely recognized as one of the leading postmodern theorists in the world today, and his writings have provoked considerable discussion on deconstructing modern thought.

He used this term to describe the transformations that are taking place in our postindustrial, electronic world today.[66] He defined the main feature of postmodernism "as incredulity toward metanarratives."[67] By metanarratives he means the idea that there is a universal truth that can be communicated between "the sender and the addressee of a statement" that is intellectually binding for all rational minds. He refers to this modernist idea of rational communication as "the Enlightenment narrative."[68] Supposedly this modernist metanarrative has "a good ethico-political end—universal peace." Lyotard rejects this universalist assumption, claiming that one method or one set of categories and values is no better than another set. This modernist appeal to a rational foundation for universal truth (known as "foundationalism") reflects a dysfunctional attitude that he called "terroristic" and "totalitarian." He believed that "each of us lives at the intersection" of the modern and postmodern worlds, and as a result metanarratives are increasingly being set aside.

He showed that a distrust of metanarratives began with modern science: "Science has always been in conflict with narratives. Judged by the yardstick of science, the majority of them prove to be fables."[69] He noted that modern science itself sought to justify and legitimate its own method of seeking for universal truth through turning to philosophical reflection. But postmodernism sees this secular "metadiscourse" (creating a non-religious knowledge of universal morality and justice through rational reflection) as just one more fable among many others.[70] If modern thought deconstructed religious narratives as fable, postmodern thought is deconstructing the modern idea of metadiscourse as just another fable.

Lyotard believed the process of reconstructing the idea of universal truth in a secular, non-religious way was completed by the end of the 1950s, and subsequently modernism is being deconstructed also as naïve and authoritarian.[71] Postmodernism thus champions a plurality of narratives and viewpoints, none of which can claim to be absolute. Lyotard's views have occasioned considerable debate across the university curriculum, but his views of postmodernism do not in themselves have the negative consequences for religious faith that might seem to be obvious upon first reflection. On the contrary, Christian theology is not well served by modernist epistemology. For example, Lyotard's refutation of the modernist claim to possess universal truth based on foundationalist principles implicitly demonstrates the failure of liberal theology. This is because theological liberalism assumed that the significance of Jesus was his embodiment of the universal principle of morality based on a rationalistic reinterpretation of the gospels rather than on the basis of the history of salvation.

Notes

1. Herbert Butterfield, *The Origins of Modern Science* (New York: Macmillan Company, 1959), p. 3.

2. Ibid.

3. Cf. A. Shadowitz, *Special Relativity* (Philadelphia: W. B. Saunders Company, 1968); R. G. Mitchell, *Einstein and Christ, A New Approach to the*

Defence of the Christian Religion (Edinburgh: Scottish Academic Press, 1987).

4. Cf. Stephen Hawking, *A Brief History of Time* (London: Bantam Books, 1988); Steven Weinberg, *The First Three Minutes: A Modern View of the Origin of the Universe* (New York: Basic Books, 1977).

5. Cf. John Polkinghorne, *The Quantum World* (London: Longman, 1984)

6. Ibid., p. 59.

7. Cf. Bernstein, *Beyond Objectivism and Subjectivism*, pp. 20. Richard Rorty, *Philosophy and the Mirror of Nature*, pp. 322-356. David D. Roberts, *Nothing but History: Reconstruction and Extremity After Metaphysics* (Berkeley: University of California Press, 1995), p. 8.

8. Cf. Richard J. Bernstein, *Beyond Objectivism and Subjectivism*, pp. 54ff.

9. Cf. Thomas S. Kuhn, The *Structure of Scientific Revolutions* (University of Chicago Press, 1974). Cf. Bernstein, *Beyond Objectivism and Subjectivism*, pp. 51ff.

10. Bernstein, *Beyond Objectivism and Subjectivism*, p. 2.

11. Ramberg, Bjørn, "Richard Rorty", *The Stanford Encyclopedia of Philosophy (Summer 2002 Edition)*, Edward N. Zalta (ed.). Http://plato.stanford. edu/archives/sum2002/entries/rorty (19 April 2004)

12. Richard Rorty, *Philosophy and the Mirror of Nature*, pp. 8, 257ff. Cf. Richard J. Bernstein, *Beyond Objectivism and Subjectivism*, pp. 197-207.

13. Rorty, *Philosophy and the Mirror of Nature*, p. 12. See especially the chapter on "The Invention of the Mind."

14. Ibid., p. 9.

15. Ibid., pp. 44ff.

16. Ibid., p. 47.

17. Ibid., p. 126.

18. Ibid., pp.3ff.

19. Ibid., pp. 126-127.

20. Ibid., p. 9ff.

21. Ibid., p. 12.

22. Ibid., pp. 299ff.

23. Ibid., p. 13.

24. Ibid., p. 13.

25. Ibid., p. 315.

26. Ibid., p. 316.

27. Ibid., p. 317.

28. Ibid., p. 315.

29. Ibid., pp. 357-365.

30. Ibid., p. 364.

31. Ibid., p. 315.

32. Ibid., p. 373.

33. Ibid., p. 319.

34. Ibid., p. 325.

35. Ibid., p. 379.

36. Thomas Torrance, "Introduction," *Belief in Science and in Christian Life, The*

Relevance of Michael Polanyi's Thought for Christian Faith, ed. Thomas Torrance (Eugene, OR: Wipf and Stock Publishers, 1998), p. xiii.

37. Http://griffon.mwsc.edu/~polanyi/guide/3pprs.htm (19 April 2004).

38. Cf. Thomas Langford, "Michael Polanyi and The Task of Theology," *Journal of Religion* 46 (1.1) January 1966, 45-55.

39. Jerry Gill, *The Tacit Mode,* p. 10. For a review of recent literature on the thought of Polanyi, see Jerry Gill, *The Tacit Mode,* pp. 157-175.

40. Michael Polanyi, *Personal Knowledge* (University of Chicago Press, 1958), p. 9; cf. Thomas Torrance, "The Framework of Belief," *Belief in Science and in Christian Life,* p. 7.

41. Michael Polanyi, *Personal Knowledge,* p. 312.

42. Polanyi, *The Study of Man* (Chicago: University of Chicago Press, 1959), pp. 58ff. Cf. John C. Puddefoot, "Indwelling: Formal and Non-Formal Elements in Faith and Life," *Belief in Science and in Christian Life,* pp. 28-48.

43. Polanyi, *The Study of Man,* p. 26.

44. Cf. Polanyi, *Personal Knowledge,* pp. 3-17; Polanyi, "From Copernicus to Einstein," *Encounter* (September 1955), 54-63.

45. Michael Polanyi, *The Study of Man,* pp. 30-31.

46. Jerry Gill, *The Possibility of Religious Knowledge* (Grand Rapids: Wm. B. Eerdmans, 1971), pp. 117-145. More recently, Gill has used the image of an axis to describe the various dimensions of knowing in Polanyi's philosophy. *The Tacit Mode,* pp. 57, 91, 154.

47. Michael Polanyi, *The Study of Man,* pp. 16-17.

48. Ibid., p. 13.

49. Rorty, *Philosophy and the Mirror of Nature,* pp. 225, 227, 328.

50. Michael Polanyi, *Meaning,* pp. 56-57.

51. Cf. John Barr, "Conversion and Penitence," *Belief in Science and in Christian Life,* p. 49.

52. Rorty, *Contingency,* pp. 4-5.

53. Polanyi, *The Study of Man,* pp. 21ff.

54. Ibid., p. 22.

55. *Personal Knowledge,* pp. 281, 405.

56. *Belief in Science and in Christian Life,* p. 148. Jerry Gill believes that Torrance has largely misunderstood the religious implications of Polanyi's philosophy. Gill reviews the literature on this issue, concluding with Harry Prosch "that there is no evidence in any of Polanyi's writings for Torrance's conflation of his own ideas with those of Polanyi." *The Tacit Mode,* p. 172. I personally think this is an exaggerated assessment, though perhaps Torrance overworks the concept of reality as self-disclosing itself in the act of knowing. Cf. *Belief in Science and in Christian Life,* p. 15 where Torrance speaks of reality "disclosing itself." This tends to be more Barthian than Polanyian, but Torrance is right to argue that Polanyi assumes that there is a rational structure in reality which is intelligible to the mind. However, Polanyi also emphasizes that one's personal and passionate involvement is the decisive factor in knowing, not the self-disclosure of an

objective reality mirroring itself in self-consciousness.

57. Cf. Thomas Langford, "Michael Polanyi and the Task of Theology," *Journal of Religion* 46 (1.1) January 1966, 45-55.

58. Polanyi, *The Study of Man*, p. 41.

59. *Belief in Science and in Christian Life* is devoted to this comparison between science and theology as it relates to the thought of Polanyi.

60. *Personal Knowledge*, p. 281.

61. Cf. Pannenberg, "An Autobiographical Sketch," *The Theology of Wolfhart Pannenberg*, ed. Carl E. Braaten and Philip Clayton (Minneapolis: Augsburg Publishing House, 1988).

62. David Griffin, "Series Introduction," to Jerry Gill, *The Tacit Mode, Michael Polanyi's Postmodern Philosophy*, p. xi.

63. Griffin, "Series Introduction," to Jerry Gill, *The Tacit Mode*, p. xi.

64. Cf. Jerry H. Gill, *The Tacit Mode, Michael Polanyi's Postmodern Philosophy*, p. 1.

65. Jean-Francois Lyotard, *The Postmodern Condition: A Report on Knowledge*, trans. Geoff Bennington and Brian Massumi (Minneapolis: University of Minneapolis University, 1984), p. xxiii.

66. Ibid., p. 3

67. Ibid., p. xxiv.

68. Ibid.xxiii.

69. Ibid.

70. Ibid.

71. Ibid., p. 3.

5

Pannenberg's Theology of Universal History

If theology is to be true to itself, it is doubtful that it should begin with a foundationalist approach to truth. Nor should it begin with the presuppositions of any particular philosophy. The methodological point of departure for Christian reflection is the narrative of what has been revealed in salvation history. Wolfhart Pannenberg well stated this case: "Christian doctrine is from first to last a historical construct. Its content rests on the historical revelation of God in the historical figure of Jesus Christ and on the precise evaluation, by historical interpretation alone, of the testimony that early Christian proclamation gives to this figure."[1]

Pannenberg's theology of history has led some to think that he is a historicist,[2] but this is not an accurate representation of his theology. Leopold von Ranke, professor of history at the University of Berlin from 1825 until 1871, is recognized as one of the first historicists. His influence on many historians earned him the title, "the greatest German historian." He is also known as "the father of the objective writing of history" and "the founder of the science of history."[3] Von Ranke developed his view of history in opposition to Hegel's idea of universal history. He believed that the historian should write history "as it really happened,"[4] and this meant discovering the individual facts of history. This also entailed the method of discovering the past as it really happened independent of personal presuppositions. This neo-Kantian view of history was dominant in the 19th century, which operated with a dualism of fact and value. Von Ranke's famous pupil, Wilhelm Dilthey, asserted the possibility of an objectivism of historical knowledge on the grounds that the historian is able to enter the mind of the author.[5] Pannenberg has particularly defeated this historicist view of historical objectivism.[6]

Pannenberg has shown that the historicism of Ernst Troeltsch (1865-1923) represents a serious challenge to Christian faith and that Troeltsch gave the clearest formulation to the problem of critical history for faith.

He argued that history is a closed web of cause-effect. All events are contingent and are on the same plane. There is nothing absolutely unique in history, and thus Jesus Christ as a human being can be explained in the same natural way that any other human being can be, namely, that he is the product of past events which shaped who he is. The principle of analogy was another fundamental assumption of Troeltsch's historicism. The past is to be explained on the analogy of what is known to be possible by present experience. Because we know today that resurrections are physically impossible, we must conclude that Jesus himself was not raised from the dead.[7] Pannenberg has been the most effective critic of historicism, showing that the guiding principles of the modern historical method entail presuppositions that are based on false notions of objectivism, irrefutable rationality, and the absolutizing of human subjectivity. He shows that modern historicism is largely philosophical positivism applied to historical studies.

A new appreciation for history is being promoted in what is being called the new historicism of postmodernism.[8] The new historicism is still enmeshed in the relativism of modernist historicism, but its rejection of the modernist view of causality in favor of recognizing discontinuities ("gaps") in history can be construed as being unwittingly friendlier toward religion in general and Christianity in particular. David D. Roberts, Professor of History at the University of Georgia, declares that we now have moved beyond foundationalism to a post-Hegelian view that there is *Nothing but History*, as his book is titled. The demise of metaphysics means history is "left standing alone, naked, for the first time—as all there is."[9] This view is post-Hegelian in the sense that radical contingency is affirmed without metaphysics and without the idea of universal reason (or God) lurking in the background. In rejecting metaphysics, postmodernism maintains, "there are only historical ways of knowing."[10]

Pannenberg's theology of history incorporates two major themes of postmodernism—"anti-foundationalism," as Rorty has called it, and historical contingency. Pannenberg does not directly discuss postmodernism. However, his idea of history shows that he incorporates constructive elements of both modernism and postmodernism, while transcending them. He agrees with modernism in the sense that history is contingent; he agrees with postmodernism in rejecting foundationalism. Like postmodernism, Pannenberg rejects the Hegelian notion that history is the reflection of a logically-fixed idea. He further agrees with the postmodernism that there are only historical ways of knowing. However, he moves beyond the postmodernist assumption that nothing universally true could emerge out of history. If postmodernism predetermines that nothing universally true can emerge out of history, this is a universal, metaphysical principle itself and inconsistently is a form of foundationalism. Pannenberg is more consistent in rejecting foundationalism by insisting that the appropriate attitude is to be open to what can be learned from history.

Reality as History

Pannenberg has shown that the historical character of truth has its source in the Old Testament as opposed to the classical Greek idea of truth.[11] Truth for the Greek was timeless in contrast to the Israelite view of the historicality of truth. The Hebrew word for truth is *emeth*. It means "standing firm, establishing, supporting, bearing."[12] It does not entail timelessness, but rather it is a recurring, temporal event, thereby indicating its reliability. A person's word is true, for example, if it shows itself to be reliable over the course of time. Thus, futurity is a fundamental feature of the Hebrew meaning of *emeth*. Hans von Soden shows that truth for the Israelites was a "reality (which) is regarded as history not something that in some way or another lies under or behind things, and is discovered by penetrating into their interior depths; rather, truth is that which will show itself in the future."[?]

The Greek idea of truth is *alētheuein*, unconcealment, i.e., a letting-be-seen. Since the physical senses prevent the genuine "unconcealment" of what is, *logos* as rational thought must reach behind the appearance to the unchanging reality. Just as Being is unchanging, so is truth. This unchangeable unity of truth and of what-is (Being) is distinguished from the changing multiplicity of appearances. This timelessness of truth and Being is thus opposed to the Israelite *emeth*, which emphasizes the historical manifestation of faithfulness and constancy. Thus, the happened-ness of truth, i.e., the event that constitutes the revelation of what-is, is of no material importance for the Greek. On the contrary, truth is the enduring, unchanging, timeless attribute of what-is.

For the Israelite, the essence of truth was knowledge of the enduring and constant, but it was knowledge based upon the continuing experience of the faithfulness of God's historical manifestations. It is this historical aspect of truth that stands over against the Greek concept of *logos* (as rational thought) through which the truth of being was uncovered. For the Israelite, one could only attain stability in the midst of the flux of change through entrusting oneself to God. Here faith (*he͜emin*) and truth (*emeth*) are closely related, as it is suggested by their having the same stem. That one attains stability through trust points out that truth will be seen to be reliable from the future. However, this future verification of truth does not eliminate the *present* knowledge of truth. That the truth of Jahweh is the unchanging and constant reality is not axiomatic, however. It is not a logical necessity from the standpoint of thought. That-which-is is not an abstract identity for the Israelite; rather the constancy of God is known on the basis of his historical activity. "He has shown his people the power of his works, in giving them the heritage of the nations. The works of his hands are faithful and just; all his precepts are trustworthy, they are established for ever and ever, to be performed with faithfulness and uprightness" (Psalm 111:6-8). Even the created order has its unity in the truth of God: "Thy faithfulness endures to all generations; thou hast established the earth, and it stands fast" (Psalm 119:90). Pannenberg shows that the biblical idea of constancy in nature, in the nations, or in the individual has its basis in the "truth of God."[14]

This means that truth is historically mediated. The Greek quest for the timeless unity of truth and true Being stands in contrast to the Old Testament insistence upon the historicality of truth, i.e., that the truth of what-is is mediated historically. The Greek idea of truth with its emphasis upon what-is is not excluded in the biblically derived meaning of reality, but is absorbed and modified. In fact, that the Greeks defined Being (what-is) as the constant and enduring reality explains why Hellenistic Judaism and early Christianity connected the God of the Bible with the Greek idea of true Being.[15]

However, the Greek dualism of true Being (subject) and changing sense-appearance (object) is overcome in the biblical meaning of truth. Instead of God as true Being described in terms of timelessness, God's truth is revealed historically, which truth is not exhausted in the present but always points to the future. The biblical God is distinct from creation as one who acts freely and contingently upon it in contrast to the Greek understanding of true Being in terms of a timeless cosmos. The Israelite view holds to the permanency of truth (namely, God) while at the same including those aspects that are rejected in the Greek view (as in Parmenides and Plato)—that is, changing sense-appearance—as true as well.[16]

However, since thought is distinguished from sense-experience, the problem arises how to bridge the gap between the two aspects. This question again raises the problem whether truth is something that comes under human control or whether truth is the *passive* reception of what presents itself to the senses. The question is not quite properly framed in this way, for in either case one may fall either into a dualistic definition of reality in which one can only know what merely appears in contrast to what really is, or else one may fall into the abyss of Hume's metaphysical agnosticism.

The dualism of subject and object is what led to the modernist correspondence theory of truth that ideas mirror facts, which postmodernism refutes. Rather, truth is multidimensional—relational, historical, and salvific. Truth is relational in the sense that the distinction between subject and object is preserved without divorcing these two poles. As Polanyi put it, the subject-object poles form a continuum, not a gap. There are no mere historical facts and there are no mere interpretations apart from facts; rather, a historical fact is the narration of an event interpreted in its larger context. Instead of an interpretation intellectually mirroring an event in the modernist sense, the meaning of an event emerges out of the lived context in which it happens.

Pannenberg was one of the first theologians today to criticize the way the subject-object divorce has been allowed to confuse a proper interpretation of Christian faith. He shows that the "splitting up of historical consciousness into a detection of facts and an evaluation of them (or into history as known and history as experienced) is intolerable to Christian faith." This dualism is largely responsible for the modernist interpretation of Jesus' resurrection as a subjective concept lacking objectively validity. Pannenberg also rejects this dualism because it represents "an outmoded and questionable historical method." He notes that it served as the basis of positivism and historicism—the assumption that the historian can discover and present bare, objective facts of history without being influenced by any subjective interpretation.[17]

Pannenberg insists upon the primordial unity of fact and meaning, event and interpretation. Every event imposes its own meaning to each inquirer. Not every event possesses equal clarity, but its clarity will be disclosed in proportion to the knowledge that the historian gains of its context and tradition and understands its connection and interests for the present.[18]

Pannenberg is not resorting to a modernist epistemology in which the mind mirrors reality. This context of tradition extends from the present moment of each particular inquirer into the past event. One must not simply inquire into the past as though it were a dead past. The historian is no cemetery caretaker.[19] This reciprocal relationship of past and present means that our present thought-world is not sacrificed to a previous worldview, but at the same time our own worldview is not inflexible or absolute. Pannenberg is not embracing an absolute relativism of historical knowledge, rather he is pointing out that any one event has its inherent meaning only as it is seen in the context of universal history. Obviously truth in any absolute sense of the word cannot be rationally comprehended by finite man, but this does not minimize the fact that the greater a knowledge of the traditio-historical context of any event is, the greater one's understanding of the event will be.

Pannenberg is careful to guard against permitting one's own subjective interpretation to be injected into an event of the past. Although an event must be interpreted in the context of universal history, this does not mean one can inject whatever interpretation one likes into the event. "If we are to take these facts seriously, nothing ought to be inserted so as to allow them to be seen in a way different from what would naturally emerge."[20]

That one does not see the events correctly does not mean that they are beyond human reason to know. It could be that one does not have sufficient historical data to see the meaning of an event. At any rate, insofar as the meaning of the Christ event is concerned, that certain people do not see Jesus as the revelation of God does not indicate this unique event is above reason to know. "If the problem is not thought of in this way, then the Christian truth is made into a truth for the in-group, and the church becomes a gnostic community."[21]

One might ask if the revelatory events are open for anyone who has eyes to see and if the interpretation of these events is self-evident to historical reason, why is there no general consensus of opinion concerning the revelation of God in Jesus of Nazareth? Pannenberg answers this question in reference to Paul's statement that "the god of this world has blinded the minds of the unbelievers" (2 Cor. 4:4).[22] Unbelief is the refusal to accept the "open truth" of the gospel (2 Cor. 4:2).[23] Pannenberg thus shows that faith and knowledge are related. The knowledge of revelation is linked to faith as the announcement of the good news, but it is "the resulting faith in God that secures participation in salvation."[24] The knowledge of revelation is thus impossible apart from the act of divine worship.

Theology and the Historical Method

Pannenberg has readjusted the modern concept of historical method, showing that it has been unnecessarily linked with rationalistic presuppositions that arbitrarily disallow the realism of salvation history. The reason why historical criticism in biblical studies has been seen to be so destructive of faith is because it has been practiced by those who believe that God does not really act in the history of the world. Freed from these prior conceptions, Pannenberg believes that the historical method is friendly toward the idea of the historical revelation of God in Jesus.[25]

His use of the historical method assumes that faith and knowledge are closely related. For example, Pannenberg shows that for the Reformers faith has three inseparable distinctions—*notitia* (insight), *assensus* (assent), and *fiducia* (trust). Pannenberg insists that the acceptance of Christian doctrine (*notitia*) is directly related to one's willingness (*assensus*) to trust in Christ (*fiducia*).[26] Unless one is willing to accept the report of the good news that Jesus is the risen Lord and to commit oneself to a trusting relationship with Christ, then one will also lose the insight (knowledge) of the historical fact of Jesus' resurrection from the dead.[27] Pannenberg maintains that only believers who worship Jesus can affirm that he was raised from the dead. He also allows that in some instances one may have the insight that Jesus was really raised from the dead but then subsequently lose that insight through lack of trust in, and worship of, Jesus.[28]

Here again it is evident that Pannenberg does not accept the modernist view that knowledge is simply a correspondence of intellectual ideas with objects. He makes a distinction between the logic of faith and the psychology of faith.[29] In principle, there is also a distinction between perception and reality. One's faith-perception that Jesus is the Son of God needs to be corroborated with the logic of reality, but this corroboration cannot take place merely in an intellectualistic way. Knowing involves in an interaction of *notitia, assensus,* and *fiducia.*

Thus, "Christian faith must not be equated with a merely subjective conviction that would allegedly compensate for the uncertainty of our historical knowledge about Jesus."[30] This would only make faith indistinguishable from superstition. Pannenberg thus sees the task of the theologian to be one of critically assessing the truth-claim of Christian faith. He notes, "for much too long a time faith has been misunderstood to be subjectivity's fortress into which Christianity could retreat from the attacks of scientific knowledge." The consequence of this retreat into pious subjectivity has been a loss of the consciousness of Christian truth.[31]

Pannenberg says "faith can breathe freely only when it can be certain, even in the field of scientific research, that its foundation is true."[32] For example, the historical character of the resurrection of Jesus (without which Pannenberg argues that there can be no Christology) cannot be ruled out *a priori* on modern presuppositions. It cannot be deprived of its historical past-ness and then re-interpreted existentially as Bultmann wanted to do. If there is any present significance to the resurrection kerygma, then it must be seen as telling us something about a real event of the past.

Pannenberg's Theology of the Resurrection

In arguing for the bodily resurrection of Jesus, Pannenberg pursues a closely reasoned argument which includes: (1) delineating the Old Testament and Jewish eschatological expectation of the general resurrection of the dead, (2) a historical-critical analysis of the resurrection traditions, (3) an exegesis of the resurrection texts, (4) a philosophical reflection on the possibility of Jesus' resurrection, and (5) anthropological considerations concerning the human hope for life beyond death.[33]

We will consider two of these arguments. First, Pannenberg believes the language of the Old Testament and the Jewish eschatological hope show that the expectation of the general resurrection of the dead was already present in the Jewish community. He also believes this expectation entailed an understanding of the difference between eternal, imperishable life on the one hand, and temporal, transitory life in this world, on the other hand. Hence the encounters with the risen Lord were expressed in already-existing thought-patterns, such as "resurrection from the dead," "rising from sleep," etc. (Isa. 26:19; Dan. 12:2; 1 Thess. 4:13ff; 1 Cor. 11:30; 15:6, 20, 51). The disciples did not have to invent a conceptuality of the resurrection when they reported that Jesus was raised from the dead. The resurrection of Jesus was described, not as a resuscitation of dead body, but the transformation of an old body into a "spiritual body" (1 Cor. 15:35-56). The early Christian community understood the difference between "the intended reality" on the one hand, and "the mode in which it is expressed in language," on the other hand.[34] Pannenberg's point is that the disciples knew how to express the reality of Jesus' resurrection without resorting to mythological conceptions. Without intending to negate the factuality of Jesus' resurrection, Pannenberg designates it as a "metaphor." Although the event happened in space-time, the language itself is a figure of speech because it speaks of a reality beyond human experience. Further, the term, "resurrection of the dead," is an "absolute metaphor," for it is an absolutely unique expression that cannot be interchanged with other images and expressions because there is nothing like it that has emerged in the history of the world.[35]

The second factor to be considered in establishing the resurrection as a historical event is the Pauline account of the appearances of the risen Lord to specific members of the Christian community (1 Cor. 15:1-11). Pannenberg believes the account of the appearances of Jesus in the four Gospels are legendary and historically unacceptable,[36] but he finds strong historical evidence of such appearances in Paul. This is because Paul gives a thoughtful and historical defense of the resurrection, using eyewitness testimony and a responsible use of a carefully formulated tradition, which he drew from. The nearness of Paul to the actual event and his ability to check out the information with numerous eyewitnesses sufficiently prove that Jesus was really raised from the dead instead of it being the result of mythical imagination and legend.[37]

The Historical-Critical Method and Jesus' Resurrection

The question arises whether Pannenberg has in fact "proven" the resurrection itself, or proven that Paul and those to whom he appeals as witnesses, whose testimony could be checked by Paul's contemporaries, merely *said* Jesus was raised on the basis of their having *remembered* certain appearances of the risen Lord. If one understands history in R. G. Collingwood's sense, then Pannenberg's proof is not a historical demonstration of the resurrection. Collingwood's classic work, *The Idea of History* (1946), argued that what is merely remembered does not qualify as scientific history. Paul's statement of the resurrection is based on the "memory" of those who witnessed the appearances of the risen Lord, but there was no present concrete evidence that Paul could appeal to, excepting of course the empty tomb, which Paul does not mention.

Collingwood, whose epistemology of history Pannenberg in general appreciates,[38] defined scientific historical knowledge in terms of what can be conclusively known comparable to the certainty that one can attain in mathematics. It leaves "nothing to caprice," and allows "no alternative conclusion, but proved its points as conclusively as a demonstration in mathematics."[39] However, Collingwood does not define all reality as history.[40] A biography is not defined as historical knowledge because it relies on memory and not concrete evidence. To be sure, Collingwood does not deny that a biography is genuine knowledge, but it is not historical knowledge because there is no immediate appeal to tangible evidence but only an appeal to one's memory.[41]

Collingwood defined historical knowledge in a very restricted sense: "If I say 'I remember writing a letter to So-and-so last week', that is a statement of memory, but it is not an historical statement. But if I can add 'and my memory is not deceiving me; because here is his reply', then I am basing a statement about the past on evidence; I am talking history."[42] Thus, scientific historical knowledge is imaginatively re-enacting the past on the basis of what is currently given as concrete evidence.

On the other hand, whenever it is admitted that historical conclusion represent degrees of probability, then Collingwood said that one is resorting to scissor-and-paste history, which relies on memory and authority of others.[43] However, Collingwood affirmed that we may accept as true some things even though we cannot appeal to the grounds upon which they are based. But this "information" is not scientific historical knowledge, even though it may be said that such is real knowledge and not mere belief.[44]

When Pannenberg states that the resurrection of Jesus has good historical foundation on the basis of those who saw the appearances of the risen Lord and that faith has its point of departure "on an event which we can know historically only with probability,"[45] then he is not providing a scientific historical demonstration of Jesus' bodily resurrection according to Collingwood's definition of history, rather he is historically demonstrating that Paul and the early Christian community *said* that Jesus was raised on the basis of their memory of his having appeared to them. If this is to be called a historical demonstration, then in Collingwood's terms this is scissor-and-paste history, based on the memory and authority of those who reported the appearances.

It is because theology has to deal with degrees of historical probabilities that causes the real rub for faith. This is why Kierkegaard and subsequent neo-orthodox theology refused to put faith at the mercy of historical research. For Kierkegaard, faith has its point of reference in history, but its sole condition is found in God. Faith is thus solely the work of God.[46] Pannenberg refutes this dichotomy of faith and history. He distinguishes between the certainty of faith and the certainty of historical knowledge and shows that they lie on different levels;[47] nevertheless, his exclusively critical-historical approach is at best problematic from an apologetic standpoint, if one assumes the modernist notion of history as seen in Collingwood's definition of scientific history. Pannenberg is surely right to resist this criterion of absolute knowledge as a definition of scientific history. However, even from the standpoint of Collingwood's epistemology of scientific history, Paul's re-enactment of the resurrection event based on the memory of the apostles, along with the concrete evidence of the empty tomb, qualify the resurrection of Jesus as "scientific knowledge." Certainly without the tradition of the empty tomb, Jesus' resurrection would be problematic even for believers today. Memories can be confusing, and hence the concrete evidence of the empty tomb was a necessary confirmation.

Pannenberg appeals to the tradition of the empty tomb and sees in this tradition a valid historical account.[48] Consequently, Pannenberg argues the resurrection event is historically demonstrated (even according to Collingwood's idea of "scientific" history) because there is not only the tradition of the appearances of the risen Lord, but also the tradition of the empty tomb as well. Unless the tomb was empty, the claim that Jesus was raised would have been immediately disproved by going to his tomb and producing his body as evidence. To be sure, today we do not have access to the empty tomb, but we do have access to the tradition that reported it. This tradition was not based on a memory, but upon physical evidence. Scientific, historical knowledge based on what is concrete evidence (and not mere memory) can thus be claimed for the resurrection event itself because there is good reason to accept the reliability of this tradition. But on the other hand, when Pannenberg argues that the Jewish apocalyptic expectation (which provided the language for expressing what is meant by the resurrection) and the Pauline kerygma constitute in themselves a historical demonstration,[49] it is problematic. Only if the tradition of the empty tomb can be supported (which Pannenberg argues in favor of) can the resurrection in theory be called a "scientific" historical demonstration. Even so, Pannenberg is right to say that historical demonstrations can only entail strong probabilities, not absolute certainty.

Collingwood's definition of "historical knowledge" has too much in common with positivistic historiography with its assumption that facts can be established with irrefutable proof. The suspicion arises whether or not Collingwood's so-called "scientific" history is a realistic assessment of what constitutes a historical demonstration. History should be "wholly a reasoned knowledge of what is transient and concrete," but is it really possible to assert that "scientific" history proves "its points as conclusively as a demonstration in mathematics"? Can historical knowledge ever advance beyond the concept of probability? Collingwood failed to appreciate that historical evidence and historical judgment are not the same. One's judgments about the historical evidence is always conditioned by varying degrees of probability.[50] In his criticism of Collingwood, Haskell Fain has observed: "A body of evidence may oblige assent; it can never compel it."[51]

In contrast to Collingwood's epistemology and from a more realistic assessment of what constitutes historical knowledge, the believer can speak of the resurrection as a historical event on the basis of Jesus' appearance to the disciples and can refer to this knowledge as *historical* knowledge because the appearances were occurrences that happened in space-time. At the same time it is to be acknowledged in accordance with Collingwood's epistemology that there can be no "scientific" historical verifiability of the resurrection merely from the standpoint of the Pauline kerygma, especially since Paul (1 Cor. 15:1-11) only appeals to the memory of those who witnessed the appearances of the resurrected Lord. However, the tradition of the empty tomb provides an important piece of additional information, showing that that the resurrection was an empirical event and not based upon mere memory. In the light of the appearances of the risen Lord and the tradition of the empty tomb, one can argue that there is sufficient "scientific" evidence for the resurrection. To disbelieve that Jesus was raised from the dead reflects a particular worldview that has prejudged the evidence on the basis that miracles are impossible rather than a fair and balanced assessment of what Paul's resurrection kerygma and the tradition of the empty tomb actually report.

Notes

1. Pannenberg, *ST*, p. x.

2. Cf. Robert North, "Pannenberg's Historicizing Exegesis," *The Heythrop Journal*, 2.4: 377-400.

3. Cf. Leopold von Ranke, *History of the Popes*, trans. E. Fowler, with an introduction by William Clark (New York: Colonial Press, 1901), 1:xvi. Cf. David D. Roberts, *Nothing but History: Reconstruction and Extremity After Metaphysics*, p. 31.

4. Leopold von Ranke, "Preface: *Histories of the Latin and Germanic Nations from 1494-1514*," trans. Fritz Stern, in *The Varieties of History: From Voltaire to the Present*, ed. Fritz Stern (Cleveland: World, Meridian, 1956), p. 57; cf Roberts, *Nothing but History*, p. 31 n.19.

5. Hans-Georg Gadamer, *Truth and Method*, trans. Garrett Barden and John Cumming (New York: Seabury Press, 1975), pp. 193ff., 266ff.

6. Pannenberg, "Redemptive Event and History," *Basic Questions in Theology*, 1:15-80.

7. Ibid., 1:38-50.

8. David D. Roberts, *Nothing But History: Reconstruction and Extremity after Metaphysics*, p. 2; Claes G. Ryn, "Defining Historicism," *Humanitas*, 11. (1998); Judith Newton, "History As Usual?: Feminism and the "New Historicism,'" *Cultural Critique* 9 (1988): 87-121.

9. Roberts, *Nothing But History*, p. 9.

10. Ibid., p. 8

11. Pannenberg, *Basic Questions in Theology*, trans. G. H. Kehm (London: SCM Press, Ltd., 1971), 2:1-17.

12. Ibid., p. 3.

13. *Was ist Wahrheit? Vom geschichtlichen Begriff der Wahrheit*, Marburger akademische Reden 46 (Marburg, 1927), cited in *Basic Questions in Theology*, 1:3.

14. *Basic Questions in Theology*, 1:9.

15. Ibid.

16. Ibid., 1:9-10.

17. "The Revelation of God in Jesus of Nazareth," *Theology As History*, p. 126. Cf. *Basic Questions in Theology*, 1:8.

18. "The Revelation of God in Jesus of Nazareth," *Theology As History*, p. 127.

19. Pannenberg, *History and Hermeneutic*, p. 125.

20. "The Revelation of God in Jesus of Nazareth," *Revelation as History*, p. 137.

21. Ibid.

22. Ibid, p. 136.

23. Ibid, p. 136.

24. Ibid, p. 139.

25. Pannenberg, "Redemptive Event and History," *Basic Questions in Theology*, 1:38-50.

26. Pannenberg, "Insight and Faith," *Basic Questions in Theology*, 2:30-34.

27. Pannenberg, *Faith and Reality* (Philadelphia: Westminster Press, 1977), p. 66. Cf. "Theta Phi Panel Discussion with Wolfhart Panneberg," *The Asbury Theological Journal* 46.2 (Fall 1991): 24-25.

28. Pannenberg, *Faith and Reality*, pp. 66-67.

29. Pannneberg, "Insight and Faith," *Basic Questions in Theology*, 2:30ff.

30. Pannenberg, "The Revelation of God in Jesus of Nazareth," *Theology As History*, p. 131.

31. Ibid.

32. Ibid.

33. *Jesus—God and Man*, pp. 53-114. N. T. Wright misunderstands Pannenberg's theology of the resurrection. Wright complains that Pannenberg makes too much of the connection between the resurrection and the incarnation. N. T. Wright, *The Resurrection of the Son of God* (Minneapolis: Fortress Press, 2003), pp.24-25.Wright affirms there is a connection, but only in conjunction with his teachings. The resurrection in itself or the teachings of Jesus per se will not serve as the basis of Jesus' being confirmed as the Son of God. Ibid. pp.243-

245. This is the same argument in Pannenberg, except that Pannenberg gives an even more detailed discussion of this connections showing how it must be rooted in the Old Testament view of history, creation, and divine transcendence. Cf. Pannenberg, *Jesus–God and Man*, pp. 135, 153.

34. Ibid., p. 75.

35. Ibid., p. 187.

36. *Jesus–God and Man*, p. 89.

37. Ibid., p. 91.

38. *Basic Questions in Theology*, 1:70-72, 78-80.

39. Collingwood, *The Idea of History*, p. 262.

40. Ibid., pp. 210, 302.

41. Ibid., p. 304.

42. Ibid., pp. 252-253.

43. Ibid., pp. 257-263.

44. Ibid., pp. 256-257.

45. "Response to the Discussion," *Theology As History*, p. 273.

46 Søren Kierkegaard, *Philosophical Fragments*, translated by David F. Swenson with an introduction and Howard V. Hong with a new introduction and commentary by Niels Thulstrup (Princeton: Princeton University Press, 1962), p. 55.

47. "Response to the Discussion," *Theology As History*, p. 273.

48. Søren Kierkegaard, *Philosophical Fragments*, translated by David F. Swenson with an introduction and Howard V. Hong with a new introduction and commentary by Niels Thulstrup (Princeton: Princeton University Press, 1962), p. 55.

49. Ibid.

50. *Jesus-God and Man*, pp. 99-106.

51. Ibid., p. 98.

52. Cf. Haskell Fain, *Between Philosophy and History* (Princeton: Princeton University Press, 1970), pp. 154-155.

53. Ibid., p. 184.

6

Critical and Post-Critical Hermeneutics

The word "hermeneutics" is derived from the Greek word, *hermeneia*, which is related to the name of Hermes who was the messenger of the gods in Greek mythology.[1] The meaning of the Greek verb *hermeneuein* corresponds to the Latin word *interpretari*, to interpret. Various forms of the word *hermeneuein* are found in the New Testament (Matthew 1:23; Mark 5:41; Luke 24:27; John 9:7; Acts 4:36; 1 Cor. 12:10; Heb. 7:2). The New Testament does not formally reflect on a method of interpretation because its primary interest is being a witness to the events of revelation. As a formal term to describe the process of interpretation, hermeneutics was first used in 1654.[2]

Pre-Critical Hermeneutics

The development of the formal theory of hermeneutics can be traced back to the early Greek philosophers, which they called grammar and rhetoric.[3] It was systematically formulated in the fifth century B.C. by a group of itinerant teachers, called sophists, who were the professional instructors of Greece for many years.[4] They largely popularized the teaching of previous philosophers, but they generally embraced a skeptical view of truth and morality and emphasized persuasive expressions of rhetoric as the key to success in life. The sophists eventually lost their popularity largely because they drew criticism from Socrates, Plato, and Aristotle over the practice of charging a fee for their teaching and for playing "fast and loose" with the truth by emphasizing persuasive speech rather than truthful speech.[5] "Sophistry" is a term that is derived from the sophists and is a derogatory term to describe the practice of deceptive and false reasoning. Aristotle placed the theory of interpretation on a firmer foundation in *Rhetoric* and *Poetics* by offering formal rules of literary interpretation. In the course of its further development hermeneutics came to include various aspects—grammatical, historical, aesthetic-rhetorical, and impartial interpretation.⁶

Christian theology developed its own theories of interpretation of the biblical texts, although the New Testament does not engage in a formal theory of hermeneutics. Borrowing from Greek philosophy with its practice of allegorizing its "bible" (the religious texts of Homer and Hesiod), the early Christian Fathers often used allegory as a method of interpreting the Old Testament in order to show that it was a foreshadowing of the coming of Jesus.⁷ Allegory was often overdone by the early Christian interpreters by reading too much symbolic meaning into a biblical text and over-spiritualizing it, but they avoided making Christianity a cultic religion because they retained the realism of the history of salvation as the primary source of faith.

In the medieval period, the Roman Catholic Church assumed that it had the exclusive gift to interpret the Bible. Martin Luther challenged this claim, and insisted that anyone could rightly interpret the Bible according to the clear sense of the text. He developed the concept of the *outer* and *inner* clarity of Scripture. The "outer clarity" means the New Testament teaching about Jesus Christ is clear enough for anyone to understand, and the subjective illumination of the Holy Spirit provides an "inner clarity" of its truthfulness.⁸ In the seventeenth century following Luther, High Lutheran Orthodoxy emphasized the grammatical and historical rules of interpretation and assumed largely an intellectualist interpretation of Christian faith, based on Luther's idea of the outer clarity of Scripture.⁹ To be a Christian allegedly entailed first and foremost a right understanding of the Bible. Luther's idea of the subjective illumination of the Holy Spirit was largely ignored, but a movement known as Pietism emerged as a protest to this one-sided emphasis.

The pietists said that Lutheran orthodoxy had neglected Luther's emphasis upon the interpretative role of the Holy Spirit.¹⁰ Pietism focused on a devotional study of the Bible, believing that the inner meaning of Scripture is largely attained through the illumination of the Spirit. Three of the greatest pietists were Philip Jacob Spener, A. H. Francke, and Bengel (whose commentary on the Bible greatly influenced John Wesley).¹¹

While the Continental reformers (Luther and Calvin) affirmed the sole authority of Scripture as the basis of faith, the English reformers retained the role of tradition and reason as supplementary sources for interpreting Scripture. Richard Hooker (1554-1600) in *The Laws of Ecclesiastical Polity* helped to develop the three elements of High Anglican methodology—that *Scripture* was properly interpreted by the *tradition* of the early Greek Fathers and that the early creeds based on Scripture were consistent with *reason*.[12]

Although a High Anglican priest who emphasized Christian antiquity and reason, John Wesley (1703-1789) incorporated personal experience as an additional source for interpreting Scripture. The Moravian pietists contributed to Wesley's methodological use of experience. They had taught Wesley during his early years as an Anglican priest to expect the internal witness of the Spirit and a feeling of assurance as a confirming experience that one is justified by faith. Wesley often used the term, "experimental religion," by which he meant that one's beliefs would be confirmed in personal experience.[13] He did not believe that experience could "establish" a doctrine of Scripture, but rather he believed that experience would "confirm" that one had rightly interpreted the Bible. Although experience could not *establish* a doctrine that is not based on the Scriptures, Wesley believed experience could *disconfirm* an interpretation of Scripture.[14] If one's interpretation of a particular text contradicts experience, Wesley believed this was clear evidence that one had misunderstood the biblical text.

Drawing from Anglican and Pietistic sources, Wesley gave hermeneutical significance to these four means of doing theology—Scripture, tradition (limited to the first three hundred years of Church history), reason, and experience. However, Wesley held to the *sola scriptura* principle in the sense that the Bible contained the original revelation. He believed that Scripture must be interpreted according to the plain sense of the texts and by the principle that "Scripture interprets Scripture."[15] At the same time, tradition, reason, and experience were resources to help interpret the Scriptures.

Although Wesley's four means of doing theology are still relevant, his hermeneutics largely assumed a pre-critical perspective.[16] For him, the task of interpreting Scripture was a process of determining the whole sense of the text through comparing the various parts of the texts with each other, but he largely ignored the rise of critical history which was only beginning to affect the way theology was being done in his day. Wesley's four means of theology saved him from extreme literalism, but hermeneutical theory took on a new dimension in the eighteenth century as Enlightenment criticism rejected the traditional doctrines of the Church on the ground that they were based on a naïve and literalistic interpretation of the Bible. After the Enlightenment, it was no longer possible to assume that one can have an understanding of the biblical text merely through a literal-grammatical exegesis of the text, for very complex epistemological and methodological procedures are tacitly involved in the hermeneutical process.

Schleiermacher—The Psychologizing of Hermeneutics and Authorial Intent

Although Wesley was influenced by Moravian Pietism and became the founder of a new denomination that was to become one of the largest Protestant Churches in the modern world, it was a Moravian pietist, Friedrich Schleiermacher (1768-1834), who was to become the founder of modern theology with an emphasis on experience as the basis of doing theology. The methodologically decisive means of doing theology is a feeling of divine dependence, which is deeply imbedded in our intuitive sense of reality.[17] If experience could either confirm or disconfirm our understanding of the doctrines of Scripture for Wesley, for Schleiermacher religious experience was more basic than Scripture for establishing the doctrines of faith. As a result of the Enlightenment criticism of biblical inspiration, Schleiermacher rejected the *sola scriptura* principle.[18]

Kant's critical philosophy had undermined belief in miracles and supernaturalism as an irrational interference in human affairs. Schleiermacher accepted Kant's criticism of miracles, but in his books, *On Religion* and *Christian Faith*, he retained his belief that the scriptures had enduring relevance. Although Enlightenment criticism had de-constructed traditional Christian doctrine, Schleiermacher sought to reformulate it for thoughtful, enlightened people. His reformulation of Christian doctrine presupposed a new theory of hermeneutics that went beyond traditional hermeneutics as literal-grammatical exegesis. This earned him the title, "the father of modern theology."[19]

Schleiermacher's pioneering work in hermeneutics was to have far-reaching influence in theology. He showed that the interpretation of literary documents could not be successful until the formal and logical rules of philology included the general question of epistemology.[20] Philology is the formal study of the social and historical development of languages and the rules of grammar that determine meaning. The addition of epistemology showed that hermeneutics is more than a skill to be acquired; rather interpretation is also an "art."

Schleiermacher's interest in hermeneutics was sparked by his attempt to replace the traditional theory of biblical inspiration.[21] His hermeneutical theory, however, was developed in connection with his work as a

Platonic scholar, critically reconstructing and ascertaining the authenticity of historical documents and distinguishing between the Platonic and pseudo-Platonic dialogues. He came to see in the course of this work that criticism must be supplemented with the art of understanding–that the true understanding of historical documents demands more than a mere following of certain rigid rules of grammar and philology.[22] Schleiermacher stressed that hermeneutics and criticism are inseparably related so that the practice of one presupposes the practice of the other.[23]

Schleiermacher did not intend to diminish the significance of the rules of grammar and philology. He stressed the following conditions as the basic rules of hermeneutics: (1) a knowledge of languages,[24] (2) a knowledge of the subject matter,[25] (3) a knowledge of the historical conditioning of the language and the author,[26] (4) a knowledge of the author's style of writing and linguistic usage,[27] (5) a knowledge of the individual parts in the light of their whole context,[28] and (6) a special talent for discerning human nature.[29]

In addition to these basic rules, however, he pointed to the epistemological need for a psychological interpretation of texts.[30] This psychological interpretation means that one must re-enact the selfhood of the author to gain an understanding of the text.[31] Schleiermacher spoke of this re-enactment as a divination[32] and "a right feeling."[33] It is this psychological interpretation that makes hermeneutics an art rather than a mere scientific study.[34] The underlying presupposition of the psychological interpretation is that what is peculiar to any one individual is capable of being subjectively appropriated by another because of their common receptiveness to the same peculiarities. In this way, one can transform oneself into a corresponding subjective feeling of another, thus re-enacting in the present what was the selfhood of another in the past.[35]

When the task of the grammatical-historical and the psychological aspects of hermeneutics has been completed, Schleiermacher believed it is possible for interpreters to understand authors ever better than authors understood themselves. He claimed the interpreter has this advantage, for he brings to conscious awareness much of what was not consciously recognized by the author.[36] Hence authorial intent became a basic premise of modern hermeneutics and this was more important that what the author reported as objective history.

Dilthey: The Critique of Historical Reason

Wilhelm Dilthey (1833-1911) was the son of a Reformed theologian. He studied theology at Heidelberg and later at Berlin where he transferred to philosophy. He is remembered primarily for his work in developing a methodology of the humanities. He formally defined hermeneutics as the "art of understanding" which "has its centre in the exegesis or *interpretation of the remains of human existence, which are contained in writings.*"[37] He expanded on Schleiermacher's theory of hermeneutics and extended it into fields of inquiry other than literary documents. For example, he noted that there was an archaeological hermeneutics, or a hermeneutics whose objects were paintings, statues, etc.[38]

Dilthey pointed out that Schleiermacher was the first to extend hermeneutics beyond mere "philological virtuosity" to a "philosophical possibility."[39] He acknowledged his indebtedness to Schleiermacher and pointed out that all subsequent development in the art of interpretation depended on Schleiermacher's re-orientation of philology toward epistemology.[40]

Dilthey distinguished between the epistemology of the natural sciences and the epistemology of the human sciences. The method of the natural sciences focuses on what one perceives of the natural world. Assuming Kant's distinction between reality and appearance,[41] Dilthey concluded that the natural world is "a mere shadow cast by a reality hidden from us."[42] This skeptical conclusion about the possibility of knowing the natural world is offset by a confident assertion that one can know the world of human action as it really is because one can know the world of the mind in its very essence.[43] Obtaining this objective knowledge is the task of historiography and is possible because a human being is history in the primary sense of the word. Dilthey wrote: "So now appears the first significant moment for the solution of the epistemology of history: the first condition for the possibility of the historical sciences lies in the fact I myself am a historic being, that the one who investigates history is the same one who makes history."[44] He further said: "We are first historic beings before we are observers of history, and only because we are the former do we become the latter."[45] Because the mind can understand what it has created, one can thus know history as-it-really-is.[46]

The natural sciences distinguish between *reality* and *appearance,* while the human sciences distinguish between *inner* and *outer.*[47] The inner and outer aspects of the human sciences are based on the connection between human beings and the physical world. A human being does not exist as an independent subject over against the world as an independent object. He said: "The historical world is always there, and the individual observes it not only from the outside, but he is interwoven with it....It is not possible to isolate these relationships."[48]

Because a human being in the primary sense of the word is history, the task of the historian is to unfold the possibilities of human existence. Hermeneutics thus plays a vital role for discovering the meaning of existence, for happiness depends in a large measure upon an understanding of oneself in the light of what others are and have been. Without this historical understanding, understanding oneself and one's possibilities are severely restricted.[49] Dilthey believed the weakness of the philosophy of Descartes was its ahistorical premise that knowing involved mere introspection. By looking inward and analyzing the ideas of the mind that were supposedly inborn, Descartes assumed that one could know the ultimate meaning of human life and the world. As opposed to this, Dilthey assumed we know ourselves only as we know our history.

As distinct from Kant's *Critique of Pure Reason*, Dilthey called for "a critique of historical reason." This critique would do for historical science what Kant's *Critique of Pure Reason* did for the natural sciences.[50] Dilthey wanted to lift historical studies out of bondage to the natural sciences and hence he called for a rethinking of epistemology in which inner experience (i.e., the facts of consciousness) would become the point of departure of historical study.[51]

If Kant's critique of reason failed to provide for an epistemology of history,[52] Dilthey believed traditional hermeneutics also failed. He believed that Schleiermacher was the first to provide an adequate basis for hermeneutics because his "analysis of understanding" showed that the exegesis of literary texts required a psychological reenactment of the author.[53] Dilthey believed that beginning with Schleiermacher's "analysis of understanding" he could develop "a critique of historical reason," which would correct the epistemological shortcoming of Kant's *Critique of Pure Reason*.[54]

Understanding thus takes on a new meaning with Dilthey, as opposed to Kant's concept of understanding. Understanding the objects of the senses means understanding the way that mental life has objectified itself in the events of world history. Dilthey wrote: "But the existence of others in the first instance is given to us only from without, in facts of sensation, in gestures, sounds, and actions."[55] Strictly speaking, Dilthey said that one does not understand nature; rather one explains it.[56] On the other hand, understanding (as distinct from explanation) is the art of seeing the inner reality behind the external signs. Dilthey said: "We call the process in which, from signs given outwardly to the senses, we know an inner reality, by the name of *understanding*."[57] He continued: "We mean, then, by understanding, the process in which from signs given to the sense we come to know a psychic reality whose manifestation they are."[58] Historical knowledge thus comes about as a result of *understanding* the world of the mind. Historical knowledge is the identity of subject and object, "a rediscovery of the I in the Thou."[59] He said: "The knowing subject is here one with its object, and this object is the same on all levels of objectification."[60] The object of historical knowledge, for Dilthey, is thus not a mere physical object to be perceived by the senses, as with Kant; rather, it is an external sign of an inner reality.

Understanding for Dilthey thus does not mean the analysis of texts pure and simple. It is not the application of a list of formal and logical rules of grammar and philology. Neither is it mere *explanation*, which is the method of natural science. Rather, *understanding* is a re-enactment, a reliving, a reproduction of the inner life of another.[61] This art of imaginatively projecting oneself into another is likewise called by Dilthey (as with Schleiermacher) a divinization.[62] Reliving the "inner affinity and sympathy"[63] with the author makes possible the objectivity of knowledge and is the central task of hermeneutics, while the objectivity of knowledge for the natural sciences depends upon the testing of hypotheses with mathematical exactitude.[64] Hermeneutics does for history what mathematics does for the natural sciences.[65]

In summary, Dilthey contended that historical knowledge is understanding, not in the sense of "rational comprehension,"[66] but as the art of imaginatively projecting oneself into the life work of another person. The most subjective approach functions as the proper epistemological basis of the human sciences.[67] This insistence upon knowing the psychology of the author reflected his historicist concern to have objective knowledge. Only if one could get inside the mind of the author could one really understand objectively the meaning of the text. He thus defined the science of hermeneutics as "the *technique* of the *exegesis* of written records."[68] The significance of the historical method for Dilthey lies in the fact that one can understand the essence of humanity only through the knowledge of history. Dilthey thus connected historical method and hermeneutics, and he laid the foundation for rethinking the way theology was to be done in the modern world by shifting theology away from mere objective historical facts to inner meaning and subjectivity. He also set the stage for hermeneutics to replace epistemology in the postmodern world.

Bultmann: The Pre-Understanding of Human Existence

Rudolf Bultmann (1884–1976) was a professor at the University of Marburg (German) for over 30 years and is recognized as one of the most significant New Testament scholars in the 20th century, but he is remembered primarily for his demythologizing exegesis of the New Testament. He believed the gospels were not history but theology presented in story-form. Hence the gospels could not be read as a real record of the life of Jesus; rather the gospels presented a mythical understanding of the world, which biblical theologians today must reinterpret in a non-mythical way.

Like Schleiermacher and Dilthey, Bultmann pointed out that the central problem of hermeneutics is epistemological.[69] We noted that Schleiermacher introduced a psychological interpretation as a main component of hermeneutics. Dilthey believed that because one's essence is history and because what one creates is history, one can know history as-it-really-is. Thus, the hermeneutical task is for the interpreter to project oneself into the mind of the author and to gain an understanding of a historical text by re-thinking what the author thought. If the decisive feature of modern thought was an emphasis upon human subjectivity, then Schleiermacher and Dilthey were clearly modernist. Their subjectivizing of hermeneutics was an important source of Bultmann's hermeneutical theory, but the most immediate as well as the most important influence upon Bultmann was Martin Heidegger.

Heidegger developed a theory of hermeneutics based on the concept of one's historicity, which is a term he used to refer to the possibilities of human existence. For Dilthey, the purpose of historical study is to furnish examples of what human beings have been in the past in order to deepen one understanding of oneself. For Heidegger, the function of historical science is to unfold what is existentially meaningful history that can be repeated today. The hermeneutical task is thus guided by a prior interest in human existence. This "pre-understanding" of what constitutes authentic existence served as the basis of Bultmann's existentialist exegesis of the New Testament.[70]

As opposed to Schleiermacher and Dilthey, Bultmann stressed the subject matter of the text, which the interpreter shares with the author, instead of trying psychologically to reconstruct the selfhood of the

author. The subject matter is thus the presupposition for a proper understanding of a text.[71] This common relationship of author and interpreter
to the same subject matter underscores for Bultmann "that every interpretation is guided by a particular purpose."[72] This particular purpose
Bultmann called a "pre-understanding."[73] However, he intended to overcome the one-sided "pre-understanding" of Schleiermacher and Dilthey
with their heavy emphasis upon the psychological aspect of hermeneutics. Rather, Bultmann argued that what is important is "the putting of
the question," i.e., what does the contemporary interpreter wish to
understand in the text?[74] For example, when one seeks to understand
mathematical, medical, musical, political, military, astronomical texts,
etc., it is not necessary to reproduce imaginatively the selfhood of an
author. Rather, what is important is a prior knowledge of mathematics,
astronomy, politics, military strategy, music, medicine, etc.[75] Likewise, if
the putting of the question relates to "*history as the sphere of life in which
human existence moves,* in which it attains understanding of itself and of
its own particular possibilities," then what is necessary is a prior understanding of human existence.[76] So the point of interpreting the biblical
text for today is not to discover what the authors' psychological state of
mind was or what they believed about the world, but to reconstruct their
true existential quest for meaning. The hermeneutical task is thus to discern the intent of the biblical authors by focusing on their need to understand themselves and to discover their purpose for living.

In this respect, Bultmann was highly indebted to the existentialist philosophy of Heidegger, which served as the basis of his "pre-understanding" the way that the gospels should be interpreted. If Augustine relied
heavily upon neo-Platonic philosophy, if Thomas Aquinas relied heavily
upon Aristotelian philosophy, and if modern liberalism relied heavily
upon Kantian philosophy, then Bultmann relied heavily upon the existentialist philosophy of Heidegger for his interpretation of the gospels.
Augustine and Aquinas were interested primarily in only *translating* the
gospel in categories that would be intelligible to their contemporaries,
but liberal theology and the existentialist theology of Bultmann intended to *transform* the gospel into a new meaning based on modern ways
of thinking. Bultmann saw his theological task to extract from the
gospels all remnants of mythical thinking and to reinterpret it according
to Heidegger's philosophy of existence. By mythical thinking, he of
course meant any idea of divine intervention in the world and in human
history. The hermeneutical key for demythologizing the gospels was to
separate the Jesus of history from the Christ of faith. Faith in Christ was

a symbolic expression for authentic existence (a true self-understanding of one's potentialities), whereas the Jesus of history was just a man like the rest of humanity without special divine qualities. The gospel accounts confused this distinction, but allegedly thanks to Heidegger's existentialist philosophy, the biblical exegete today can sort out this difference. [77]

Bultmann did not think that a "prior understanding" of existentialism as the means for interpreting the gospels meant that he merely subjectivized historical knowledge. Bultmann believed historical knowledge cannot achieve objectivity in the sense that natural science can, for human existence is a different kind of reality than the physical objects of natural science. On the other hand, the interpreter can achieve objectivity of knowledge when one properly frames the question to be asked of a text, and then methodically pursues this question.[78] Bultmann's hermeneutics thus selected the existentialist themes in the New Testament as the way to connect the gospel to the modern mind.

He noted that it is impossible for one to eliminate one's own subjective standpoint in order to achieve objectivity of knowledge, for it is only through subjectivity that the objectivity of knowledge can be attained, i.e., "only those who are stirred by the question of their own existence can hear the claim which the text makes."[79] What must, however, be eliminated is one's own personal prejudices in order to avoid forcing on to the texts an alien interpretation, coercing the text arbitrarily to fit one's own preconceived ideas.[80] Furthermore, because historical texts can be methodically questioned from many different perspectives and from a number of different kinds of interest, one must guard against making any individual "putting of the question" absolute, for this would distort the objectivity of historical knowledge.[81]

Bultmann's reflection on the task of New Testament exegesis, however, led him back to Schleiermacher's and Dilthey's existential narrowing down of hermeneutics. The goal of his hermeneutical theory is to make a scientific exegesis of the New Testament in the light of one's prior understanding of human existence. Bultmann acknowledged that one does not obtain this existential knowledge from the New Testament, which is solely concerned with an actual understanding of human existence. Rather, it comes about through philosophical reflection.[82] Without this prior understanding of human existence, Bultmann believed the exegete would have "to read the biblical writings as a compendium of dogmatic pronouncements, or as 'sources' for the reconstruction of a section of past history," thus reducing the significance of the Scriptures by forbidding it to "speak as a power which has something to say to the present, to present-day existence."[83]

The New Hermeneutic of Gerhard Ebeling and Ernst Fuchs

Gerhard Ebeling (1912–2001) of the University of Zurich and Ernst Fuchs (1903–1983) of the University of Marburg jointly worked out[84] what is called "The New Hermeneutic."[85] Ebeling and Fuchs intended to move beyond the existentialist exegesis (demythologizing) of their teacher, Rudolf Bultmann.[86] As noted above, Bultmann adapted the early Heidegger's existentialist philosophy with the intent of going behind the objectifying language of the New Testament to discover the primordial thinking (i.e., existential intention) of the biblical writers, thus showing that the primary intention of the New Testament was to express an understanding of authentic existence. On the other hand, Ebeling and Fuchs adapted the later Heidegger's ontological investigation of authentic language, which discloses Being, i.e., language lets Being be. The change of emphasis was thus from "existence" in Bultmann to "language" in Ebeling and Fuchs.[87] For Bultmann the emphasis was upon the distinction between authentic and inauthentic existence, but with Ebeling and Fuchs the emphasis was upon the distinction between everyday language corrupted by the subject-object split and the uncorrupted language of being.[88]

Ebeling defined hermeneutics as the theory of understanding the function of words.[89] The task of hermeneutics is to remove "hindrances" which obscure the word. The scope of hermeneutics includes linguistics and a grammatical understanding of texts as well as the general problem of historical understanding.[90] Theological hermeneutics in particular is defined as focusing on the word-event in which faith happens. This word event of faith transcends the subject-object split of everyday language and thus does not entail the idea of specific information about other-worldy realities and objective facts. If one seeks for an objective fact behind the words, this would be to confuse the nature of authentic faith. Faith is an understanding of oneself through words contained in the biblical texts, not an intellectual acceptance of historical information.[91] Another way to explain the nature of faith is to say that words generate imagery that provokes an understanding of oneself. Although the words may appear to contain objective information, this is secondary to the nature of the biblical texts. Personal insight, self-understanding, and authentic existence are the meaning of faith. For example, to think of the

Easter faith as a real event involving an empty tomb is to slide back into the subject-object split of everyday language, according to Ebeling's view of theological hermeneutics.

The task of hermeneutics as removing those hindrances which obscure the mediation of reality through language corresponds closely to Heidegger's concept of language as the "house of Being," i.e., language lets Being be. Understanding takes place *through* language, but this understanding is not about objective facts or miraculous revelations in history. In this sense, language is performative, not informative. [92] Ebeling explained the performatory function of language in this way: "The basic structure of word is therefore not statement—that is an abstract variety of the word-event—but apprisal, certainly not in the colourless sense of information, but in the pregnant sense of participation and communication."[93] Simply put, words are primarily expressive of personal insight, not reports of what is true about the world or external history.

Ebeling and Fuchs thus wanted to re-adjust Bultmann's program of demythologizing.[94] Unlike Bultmann, Ebeling and Fuchs wanted to get back to the real Jesus of history to show that he personally appropriated authentic existence and thus served as a witness of faith. They believed this task was possible because the nature of language permitted it. If Bultmann believed the meaning of authentic existence was embedded in the mythological language of the gospels, Ebeling and Fuchs believed that Jesus' self-understanding as a person of faith was also embedded in the text. This is why they believed it was possible to discover in a limited sense who the real Jesus of history was.[95]

The historical Jesus, they believed, is the word of God because his preaching made God present to his hearers. Thus, by getting back to the preaching of the historical Jesus, one gets back to *authentic language*—the language of faith.[96] Jesus' word is called a gift that was given to his hearers, and thus by clinging to his word the hearers have a model of faith to take along with them.[97] Subsequent to his crucifixion, Jesus became adorned with honorific titles by the primitive church and they replaced Jesus' preaching with his person as the object of faith.[98] The task of theological hermeneutics is to reconstruct the real Jesus that lies behind this mythologizing of Jesus as the supernatural Son of God. Ebeling and Fuchs believed that the real Jesus is not the object of faith, but a model of faith. To believe in Jesus is to believe in Jesus' message of love.[99] Jesus' message as the word of God is significant, not because of its content, but because it shows that we are accepted as persons of worth. The phenomenon of language is that one speaks not so much to be understood, but because one understands. Fuchs writes: *"At home one does not speak so that people may understand, but because people understand!"*[100] Language thus does not create anything new, and its purpose is not to be informative, but to mediate understanding. Language "announces what it is time for."[101] The significance of Jesus' parables and his language is that his message announces that now God has come forward and has enabled us to love one another because we "clothe ourselves" with Jesus words.[102]

The New Hermeneutic says that the New Testament is *"a textbook in hermeneutic.* It teaches the hermeneutic of faith—in brief, the language of faith—and it encourages us to try out this language ourselves, so that we may become familiar with—God."[103] The ultimate task of theological hermeneutics is thus to bring the believer to an understanding of the historical Jesus as a word-event, (Ebeling), or language event (Fuchs).[104] It is this "event" which is the saving event, for what came to expression in Jesus was faith, and to have faith in Jesus means to re-experience Jesus' decision of faith. Faith in Jesus has nothing to do with a real historical event, such as the empty tomb, or other real events, such as Jesus being in his own person both God and man. The significance of the historical Jesus is that he used words, which bring us into communion with God. However, the word of God is not connected with the idea of an objective divine Person who transcends the world as its creator *ex nihilo*. It has nothing to do with words of information about the world or history. This would be to fall back into the subject-object split of everyday language. Faith is rather an existential understanding, an understanding of one's true potential being realized in the word-event.

Bultmann rejected the theology and methodology of the New Hermeneutic. He especially rejected the idea that the historical Jesus was a witness of faith. Instead Bultmann observed that Jesus was not listed as a witness of faith in Hebrews 11. Rather, Jesus was listed as the perfecter of faith (Heb. 12:2). To be sure, Bultmann did not believe that the Jesus of history was an object of faith, although he recognized that Jesus was presented as such in the biblical text. His point against his students, Ebeling and Fuchs, was that there could be no continuity between the Jesus of history and the Christ of faith. Unfortunately, the hermeneutics of Ebeling and Fuchs, as well as Bultmann, does not transcend the subject-object split, but rather they divorce the *meaning* of the risen Christ from the *fact* of the historical Jesus, while re-interpreting the Christ of faith in existentialist terms as if the risen Lord were merely a symbolic image and not a real, tangible human life.

Pannenberg and the Integration of History and Hermeneutics

Wolfhart Pannenberg believes that the historical distance between text and interpreter cannot be bridged merely in a psychological or existentialist way.[105] While Bultmann's hermeneutical approach intended to take seriously the historicity of both the author and interpreter and the claim that the text lays upon the hearer, it failed to grasp the comprehensive historical situation because it denied the realism of salvation history.[106]

Pannenberg's chief merit lies in his attempt to integrate historical reflection and theology. There can be no bridging of the historical past and the present in terms of a mere psychological or existential narrowing down of the problem. Furthermore, the probabilities of historical knowledge have a significant bearing upon the reality of faith.

If Bultmann denied any meaning in history as a temporal course of events because one cannot know the end, Pannenberg constructs a theology of universal history on the very basis that we can know the end of history since it proleptically occurred in the resurrection of Jesus of Nazareth. He thus intends to integrate hermeneutics and history.

First, Pannenberg proposes the convergence of history and hermeneutics into a universal-historical perspective. Historical study must not think of its task in mere terms of going *behind* the texts to ascertain bare facts. Rather, historical study in effect goes *beyond* the actual texts when it goes *behind* them, for what lies behind the texts cannot be understood as "an isolated datum, but reveals itself only within a universal context of events and meaning, only in terms of a universal history, which also embraces the era of the investigator."[107] The task of the historian is not restricted to the "dead remains of the past."[108] On the contrary, historical interrogation includes the historian's relationship to the subject matter, for the "object is already viewed from the perspective of the present time."[109] This is not to embrace a historical relativism in which it would be impossible to gain an objective knowledge of what happened. To be sure, events have their own immediate environment in which they can be seen, but their true significance extends beyond this. In order to see the larger significance of an event, one must development a more inclusive context than the immediate surroundings. This larger context includes both its past history and its future implications.[110]

If historical study restricts its interest solely to what happened in the past, then it becomes a subsidiary science to hermeneutics.[111] Going behind the texts to the actual course of events to which the texts refer is the central task of historical study in itself. But, it must not stop there. Rather, its interrogation must be viewed from the standpoint of the present interrogator's era, if the true significance of the past is to be given its due credit. Bridging the past texts and the present era of the investigator is the central task of hermeneutics. The need for this bridge originally gave rise to the need of historical study itself.[112] Pannenberg points out that the distinction between the historical investigation of going behind the texts and the constructing of hermeneutical bridges to the present can at best claim only tentative legitimacy, for both history and hermeneutics form a single theme.[113]

Because transmitted texts have a relevance that extends beyond their immediate historical setting is why there is a relative independence of hermeneutics from historical study.[114] Such is the case for example with the Pauline letters. Their significance is not exhausted in mere terms of historical study; they have a present day relevance concerning one's condition before God. A further example is the history of Herodotus who intended his history to be a memorial to the heroic deeds of his age, which in turn would be an example for all humankind.[115] Pannenberg writes: "Historiography itself never intends to describe a completed, past epoch merely as past. That would not be worth the effort. Quite the contrary, historiography is constantly guided by an interest in the present."[116] What Pannenberg calls for is not an either-or situation, but the integration of history and hermeneutics into a universal-historical method. [117]

Schleiermacher sought to reconstruct texts from the thought processes of the author without sufficient attention being given to the history of salvation, which was the primary concern of the biblical authors.[118] Dilthey limited history to what human beings had done, thus making it possible to intuit the actual meaning of texts on the basis that what humans have created humans can know. Pannenberg points out the theological weakness of defining history solely in terms of what humans have done in the past. "It is simply not the case that the historian may concern himself only with the intellectual and spiritual activity of man, and may turn everything else over to physics."[119] Dilthey constructed a faulty hermeneutical bridge because he was only interested in investigating the past in terms of its present possibilities of human existence. But if this hermeneutical task is to be accomplished, then it must go beyond "intuition" to an examination of not what human beings have done but what happened to them as well.

Pannenberg believes that Bultmann's emphasis upon the "claim" which the transmitted texts make upon the investigator in principle overcame his existentialist "pre-understanding."[120] To be sure, Bultmann's "preunderstanding" did not intend to suggest that the text cannot speak anew. He stressed the claim, which the text makes upon the hearer. However, Bultmann limited the "claim" of the biblical texts in terms of what they suggests as possibilities of authentic existence. Pannenberg shows that the biblical texts are interested in more than human existence in an abstract way. They speak also of God, the world, and history. God mediates God's very self to humans not only through an existential encounter, but through the world and history. Human beings cannot understand themselves in isolation from the whole of reality. Pannenberg argues that the possibilities of human existence always entails questions concerning the nature of the world, society, and ultimately questions about God. In fact, one's relationship to the world, to society and to God permits one to understand oneself. Overcoming the subject-object split thus does not mean that one is committed to be silent about the world, society, and God, but rather it means a proper integration of oneself to one's larger world; hence the importance of the idea of universal history. [121]

Pannenberg further shows that the "past cannot be deprived of its past-ness" and then be re-interpreted as possibilities of present authentic existence. Instead, the past "must be related to the present precisely as what is past."[122] If a text makes a claim upon the interpreter, one cannot set up arbitrary limits around the claim and allow it to say only what one wants it to say. The text must be allowed to speak for itself in all of the particularity of what is past. [123]

In pointing out the convergence of history and hermeneutics, Pannenberg uses Gadamer's expression, "the fusing of horizons," which describes the meeting between the horizon of the past text and the present horizon of the interpreter.[124] But Gadamer speaks of the texts in terms of words alone (the linguisticality of reality) and says that the mediation of the past text to the present is strictly an accomplishment of language. Gadamer, like Ebeling and Fuchs, devalues the assertive character of language in an attempt to preserve "the unspoken horizon" behind the text.[125] However, Pannenberg argues that even the unspoken meaning of events in the past must be made into statements and cannot simply be comprehended in terms of a mere claim, which the text makes upon the hearer as an encounter of an "I" with a "thou." Though the hermeneutical task is a linguistic process, the fusing of horizons of the past and the present is not an accomplishment of language alone, but rather, it is mediated historically. The fusing of horizons is the accomplishment of a new understanding, which in turn gives rise to a new way of speaking.[126] Through assertions, statements, and content the past is mediated to the present. Truth is itself historical.

In broadening hermeneutics into a universal-historical perspective, Pannenberg is not adopting the Hegelian idea of a total mediation of present-day truth through history. Rather, on the basis of Jesus' eschatological message, the proleptic character of his resurrection, and his Israelite-Jewish background, Pannenberg develops the idea of universal history that leaves the future open, acknowledges the limitation of finite knowledge, and at the same time attempts to provide a valid epistemological access to the larger whole of reality.[1] The idea of universal history of course does not mean that the historian can know everything about history, but it does mean that the historian can know the future goal and end of history because it has proleptically occurred in Jesus of Nazareth. In the light of the revelation of the future of all things in the God of Jesus of Nazareth, Pannenberg believes the New Testament provides a hermeneutical basis for judging and evaluating the significance of the meaning of the world from the beginning of creation. This universal significance of the gospel also serves as the basis of Christian missions and evangelism.[128]

Notes

1. Cf. James M. Robinson, "Hermeneutic Since Barth," *The New Hermeneutic*, edited by James M. Robinson and John B. Cobb, Jr. (New York: Harper and Row, Publishers), pp. 1-2.

2. G. B. Madison, "Hermeneutics, Gadamer and Ricoeur," *Twentieth-Century Continental Philosophy*, ed. Richard Kearney (New York: Routledge, 1994), 290.

3. Dilthey, "Die Entstehung der Hemeneutik," *Gesammelt Schriften*, 5:321, 327. Cf. Hodges, p. 25.

4. Ibid.

5. Cf. Plato's dialog, *The Apology* (18a-20d) where Socrates defends himself against being like a sophist (ibid., 18a-20d). Cf. Plato's dialog, *Sophist*, where they are severely criticized.

6. Dilthey, "Die Entstehung der Hemeneutik," *Gesammelt Schriften*, 5:321, 327. Cf. Hodges, p. 25.

7. Ibid. Cf. Bernard Ramm, *Protestant Biblical Interpretation* (Grand Rapids: Baker Book House, 1970), pp. 24ff.

8. Cf. Pannenberg, "The Crisis of the Scripture Principle," *Basic Questions in Theology*, 1:4-6.

9. Tillich, *A History of Christian Thought*, pp. 276-283.

10. Ibid., p. 284.

11. Ibid., pp. 283-285; cf. Wesley's *Explanatory Notes Upon the New Testament* (London: Epworth Press, 1958), p. 7.

12. Cf. Donald A. D. Thorsen, *The Wesleyan Quadrilateral* (Grand Rapids: Zondervan Publishing House, 1990), pp. 39ff.

13. Wesley, *Sermons*, ed. Albert C. Outler, "Preface," 1:106

14. Wesley, *Sermons*, ed. Albert C. Outler, "The Witness of the Spirit, II," 1:297.

15. Wesley, *Sermons*, ed. Albert C. Outler, "Preface," 1:106.

16. William Abraham particularly criticizes these four criteria derived from Anglican Richard Hooker on the grounds that the canonical heritage was originally focused on soteriology, not epistemology. Based on Hooker's epistemological criteria of the scriptures, tradition, and reason, Albert Outler developed the concept of the quadrilateral for United Methodists. Abraham argues this emphasis displaced the soteriological focus of early Methodism. He believes that "Pietism, early Methodism, and Pentecostalism represent a Protestant underworld of protest which has sought to return to a soteriological vision of the Scriptures." Eventually these protest moments were drawn away from this canonical heritage to join the mainstream emphasis on epistemology. Cf. *Canon and Criterion in Christian Theology: From the Fathers to Feminism* (New York: Oxford University Press, 1998), pp. 188-214, 474ff.

17. Cf. Paul Tillich, *A History of Christian Thought*, p. 407.

18. Hans-Georg Gadamer, "The Problem of Language in Schleiermacher's Hermeneutic," *Schleiermacher as Contemporary*, ed. Robert W. Funk (New York: Herder and Herder, 1970), pp. 69, 83-84. Cf. Schleiermacher, *Hermeneutik*, ed. Heinz Kimmerle (Heidelberg: Carl Winter, Universitätsverlag, 1959), pp. 55, 93.

19. Tillich, *A History of Christian Thought*, p. 387; cf. H. R. Mackintosh, *Types of Modern Theology* (London: Collins, 1937). Pp. 12, 36-101

20. *"Die Entstehung der Hermeneutik," Gesammelte Schriften*, 5:327-328.

21. Hans-Georg Gadamer, "The Problem of Language in Schleiermacher's Hermeneutic," *Schleiermacher as Contemporary*, ed. Robert W. Funk, pp. 69, 83–84. Cf. Schleiermacher, *Hermeneutik*, ed. Heinz Kimmerle (Heidelberg: Carl Winter, Universitätsverlag, 1959), pp. 55, 93.

22. Dilthey, *"Einleitung in Die Geisteswissenschaften," Gesammelte Schriften*, 7:95. Cf. R. R. Niebuhr, *Schleiermacher on Christ and Religion* (New York: Charles Scribner's Sons, 1964), pp. 77-78.

23. Schleiermacher, *Hermeneutik*, p. 79.

24. Ibid., pp. 82, 103, 107.

25. Ibid., p. 79.

26. Ibid., pp. 90ff.

27. Ibid., p. 108.

28. Ibid., pp. 89, 91, 95ff.

29. Ibid., p. 82.

30. *"Die Entstehung der Hermeneutik," Gesammelte Schriften*, 5:327.

31. R. R. Niebuhr, *Schleiermacher on Christ and Religion*, p. 79.

32. Schleiermacher, *Hermeneutik*, pp. 87, 109.

33. Ibid., p. 91.

34. Ibid., p. 82. Cf. R. R. Niebuhr, *Schleiermacher on Christ and Religion*, p. 85.

35. Schleiermacher, *Hermeneutik*, p. 109.

36. Ibid., pp. 87, 91.

37. Dilthey, *"Die Entstehung der Hermeneutik," Gesammelte Schriften* (Stuttgart: B. G. Teubner Verlagsgesellschaft, 1961), 5:319, trans. H. A. Hodges, "Selected Passages from Wilhelm Dilthey," *Wilhelm Dilthey: An Introduction* (London: Routledge and Kegan Paul, Ltd., 1949), p. 127.

38. *"Die Entstehung der Hermeneutik," Gesammelte Schriften*, 5:319, trans. Hodges, 127.

39. *"Die Entstehung der Hermeneutik," Gesammelte Schriften*, 5:329.

40. Ibid.

41. *"Die Entstehung der Hermeneutik," Gesammelte Schriften*, 5:317, trans. Hodges, p. 125.

42. *"Einleitung in Die Geisteswissenschaften," Gesammelte Schriften*, 1:xviii, trans. Hodges, p. 113.

43. *"Einleitung in Die Geisteswissenschaften," Gesammelte Schriften*, 1:91, trans. Hodges, p. 137.

44. *"Der Aufbau der Geschichtlichen Welt in Den Geisteswissenschaften," Gesammelte Schriften*, 7:278. Translation mine.

45. Ibid. Translation mine.

46. Ibid., p. 148. This emphasis upon the objectivity of historical knowledge (i.e., history is what humans create and what they create they can know as it really is) shows his dependence upon the ideas of Hegel.

47. *"Der Aufbau Der Geschichtlichen Welt in Den Geisteswissenschaften," Gesammelte Schriften*, 7:148, 277-278. cf. Hodges, p. 35.

48. Ibid., 7:277. Translation mine.

49. *"Der Aufbau Der Geschichtlichen Welt in Den Geisteswissenschaften," Gesammelte Schriften*, 7:86-87, trans. Hodges, p. 142. Cf. *"Die Entstehung Der Hermeneutik," Gesammelte Schriften*, 5:317.

50. *"Der Aufbau Der Geschichtlichen Welt in Den Geisteswissenschaften," Gesammelte Schriften*, 7:278.

51. *"Einleitung in Die Geisteswissenschaften," Gesammelte Schriften*, 1:xviii, trans. Hodges, p. 113.

52. *"Der Aufbau Der Geschichtlichen Welt in Den Geisteswissenschaften," Gesammelte Schriften*, 7:192, trans. Hodges, p. 115.

53. *"Die Entstehung Der Hermeneutik," Gesammelte Schriften*, 5:327-329.

54. *"Der Aufbau Der Geschichtlichen Welt in Den Geisteswissenschaften," Gesammelte Schriften*, 7:117, 278.

55. *"Die Entstehung der Hermeneutik," Gesammelte Schriften*, 5:318, trans. Hodges, pp. 125-126.

56. Ibid. *"Ideen über eine beschreibende und zergliedernde Psychologie,"*

Gesammelte Schriften, 5:172, trans. Hodges, pp. 135-136.

57. *"Die Entstehung der Hermeneutik,"* *Gesammelte Schriften,* 5:318, trans. Hodges, p. 126.

58. Ibid.

59. *"Der Aufbau der Geschichtlichen Welt in den Geisteswissenschaften,"* *Gesammelte Schriften,* 7:191, trans. Hodges, p. 114.

60. Ibid.

61. Ibid., pp. 213-214, trans. Hodges, pp. 121-126.

62. *"Der Aufbau der Geschichtlichen Welt in den Geisteswissenschaften,"* *Gesammelte Schriften,* 7:226.

63. *"Beiträge zum Studium der Individualität,"* *Gesammelte Schriften,* 5:278, trans. Hodges, p. 128

64. *"Der Aufbau der Geschichtlichen Welt in den Geisteswissenschaften,"* *Gesammelte Schriften,* 7:275, 191-192. *"Ideen uber eine Beschreibende und Zergliedernde Psychologie,"* *Gesammelte Schriften,* 7:169-170, trans Hodges, pp. 133-134.

65. Hodges, p. 84.

66. *"Beiträge zum Studium der Individualität,"* *Gesammelte Schriften,* 5:278, trans. Hodges, p. 129.

67. Ibid.

68. *"Die Entstehung der Hermeneutik,"* *Gesammelte Schriften,* 5:320, trans. Hodges, p. 128.

69. Bultmann, *History and Eschatology,* p. 110.

70. Bultmann, *Essays, Philosophical and Theological,* pp. 251-252.

71. Ibid., p. 241.

72. Ibid.

73. History and Eschatology, p. 113.

74. Ibid., p. 112. Cf. *Essays, Philosophical and Theological,* pp. 238-239.

75. *History and Eschatology,* p. 112. Cf. *Essays, Philosophical and Theological,* pp. 252ff.

76. *Essays, Philosophical and Theological,* p. 253.

77. Bultmann, "New Testament and Mythology," *Keryma and Myth,* ed Hans Werner Bartsch (New York: Harper & Row, 1961), pp. 1–44.

78. *Essays, Philosophical and Theological,* pp. 254–255.

79. Ibid., p. 256.

80. Ibid., p. 255.

81. *History and Eschatology,* pp. 118-119.

82. *Essays, Philosophical and Theological,* p. 258.

83. Ibid., pp. 258-259.

84. Ebeling, "Word of God and Hermeneutics," *Word and Faith,* p. 305n. Cf. Braaten, *History and Hermeneutics,* p. 71.

85. *The New Hermeneutic,* edited by James M. Robinson and John B. Cobb, Jr. (New York: Harper and Row, Publishers).

86. Robinson, "Hermeneutic Since Barth," *The New Hermeneutic,* p. 53.

Fuchs, "The New Testament and the Problem," *The New Hermeneutic,* pp. 115ff.
Ebeling, "Word of God and Hermeneutics," *Word and Faith,* p. 331.

87. Ebeling, "Word of God and Hermeneutics," *Word and Faith,* p. 331.

88. Robinson, "Hermeneutic Since Barth," *The New Hermeneutic,* p. 49.

89. Ibid., p. 319.

90. Ibid.

91. "Word of God and Hermeneutics," *Word and Faith,* p. 322.

92. Ibid., p. 318.

93. Ibid., p. 326.

94. "Word of God and Hermeneutics," *Word and Faith,* p. 331. Fuchs, "The New Testament and Hermeneutical Problem," *The New Hermeneutic,* pp. 116-119, 124-125.

95. Fuchs, "The New Testament and Hermeneutical Problem," *The New Hermeneutic.,* p. 136.

96. Ibid., p. 123.

97. Ibid.

98. Ibid., p. 130.

99. Ibid., pp. 135, 136.

100. Ibid., p. 124.

101. Ibid., p. 126.

102. Ibid., p. 130.

103. Ibid., p. 141.

104. Robinson, "Hermeneutic Since Barth," *The New Hermeneutic,* p. 57.

105. Wolfhart Pannenberg, "Hermeneutics and Universal History," *History and Hermeneutic,* p. 130.

106. *History and Eschatology,* p. 121.

107 *History and Hermeneutic,* p. 123.

108. Ibid., p. 125.

109. Ibid.

110. Ibid., p. 124.

111. Ibid., p. 127.

112. Ibid., p. 123.

113. Ibid.

114. Ibid., p. 127.

115. Ibid. Cf. *The History of Herodotus,* trans. George Rawlinson (London: J. M. Dent and Sons, Ltd., 1924), I, 1.

116. *History and Hermeneutic,* p. 127.

117. Ibid., p. 124.

118. Ibid., p. 128.

119. Ibid., p. 130.

120. Ibid., p. 134.

121. Ibid., pp. 132-133. Cf. *Basic Questions in Theology,* 1:3.

122. Pannenberg, *History and Hermeneutic,* p. 133.

123. Ibid., p. 134.

124. Ibid., p. 137. Cf. *Basic Questions in Theology*, 1:9.

125. H. G. Gadamer, *Warheit und Methode*, p. 444, cited by Pannenberg, History and Hermeneutic, pp. 142-143.

126. Pannenberg, *History and Hermeutic*, p. 142.

127. Ibid., p. 151. *Basic Questions in Theology*, 1:174-181.

128. *Jesus–God and Man*, pp. 70-72.

7

Paul Ricoeur:
Phenomenological Hermeneutics
and Postmodern Deconstructionism

Paul Ricoeur (b. 1913) was a French army officer at the beginning of World War II, who was captured and sent to several POW camps. While in captivity, he studied German philosophy. His interest in philosophy as well as in Christian faith was not a mere academic pursuit, but was born out of the adversities of his own life situation. He spent many years as a professor of philosophy at the Universities of Strasbourg and Paris (the Sorbonne, Nanterre), as well as other universities, including the University of Chicago where he was the successor of Paul Tillich and is now the John Nuveen Professor Emeritus in the Divinity School and the Department of Philosophy.[1]

Along with Gadamer, Ricoeur is largely responsible for the shift away from traditional epistemology to a focus on a philosophy of hermeneutics. By hermeneutics, he means that all reality can be objectified like a text, including human life because it embodies a meaning that can be objectified and interpreted. Hence human life is a text analogue, or a quasi-text.[2] Ricoeur opposes the "romantic illusion" of the empathetic (psychological) understanding of Schleiermacher and Dilthey and the positivist notion that the text is a self-contained entity independent of the subjectivity of the author and the reader.[3] Ricoeur sees the need to develop a hermeneutical theory that transcends subjectivism and objectivism.[4]

Although highly regarded as a philosopher, he has written extensively on theological issues. He has been a guest preacher in a number of churches throughout his academic career. He was reared in liberal Protestantism in the 1920's, but was subsequently influenced by Karl Barth's theology of the Word of God in 1936.[5] He was also influenced by Bultmann's demythologizing exegesis, but he believed that Bultmann too easily discarded the objective elements of the text.[6] Although primarily a philosopher, his interest in theology has never waned, and more recently he has expressed general appreciation for Moltmann's theology of hope[7] and Pannenberg's theology of history.[8]

"To Believe Again"

Ricoeur has contributed significantly to Christian theology in showing how it is possible for one to "believe again" in a post-critical age. To "believe again" does not mean that one simply sweeps away the critical thinking of the modern, Enlightenment period. To be postmodern is also to be modern in a qualified sense. If the modern historical conscious-ness seemed to make it impossible to believe in the history of salvation, Ricoeur has charted new territory beyond modern criticism, utilizing "a hermeneutic of suspicion" (as he calls it) that brings into question the religious skepticism of Marx, Nietzsche, and Freud. From these "masters of suspicion"[9] Ricoeur says we can learn about the way ideas often "mask" our illusions about God, the world, and ourselves. Ricoeur turns this suspicion back on itself, showing that we can find the true meaning of religion by stripping away the false meaning. The real significance of these masters of suspicion is that they have helped to "clear the horizon for a more authentic word, for a new reign of Truth, not only by means of a 'destructive' critique, but by the invention of an art of interpreta-tion."[10] These masters of suspicion have unmasked a false understand-ing of the text, but this critique opens the door to a more authentic meaning.

Ricoeur applies a hermeneutic of suspicion to the biblical text to open up the possibility of a "second naiveté"[11] which goes beyond the first naiveté of reading the text in an uncritical fashion. Ricoeur borrows this concept of naiveté from Heidegger's notion that phenomenology (as a method of bracketing out the nature of reality in critical reflective thinking) is not "the *naiveté* of a haphazard, 'immediate', and unreflective 'beholding'."[12] Rather, Heidegger says it is a method in which Being must "be *wrested* from the objects of phenomenology."[13] Ricoeur believes that "a second naivete" is a summons to know the God of the biblical text from a post-critical perspective. This summons comes from God and cannot be brought under the control of the interpreter. We do not dis-cover God in the text; rather we are invited through the witness of the text to enter into relationship with God. This summons is really from God who created all things and is the Lord of history. This summons is not a mere self-understanding in Bultmann's sense, although Bultmann was right to insist upon the existential priority of the claim, but he was wrong to minimize and explain away the objective meaning of the text. However, the point of the message is to know God who endows the believer with personal authenticity.

Hermeneutic Phenomenology

Following the Continental European trend, Ricoeur moved away from a modernist view of epistemology toward a philosophy of hermeneutics. He starts with Dilthey's hermeneutic—that words are forms or expressions of life. However, he turned away from Dilthey's romanticist view[14] of psychologically reconstructing the author's intellectual intent. Instead, borrowing from Heidegger's existentialism, he develops the idea of the text as "opening up" meaningful possibilities of human existence [15]

The Kantian divorce between noumena and phenomena, the subjective and the objective, was the foundation for Dilthey's dualism of understanding (*verstehen*) and explanation (*erklären*).[16] Heidegger sought to move back to a more basic question about self-understanding as opposed to a scientific explanation of things. But in so doing, he suspended the question of objectivity, choosing to define the meaning of texts as *understanding* of what constitutes the essence of our being (an existentialist ontology) as opposed to *explaining* the nature of the world outside the text (epistemology). Bultmann theologized this dualism in terms of the Jesus of history and the Christ of faith. Like Heidegger, Ricoeur rejects the modern concept of objective rationality as the basis of interpreting the meaning of a text—as if hermeneutics was a *method* of knowing competing with the assumptions of modern science.[17] And like Heidegger, Ricoeur believes the meaning of a text is existential in the sense that it focuses on what it means to exist as a human being. Ricoeur writes: "Understanding is thus no longer a mode of knowledge but a mode of being, the mode of that being which exists through understanding."[18]

So Ricoeur affirms Heidegger's ontology of being, but rejects the dualism of the objective information of the text on the one side, and its inner meaning on the other side, as if it were possible to have one without the other. Heidegger believed that through "back-tracking" to being itself (that is, to an understanding of what really is the ultimate value of life contained in a text), one could interpret directly the meaning of human existence. Ricoeur believed that this "backtracking" to being could not be achieved in such a direct manner. Instead, an understanding of the essence of human existence must begin with semantics. One must pay attention to the larger meaning and nuances of words. He insists that words are more than mere signs expressing existential meaning. Words are directed at an addressee, reporting something factual and objective as well.

Kant began with *thought*; Dilthey began with the author's *intent*; Heidegger began with *existential being*; but Ricoeur begins with *understanding* revealed through *semantics*.[19] Beginning with an appreciation of the larger purpose of words to inform as well as to inspire one to achieve self-understanding and self-acceptance, Ricoeur believes that the dualism of objectivity and subjectivity can be transcended. Ricoeur's theory of interpretation is called "phenomenological hermeneutics" or "hermeneutic phenomenology."[20] This is because he combined the "phenomenological method" of the later philosophy of Edmund Husserl (1859–1938) with existentialist hermeneutics of Heidegger,[21] who was one of Husserl's assistants at Freiburg for several years.[22]

The philosophy of phenomenology originally goes back to Kant who introduced the distinction between *noumenon* (things as they really are in their very essence) and *phenomenon* (the way things appears in our consciousness) in his *Critique of Pure Reason* (1781). However, Hegel was the first person to use phenomenology as a term to describe his philosophy in 1807 in his book, *The Phenomenology of Mind*.[23] Hegel believed that a full consciousness of the thinking self is at the same time a full consciousness of what really is true about the essence of things (ontological reality). What is known at the lowest level of consciousness, a consciousness of the sense world, is more fully developed at the highest level of rational self-consciousness, a consciousness of oneself as a thinking subject, and yet self-consciousness is based in the consciousness (knowledge) of God.[24]

Husserl stands in the idealist tradition of Continental philosophy, beginning with Descartes and running from Kant to Hegel, all of whom gave primacy to the thinking subject, although Husserl rejected the "dualism" of Kant and the "constructionism" of Hegel.[25] Husserl, however, said the self is formed as our consciousness of reality takes shape.[26] In consciousness is where all truth is measured, and here is where absolute knowledge occurs. The essence of what-is will be found only in the consciousness of phenomena, or it does not exist. Husserl's phenomenology was more of a "method" than a philosophy. As such, he did not engage in actual philosophical analysis, although he believed that if that his method was followed it would lead to irrefutable knowledge. This method has had considerable influence in philosophy among those who call themselves phenomenologists.[27] Heidegger appealed to Husserl's phenomenology as the basis of his existentialism, and agreed with the Hegelian premise that one's true existence could not be discerned without an understanding of the very nature of reality (or being itself), but Heidegger limited the concept of *being* to *human* being instead of God's being.

If premodern thought focused on the objective nature of reality as-it-is-in-itself antecedent to human experience (ontology), modern thought beginning with Descartes focused on reality as *known* (epistemology). The so-called modern "uprising of subjectivity" against the objective thinking of the premodern world culminated in Kant's theory of knowledge in which he distinguished between *noumena* and *phenomena*. This modern way of thinking about reality led to the devaluation of values as second-rate knowledge compared to what is known through scientific methodology.

Here is where Ricoeur affirms the significance of Heidegger's hermeneutics. Ricoeur called Heidegger's redefinition of ontology "a revolution in thought."[28] The goal of interpretation is not to focus on the objective being of the world, but on the human value of what it means to exist. The significance of a text, whether it is the classical Greek writings, the Scriptures, or the texts of history, lies in what it contributes to our self-understanding and authentic existence.[29] However, Ricoeur believes the significance of the text comes alive as one's self-understanding is animated by what the text says.[30] The meaning of the text is illuminated and its truth is appropriated through rationally reflecting on its meaning. Instead of an existentialist ontology limiting the meaning of the text, it actually unlocks it. So Heidegger's existentialist narrowing down of the meaning of a text to self-understanding is just as inadequate as the Kantian idea of an impersonal, irrefutable interpretation of sheer facts.

Ricoeur thinks that Heidegger failed to incorporate some of the later insights of Edmund Husserl. In particular, Ricoeur thinks the later Husserl made some suggestions for overcoming the Kantian split between fact and value. Instead of reducing everything to consciousness, Husserl embraced the external world. Instead of the phenomenological method being "locked within" mere consciousness, it included the objective world as part of "the horizon of all its intentions."[31] Ricoeur believes the range of meaning inherent in human life is the horizon out of which the real world is to be interpreted. In this way, subject and object in their original unity is restored.[32] Hermeneutics must "burrow under [the modern view of] scientific knowledge" and restore "the subject-object relation" that exists in its original unity in human consciousness. [33] This is not to suggest that one could blissfully ignore modern critical epistemology, but it does mean going beyond its fact-value dichotomy to a post-critical synthesis of event and interpretation. Simply put, human life is part of the world, and it senses a unity between its inner and external world. Hence Ricoeur believes Heidegger's dualism of *Historie* (objective facts) and *Geschichte* (inner meaning) and Bultmann's corresponding dualism of the "Jesus of history" and the "Christ of faith" are inadequate for understanding the apostolic testimony.

Biblical Language as Poetic

If there is an original unity of the inner and outer worlds, of interpretation and fact, then the literalism of modern thought must be transcended. This is why Ricoeur turned to semantics as the core of his philosophy. Language is a decisive, defining feature of human life because it is the means by which we are able to express our self-understanding. Mythopoeic thought was the primary means of expressing one's view of reality in ancient times, and thus it did not distinguish between mythical imagination and reality. Hebraic thinking and Greek philosophy made an explicit distinction between nature and spirit, thus transcending a mythical view of reality. The subject-object distinction first arose from within Hebrew religion and early Greek thought. It served as the basis for the rise of historical consciousness among the Hebrews and the rise of philosophy and scientific thinking among the Greeks.[34] In modern critical thought, an exaggerated distinction between value (subject) and fact (object) was developed, along with a correspondence theory of truth, which assumed words literally mirror objective facts.

Ricoeur proposes a post-critical view of truth, combining both the poetic, imaginative depths of reality and an empirical experience of the real world. He sees the need for a new focus on the meaning of language because modern critical thought destroyed the "first naïveté" of reading the biblical text in an unreflective way. The result has been a loss of meaning for modern people because the "fullness of language" was de-historicized. If words are stripped of their inherent power to express the meaning of their world and history, confidence in the meaning of life is eroded.

Ricoeur is not calling for a return to pre-critical thought, rather he is calling for an expanded view of the nature of language that will allow for a "second naïveté," of being "called again" [35] to believe in the reality of God's self-revealing history in Jesus Christ without reversing the insights of critical thought. Ricoeur writes:

> It is in the age when our language has become more precise, more univocal, more technical in a word, more suited to those integral formalizations which are called precisely symbolic logic, it is in this very age of discourse that we want to recharge our language, that we want to start again from the fullness of language. [36]

To remain in the abstraction of modern critical thought is like living in a desert without any surrounding beauty and life. Ricoeur says: "Beyond the desert of criticism, we wish to be called again." [37]

Ricoeur uses the term, poetics, as a general description of the nature of religious language because it allows the hearer to experience a fuller sense of reality than is possible with modern literalism. Poetic language permits the hearer to participate in, and belong to, "an order of things which precedes . . . things taken as objects opposed to a subject." [38] "To be called again" to faith in Jesus Christ is to transcend the subject-object distinction between the Jesus of history and the Christ of faith. It is to experience for ourselves today the original revelation proclaimed in the text. [39] "To be called again" does not mean to ignore the subject-object distinction in an unreflective, naïve way, but to transcend it through a reflective understanding of the nature of poetic language. Poetic language does not exclude the realism of historical events. Rather, its richness of expression includes both word and event and permits one to experience the complex unity of meaning and event.

Contemporary evangelical theology is often wary of Ricoeur's concept of poetic language. Reformed epistemology in particular embraces a modernist assumption that words mirror reality in a literal way. Kevin Vanhoozer, Research Professor of Systematic Theology at Trinity Evangelical Divinity School, has written a very fine book on the philosophy of Ricoeur, but he is uneasy with Ricoeur's theory of symbols. He wants Ricoeur to be more "literal," though Vanhoozer acknowledges that Ricoeur affirms "the realism of the resurrection event." [40] It is apparent that Vanhoozer would like for Ricoeur to be more propositional and more rationally precise in his view of revelation. This is apparent when Vanhoozer criticizes Ricoeur for not being more precise in emphasizing the fact of revelation as distinct from the meaning of revelation, [41] although he acknowledges this criticism is not "a fatal one" from an evangelical perspective. [42] Yet this is just the thing that Ricoeur set out to disallow—an extreme distinction or divorce between words and fact.

Testifying Truth

In contrast to modern critical thought that requires empirical verification and irrefutable rationality, Ricoeur shows that the truthfulness of the biblical text relies upon existential "validation" and "qualitative probability."[43] The events of salvation history are validated through personal interpretation and the logic of probability.[44] This means the foundationalist notion of absolute knowledge is impossible.[45] At the same time, he affirms the more modest claims to know based on practical rationality, thus avoiding historical relativism and nihilism.

Ricoeur believes the language of faith similar to the concept of truth given by the testimony of a witness in a courtroom.[46] A witness is one who is asked to be faithful to their perceived experience. Such a witness can only be expected to tell what they perceive, and their perceptions can be tested over against the perceptions of other witnesses. Even if scientific evidence is brought into the courtroom, a judgment is still necessary. This is why juries are split in their decisions and why decisions made by judges are reversed by higher courts. Testifying truth is largely a matter of interpretation, and interpretation is judged in terms of what the witness observed. A witness cannot be expected to give absolute proof of what is seen, but a faithful witness will tell what he or she believes to be a truthful recounting of what was perceived.[47] Ricoeur says that we never have certainty about anything, only probability, "and the probable is only pursued through a struggle of opinion."[48] Testifying truth does not claim to have irrefutable proof. Ricoeur believes that hermeneutical theory provides interpretations, not unassailable facts. Thus, he tries to avoid the extremes both of dogmatism and skepticism.[49]

Testimony is quasi-empirical because it relates what one reports as having seen or heard. The witness is the author of an action in the sense the witness is the one who reports it. The eyewitness or firsthand witness is what is meant by testimony. This testimony "is not perception itself but the report, that is, the story, the narration of the event. It consequently transfers things seen to the level of things said."[50] Testimony is moving from seeing to understanding and making a judgment about what one saw and heard.[51] The nature of testimony carries with it the possibility of being invalidated, abrogated, and defeated as unreliable.[52] The problem with Bultmann is not his attempt to see the existentialist significance of New Testament faith, but his dismissal of the relevance of the logic of historical probability for faith. Ricoeur notes in particular that Pannenberg is right to insist upon the "realism of the event of history" over against "the one-sided emphasis of Ernst Fuchs and Gerhard Ebeling."[53] Ricoeur insists that it is important "to guard ourselves against a certain narrowness of any theology of the Word which only attends to word events."[54]

A Hermeneutic of Revelation

The basic component of revelation is that it is a confession of faith, not an abstract system of doctrinal propositions. Faith is most deeply indebted to the text of Scripture, not to the theologian or the philosopher. Ricoeur insists that the original documents of faith (the scriptures) must be protected from being overrun by theological erudition in order that "the faith of Israel and then of the early church" with their variety of expressions of faith may be allowed to be heard by the reader today. Once revelation becomes a doctrinal concept its different confessional formats (prophecy, narration, wisdom, hymns, and legislative texts, supplications, and thanksgiving) are reduced to doctrinal propositions that no longer connect in the fullness of meaning with the hearer today.[55] This is why Ricoeur believes the confession of faith must begin with the original language of the community of faith, the text of scripture.

In this sense, it would be a mistake for religious discourse to begin with theological assertions, such as "God exists." This would be a mistake because theological assertions deal with the "propositional level" which is "a second degree discourse which is not conceivable without the incorporation of concepts borrowed from speculative philosophy."[56] However, revelation is more basic than second level, rational reflection. It is prereflective.[57]

The use of narrative in scripture involves more than a rational, propositional view of revelation, as if the biblical writer only intended to impart new information to the reader. The narrative confession of faith is the primary format of the Pentateuch, the Gospels, and Acts. Their focus is on the events of history, not on the writer who reports information about these happenings. It is as if the narrator does not exist because the events speak for themselves. For example, the election of Abraham, the Exodus, the Conquest, the anointing of David, the resurrection of Jesus are not presented simply as facts of the past, rather they continue to make history. They were and are events, which formed a community, and the memory of these events preserved it from the danger of losing its identity. The idea of revelation as a narrative gives the events a transcendent dimension, which is not characteristic of ordinary history.[58]

Ricoeur (like Pannenberg) is impressed with Gerhard von Rad's *Theology of the Old Testament,* and he draws from von Rad's scholarship to show "what is essential in the case of narrative discourse is the emphasis on the founding event or events as the imprint, mark, or trace of God's act."[59] He notes that the confession of faith was based primarily on the narration of the founding events, and that "God's mark is in history before being in speech."[60] This emphasis on the priority of event over interpretation was opposed in modern religious thought. For Kant, the decisive element in religion is the idea of humanity well pleasing to God, not the realism of saving events. Ricoeur shows that the biblical focus on testimony contradicts the philosophy of Kant who cites general examples and intellectual ideas as authoritative. Over against foundational principles of reason, testimony is rooted in history, and more specifically, Christian faith believes that "a moment in history is invested with an absolute character," and this testimony includes verbal "signs," which "the absolute gives of itself."[61] The original unity of word and event is thus reaffirmed in the moment of divine revelation as the text summons one to "believe again."

The Autonomous Text, Not Autonomous Reason

Ricoeur believes modern thought had difficulty relating reason and revelation because it failed to appreciate that the biblical text was a *testimony* to God's actions. Descartes began with self-consciousness, "I think therefore I am." In Descartes and the subsequent idealist tradition, self-consciousness was assumed to be autonomous and capable of developing the entire truth of reality out of its own thoughts. Ricoeur believes that the "pretension of consciousness to constitute itself is the most formidable obstacle to the idea of revelation"[62] He calls on modern thinkers to abandon their pretensions to be autonomous and to acknowledge that ideas, writings, actions, and institutions shape human consciousness through signs and symbols.[63] In particular, Ricoeur believes the autonomous self ("I think" of Descartes) ought to be replaced with the idea of the autonomous text. It is the text that shapes the self-consciousness of the believer, rather than alleged universal ideas.[64]

Ricoeur believes any philosophy that begins with human consciousness as the determinative factor in knowing will result in atheism. "Transcendental idealism of a Husserl contains implicitly the same atheistic consequences as does the idealism of consciousness of a Feuerbach." If religious truth emerges out of self-consciousness rather than out of the testifying text to the action of God in history, then consciousness is the "subject" and God is the "predicate." The consequence is that God is a self-production of human consciousness and hence God is a human self-projection. Ricoeur calls for a hermeneutical theory that is just the opposite of Feuerbach's. He rejects the pretensions of reason to establish truth upon self-consciousness.[65] One's religious consciousness is shaped by the biblical witness. The words of the Bible are signs and testimonies of God's gracious actions toward humanity, which enable us to understand ourselves and to give shape to who we are in our inner being. Ricoeur writes: "To understand oneself before the text is not to impose one's own finite capacity of understanding on it, but to expose oneself to receive from it a larger self."[66]

Ricoeur believes the premodern, authoritarian view of revelation (heteronomy) is to be given up, but the modern idea that reason offers an independent source of all truth is also to be contested. Revelation and reason must be brought together into a friendly conversation that mutually respects each other without denigrating the integrity of each. A respect for the autonomy of the text and a willingness to listen to its testimony is the place where faith and reason can meet.[67] Revelation is not to be confused with the rational attempt to verify truth literally, thus it is not in competition with reason. Revelation does not mean ""verification, but manifestation, i.e., letting what shows itself be." Here the language of revelation is poetic, not a literal correspondence of idea and reality which is known with irrefutable rationality.[68]

Ricoeur insists that a renunciation of autonomous self-consciousness is not heteronomy because it is not a denial of our wills, rather the biblical text as testimony is an appeal to our imagination to see the possibilities of the divine manifestation. "To understand oneself is to understand oneself in front of the text,"[69] and this means for the reader to suspend one's preunderstanding in order that one may receive what the text has to say as a testimony to truth.

This does not imply that the text is a fixed form of speech that does not speak beyond its original context. The text takes on an autonomous status as soon as it leaves the hands of the writer. It is no longer bound by the unwritten and psychological intention of the speaker or writer. In this sense, "the world of the text can burst the world of the author," and speak beyond its original setting. Further, "the autonomy of the text also removes this reader from the finite horizon of its original audience."[70] Authorial intent and how the first generations of hearers understood the text are not the canons of its truth; rather, the text takes on a life of its own and carries with it a meaning that transcends its original location. As such, the text is capable of speaking anew to readers far removed in time and space from its original context.[71] This is because the poetic nature of the biblical language carries with it a surplus of meaning that extends to contemporary readers. Poetic language also makes it possible for contemporary readers to participate in the reality of the biblical testimony because it is pre-reflective language and thus it holds together the original unity of interpretation and event in a way that theologically and philosophically precise language is unable to do.[72]

A Reader-Response Theory of Interpretation and the Deconstructionism of Derrida

Ricoeur's hermeneutical philosophy is one of the primary sources of what is called a reader-response theory of interpretation, but he avoids the extremes of some reader-response theorists who see the text basically as unstable and for all practical purposes non-existent until it is subjectively interpreted. Reader-response hermeneutics is like an interactive computer game. Just as one can experience virtual reality and control events on a computer through interactive technology, so one can put oneself into the text, interact with its meaning and relate it to one's own situation in an imaginative way. Reader-response theory is also reminiscent of the "Copenhagen interpretation" of quantum physics, which says that the behavior of electrons is influenced by the non-disturbing and non-intrusive observations of the scientist. Supposedly there is a hidden relationship between the knower and electrons such that the reality of electrons is influenced and determined by the subjective knowing process of the scientist.[73]

Stanley Fish, an English professor at the University of Illinois, is an example of this extreme subjectivism. His position is that the reader is immersed in an interpretative community, which has influenced the reader to see things in certain ways. He believes that the meaning of a text is indeterminate until a meaning emerges out of the interplay between the reader and the text. Hence the reader constructs a meaning out of the text, which does not exist until the reader formulates it.[74]

The deconstructionism of Jacques Derrida is also a main source of the reader-response theory of interpretation. Derrida was born in Algeria in 1930 and moved to France in 1959. In addition to spending his time at the École des Hautes Etudes in Paris, he often visits other institutions in Europe and North America. He is now one of the best-known philosophers in the world, although he may not be the most understood.[75] He borrowed the word, deconstructionism, from Heidegger whose method was to "back-track" (*destruktion*) to the meaning of Being, through tracing the etymological origins of words. Derrida noted that the French word *destruction* meant annihilation instead of conveying the idea of a genealogical study of Western philosophy. So he selected the word *deconstruction* to describe this task of unpacking the meaning of words.[76] This word included the idea of dis-assembling and dis-arranging a machine into its constituent parts. In grammar, Derrida used it to speak of the task of breaking apart a sentence so that its own constructed meaning is de-composed into pieces and parts with no overall logical consistency. To de-construct the meaning of a sentence is un-structuring, de-composing, de-stabilizing, and un-con-structing the text.[77]

Derrida was suspicious of Heidegger's goal of going back to an original moment of thinking in the beginning of Western philosophy as if the meaning of Being could be identified before it got miscopied as beings, and consequently, he de-constructed Heidegger's idea of *destruktion*. Instead of a genealogical tracing back to the beginning of Western philosophy in search of the meaning of Being, Derrida focuses on the unsettling and de-stablizing of established traditions of Western thinking through de-constructing the meaning of texts.[78] The purpose is to identify what is called *aporias*,[79] unresolved conflicts within the texts that are glossed over by non-deconstructive exegesis.

His introductory essay on deconstructionism, "Structure, Sign and Play in the Discourse of the Human Sciences," was given at international symposium at Johns Hopkins Humanities Center in 1966. It focused on deconstructing philosophical writings, highlighting how philosophy is riddled with contradictions and is historically situated, thus making them virtually useless in making universal claims about truth. Derrida believes the meanings of texts disguise themselves because of hidden meanings that are buried in human language. Texts have a surplus of meaning, and different readings emerge at different times even for the same person.[80]

This assumes that not only is the text unstable, but the human self is also an unstable reality, always changing through a process of symbolization. For who we are is always being formed by the language of our community. There is thus no such thing as an enduring, unchanging self.

We embrace different meanings as our de-centered self takes on new nuances of the changing and unstable language of our community.[81] Derrida does not mean that there is no personal center, but "the center is a function, not a being—a reality, but a function. And this function is absolutely indispensable. The subject is absolutely indispensable. I don't destroy the subject; I situate it."[82]

Derrida's point is that human knowledge is not as certain as what Western thought has assumed and that language is subtle, and even contradictory, so that all claims to knowledge are at best only interpretations. This means that for us there is no way to get outside of the text, for everything we know is textual through and through. By textual, he means that we are dependent upon words as symbols and signs of reality. This does not mean that there is no outside physical world independent of our perceptions; it only means that our perceptions cannot reflect the way the world really is since everything is a mixture of nihilism and contingency. Deconstruction does not mean destruction, and it does not say there is no meaning to the world as expressed in the text, but rather it says that meaning is a shifting interpretation based on one's relationship to the community of which one is a part. In this sense, the text has no stable meaning for the reason that oneself is also a de-centered ego whose identity is always shifting.

A widely used, postmodern term is subversion. It replaces the modernist concept of critical analysis. Modern thought intended to deconstruct the premodern Christian worldview through philosophical criticism with the intent to replace it with a secular worldview based on universal principles of reason. Modern thought assumed that reality was empirically based in the senses and its truth emerged out of the correspondence of an idea with empirical data. By contrast, postmodern thought assumes that reality is textual and its truth is as flexible and variable as human experience. Derrida's intent is to subvert the text in the sense that there is no fixed meaning, which could be replaced with a better one.[83]

Although Derrida is an atheist,[84] he has complained that his introductory essay and his subsequent writings have often been misinterpreted as advocating a Nietzschean kind of nihilism. He condemns the "facile, tedious and naively jubilatory" games that have been played mocking his idea of deconstruction. He writes: "We are not just playing here, turning this little sentence around in order to make it dazzle from every angle."[85] He complains of the "stupid and uninformed rumours" about his idea of deconstructionism. He particularly rejects the idea that his philosophy is a "linguisticism"—as if everything is simply language.[86]

Derrida's concept of deconstructionism was largely explained to the American public through Yale University theorists,[87] but Thomas Kuhn in *The Structure of Scientific Revolution* in 1962 prepared the way for its widespread acceptance.[88] While hermeneutical theory was in vogue in Continental European philosophy beginning with Schleiermacher, logical positivism (and its subsequent development in analytical philosophy) had been the dominant philosophy of the Anglo-American world. But Kuhn challenged the notion of "hard facts," contending that scientific knowledge is actually a social development in which competing interpretations (scientific paradigms) confront each other based on unstable evidence. Kuhn's epistemological relativism helped logical positivism to fade into the background with its claims of irrefutable scientific truth.[89] Its more chastened form today is called analytical philosophy, which continues to think of truth largely in terms of a correspondence theory of truth, as if words mirror objective reality. Trained in analytical philosophy himself, Richard Rorty has suggested that even analytical philosophy should give up its epistemological assumptions and embrace the hermeneutical philosophy of the European Continent.[90]

Transcending Postmodernism

Ricoeur seeks to transcend the subjectivity-objectivity polarity in terms of the hermeneutic of suspicion. One comes to a text with a critical, analytical attitude in order to avoid falling into a false meaning of the text. He advocates a "willingness to suspicion" and a "willingness to listen."[91] This dialectic points to Ricoeur's belief that there is an intrinsic relationship between the text and the reader. He rejects the idea of trying to divine the intent of the author, and rejects the relevance of trying to decide how the original audience interpreted the meaning of the text. The text stands on its feet, and the experience of the reader is a reliable means of arriving at its meaning and contemporary relevance. The purpose of Ricoeur's hermeneutic of suspicion was not simply to deconstruct the text so that the reader may abuse it with a self-indulgent interpretation; rather it was to reassert the right of the text to be heard anew in its own original, poetic language as a testimony to the revelation of God and a summons to faith.

If the hallmark of Enlightenment/modernist thought was that reason could know absolutely the nature of things based on its own reflections, then the hallmark of postmodernism is the deconstruction of this claim.

Ricoeur has shown that the idea of absolute truth and irrefutable rationality is mistaken, but he avoids relativism and nihilism often associated with postmodernism by including the logic of probability as an important component of truth. Truth, he says, can be "validated," but not "verified."

Kant's *Critique of Reason* intended to "abolish knowledge in order make room for faith" by splitting truth into a dualism of fact and value. Ricoeur's phenomenological hermeneutic intends to deny the "pretensions of reason" so that the prereflective unity of fact and value, the event of revelation and its interpretation, could once more exist. As opposed to the literalism of rationalism, Ricoeur reintroduced the priority of metaphor, poetics, and figurative language in order to appreciate the fullness of language and to experience the fullness of life.

Finally, Ricoeur's concept of surplus of meaning is an important contribution to hermeneutics. Drawing from recent developments in reading theory, Ricoeur highlights that reading is more than just repeating sounds; it is a process in which experiences and reflections in the text are brought to life again. Thus, the meaning of the text is freed to live in another context. Paradoxically as it is decontextualized, the meaning of the text is appropriated by the contemporary reader and it takes on a new significance as it speaks beyond its original context, addressing the contemporary reader. In this sense the text possesses a surplus of meaning that allows itself to be decontextualized and thus recontextualized.[92]

The idea of the surplus of meaning in the text is an extension of Ricoeur's appreciation of the existentialism of Heidegger. Because the text is guided by the often hidden existentialist interests of the reader, the reader approaches the text out of a desire to find meaningfulness. As a result, the text offers new possibilities because it inherently possesses a surplus of meaning that reveals itself to the contemporary reader. This does not mean the reader can manipulate the text for self-serving purposes, but if the text speaks today with new meaning, it does so out of the richness and overflowing fullness of its original significance. In spoken conversation, the event that is referenced is shared by the speaker and the hearer. In writing, the unity of word and event is cut off from its original setting, and the text is opened up for places and times not bound by the original event. In this sense, the text become autonomous, and its original meaning is capable of overflowing into new understandings and meanings that exceed the original context.[93]

Theology as a Growing Tradition

Ricoeur's concept of the surplus of meaning in the text is consistent with the idea of salvation history. The basic idea of salvation history is that there is an overspill of meaning in events as unnoticed aspects of previous events are brought into focus in subsequent history.[94] This surplus of meaning in the original event was discerned by the prophets in the Old Testament and by the apostles in the New Testament as they applied the word of God to their new situations.[95]

The theology of salvation history was developed with the Early Church Fathers. Irenaeus in particular developed the concept of the "whole economy of salvation" to describe the idea of salvation.[96] Irenaeus believed Jesus Christ was the recapitulation of the entire development of salvation history.[97] The call of Abraham is to be explained in the light of its future development in the history of Israel, culminating in the history of Jesus. This is why Paul says the blessing of Abraham (Gal. 3:15) had its fulfillment, not in his physical descendants, but in the sending of Jesus (Gal. 4:4) and in the sending of the Holy Spirit (Gal. 4: 6). The New Testament is consistent in its assumption that Jesus Christ is the key to understanding the history of Israel. The idea that the Old Testament can be properly interpreted independently of the history of Jesus is contrary to the apostolic witness.

The foundational events in the Old Testament were the exodus from Egypt and the conquest of Canaan. All subsequent events in the life of Israel were interpreted in the light of these events. These events were the means through which the promise of God to Abraham was to be fulfilled. This promise entailed the hope that Israel would be brought to a place where they could worship the Lord with all their heart, mind, and soul. The institution of circumcision was the ritual that symbolized this hope. The initial meaning of circumcision had an overspill of meaning in the prophetic interpretation where it came to mean an inner cleansing of rebellion against God, which had led to the exile (Jer. 4:4). The prophets spoke of a new exodus and a new conquest through which the kingdom of Israel would once more restored to the land of promise.

This prophetic expectation had an overspill of meaning in the New Testament interpretation—(1) this new exodus was accomplished through Jesus' resurrection from the dead and (2) the new conquest was fulfilled on the day of Pentecost when the Holy Spirit came to indwell the true Israel, the Church of Jesus Christ. The language of the exodus became the language of Jesus' resurrection—to be "freed" from the bondage of sin (Acts 2:24). The language of the conquest of Canaan which established the kingdom of Israel became the language of Pentecost and the founding of the Church—Jesus was "exalted" to the throne of heaven (Acts 2:33) and conquered his "enemies" (Acts 2:35). Through these two events—Easter and Pentecost—a true Israelite is one who has faith in Jesus and has been cleansed (circumcised) inwardly through the Spirit (Acts 15:8-9).

These central events—Exodus and Conquest, Easter and Pentecost—are the theological basis for interpreting the whole scope of salvation history, beginning with Abraham and continuing on—until the final revelation of God when "the Lord Jesus is revealed from heaven with his mighty angels" (2 Thess. 1:7). Although the self-revealing history of God in Jesus of Nazareth has been completed, the history of salvation continues until the final eschatological moment. The book of Acts did not have a conclusion in its history of the Church because this history is not yet finished.[98] The overspill, or surplus, of meaning in the history of salvation continues in the tradition of the church. The early creeds, such as the Nicene Creed, is an example of this tradition. The Trinitarian theology of the Cappadocian Fathers, who explained that Jesus was the second person of the Trinity, is an example of this surplus of meaning.

The criterion for the appropriateness of the ongoing theological developments in the tradition of the church is the apostolic witness and the oversight of the Holy Spirit. That is, later theological interpretations are attempts to explain previously unnoticed implications of the history of Jesus that emerge out of the contemporary experience of the church. For example, the condemnation of slavery by John Wesley was not based on explicit proof texts in Scripture. His argument was based on the overall spirit of the New Testament that all people are to be treated with respect because Jesus died for all. Paul's command to Philemon to treat his slave, Onesimus, as "a brother" surely implies the condemnation of slavery. For who would treat one's brother whom one loved as a slave? The struggle to understand the full implications of the gospel has not always come easy. This can be seen in the Christological and Trinitarian debates of the 3rd and 4th centuries. The Protestant reformers engaged in heated debate on the meaning of justification by faith and the authority of the Roman Catholic Church as they struggled intensely over the sale of Papal indulgences as being inconsistent with the gospel. The idea of sanctification during the Wesleyan revival in the 18th century was an attempt to recover the scriptural meaning of loving God perfectly, but it occasioned considerable debate over the relation between faith and good works.

Today the church is undergoing intense soul-searching over other issues such, as the ordination of women preachers and inclusive language for God. To what extent are these issues to be resolved on the basis of the surplus meaning of the biblical text? The fact that these questions have become pressing issues exemplifies what is meant by the process of salvation history, or the surplus of meaning in the biblical text. There are some issues that are absolute. For example, ethical notions such as coveting another person's spouse is always wrong; murder is always wrong; adultery is always wrong; homosexual practice is always wrong. These behaviors are explicitly condemned in Scripture because they are demeaning to one's personhood. Theological beliefs such as the doctrine of God as creator of the universe *ex nihilo,* the doctrine of the incarnation of God in Jesus of Nazareth, the resurrection of Jesus from the dead, the doctrine of the Trinity as formulated in the early creeds of the church have permanent meaning.

One issue that is gaining consensus in the Christian community is the ordination of women for ministry based on the larger meaning of gender inclusiveness implicit in the teachings of Jesus and the writings of Paul. Another feminist issue that is now being reviewed by the larger Christian community is the practice of gender-sensitive language in addressing God. On the other hand, pantheistic imagery found in radical feminism and the denial that God created all things is inconsistent with the originating events of salvation history.

The challenge of postmodernism is this—does deconstructing the pretensions of *absolute knowledge* imply that there is no *absolute truth* and no stable meaning at all in the Christian text, the Bible? David Roberts describes the general problem of the postmodern concept of truth this way: "The notion of weak, postmetaphysical truth opens up an array of questions. By definition, weak truth must get by without epistemology or any theoretical basis for adjudicating truth claims." Roberts believes, however, that unless there is some criteria for differentiating between adequate and inadequate ideas, then the idea of truth "may seem too weak to play a constructive cultural role."[99]

Ricoeur does not espouse a weak view of truth in the sense in which many postmodernists do, but rather he insists on the openness of truth and its situatedness as its comes to expression in the text and is interpreted by the contemporary reader. More fundamentally, Ricoeur has developed a theology of narrativity, showing that the past is constructed like a narrative, which can be incorporated into the narrative of the present reader. In this way, the text spills over into an open future, and thus there is a future for truth.

Ricoeur's idea of surplus meaning, however, reminds us that one cannot mistreat the text by manipulating it to say whatever we want it to say, as if all writings were unstable in their meanings. However, the solution to controversial interpretative issues is sometimes a long, painstaking process. The goal to be faithful to the Scriptures, on the one hand, and to be sensitive to the problematic issues of the contemporary world, on the other hand, are fulfilled through the oversight of the Holy Spirit over the church, but this often entails considerable conversation before consensus in the community is reached.

Notes

1. Don Ihde, *Hermeneutic Phenomenology, The Philosophy of Paul Ricoeur* (Evanston: Northwestern University Press, 1971), p. 9. Cited hereafter as *Hermeneutic Phenomenology*. Cf. Loretta Dornisch, *Faith and Philosophy in the Writings of Paul Ricoeur* (Lewiston, New York: The Edwin Mellen Press, 1990), p. 8.

2. G. B. Madison, "Hermeneutics: Gadamer and Ricoeur," *Twentieth-Century Continental Philosophy*, ed. Richard Kearney, p. 328.

3. Ibid., p. 295.

4. Ibid., p. 315.

5. Dornisch, *Faith and Philosophy in the Writings of Paul Ricoeur,* p. 271.

6. Ibid., p, 268.

7. Ricoeur, *Essays on Biblical Interpretation*, ed. Lewis S. Mudge (Philadelphia: Fortress Press, 1980), pp. 157ff.

8. Cf. Ricoeur, *Essays on Biblical Interpretation*, p. 80.

9. Paul Ricoeur, *Freud and Philosophy: An Essay on Interpretation*, trans. Denis Savage, (New Haven: Yale University Press, 1970), p. 33.

10. Ibid.

11. Paul Ricoeur, *The Symbol of Evil*, trans. E. Buchanan (New York: Harper & Row, 1967), p. 349.

12. Martin Heidegger, *Being and Time*, trans. John Macquarrie and Edward Robinson (London: SCM Press Ltd., 1962), p. 61.

13. Ibid.

14. By "romanticist," I mean the intellectual protest against Enlightenment thought which glorified reason as the ultimate criterion of truth. Romanticism in the latter half of the 18th Century sought to give subjective feelings a more prominent place in defining the meaning of truth. Cf. Barth, *Protestant Thought*, translated by Brian Cozens. (New York: Harper and Row, Publishers, 1959), p. 216.

15. Bleicher, Josef, *Contemporary Hermeneutics: Hermeneutics As Method,*

Philosophy, and Critique (Boston: Routledge & Kegan Paul, 1980), p. 229.

16. Ibid., p. 234.

17. Ricoeur, *The Conflict of Interpretation* (Evanston: Northwestern University, 1974), p. 7.

18. Ibid.,

19. Ibid., p. 11.

20. Ihde,

21. Ricoeur, *The Conflict of Interpretation*, p. 3.

22. Quentin Lauer, *Phenomenology: Its Genesis and Prospect* (New York: Harper & Row, 1965) p. 163. Cited hereafter as *Phenomenology.*

23. Ibid., p. 2; cf. Don Ihde, *Hermeneutic Phenomenology, The Philosophy of Paul Ricoeur*, p. 15.

24. Lauer, *Phenomenology* p. 2.

25. Ibid., p. 3.

26. Cf. Lewis S. Mudge, "Introduction," in Ricoeur, *Essays on Biblical Interpretation*, p. 10.

27. Lauer, *Phenomenology*, p. 128ff.

28. Ricoeur, *The Conflict of Interpretation*, p. 7.

29. Ibid.

30. Ibid.

31. Ibid., p. 9.

32. Ibid., p. 9.

33. Ibid., p. 8.

34. Cf. Henri Frankfort, Mrs. H. A. Frankfort, John A. Wilson, and Thorkild Jacobsen, *Before Philosophy* (Baltimore, MD: Penguin Books, 1964).

35. Cf. Ihde, *Hermeneutic Phenomenology*, p. 23.

36. Paul Ricoeur, *The Symbolism of Evil*, trans. Emerson Buchanan (Boston; Beacon Press, 1967), p. 349.

37. Ibid.

38. *Essays on Biblical Interpretation, p.* 101.

39. Ibid., p.145.

40. Kevin Van Hoozer, *Biblical Narrative in the Philosophy of Paul Ricoeur* (Cambridge: Cambridge University Press, 1990), p. 229.

41. Ibid., p. 278.

42. Ibid. p. 279.

43. Dornisch, *Faith and Philosophy in the Writings of Paul Ricoeur*, p. 122.

44. Ibid.

45. Paul Ricoeur, *Essays on Biblical Interpretation*, p. 152.

46. Ibid., p. 124

47. Ibid., p. 121.

48. Ibid., p. 125.

49. Dornisch, *Faith and Philosophy in the Writings of Paul Ricoeur*, p. 122-123.

50. *Essays on Biblical Interpretation*, p.123.

51. Ibid., p.123.

52. Ibid., p. 126

53. Ibid., p. 80.

54. Ibid., p. 80.

55. Ibid., pp. 74, 75.

56. Ibid., p. 90.

57. Ibid., p. 75.

58. Ibid., p. 78.

59. Ibid., p. 79.

60. Ibid.

61. Ibid., pp. 111-112.

62. Paul Ricoeur, *Interpretation Theory: Discourse and the Surplus of Meaning* (Fort Worth: Texas Christianity University Press, 1976), p. 30, cited by Dornisch, *Faith and Philosophy in the Writings of Paul Ricoeur,* p. 134.

63. Dornisch, *Faith and Philosophy in the Writings of Paul Ricoeur,* p. 134.

64. *Essays on Biblical Interpretation,* pp. 108-109.

65. Ibid., p. 109.

66. *Interpretation Theory,* p. 30. Cf. Dornisch, *Faith and Philosophy in the Writings of Paul Ricoeur,* p. 134.

67. Dornisch, *Faith and Philosophy in the Writings of Paul Ricoeur,* pp. 99, 102.

68. *Essays on Biblical Interpretation,* p. 102.

69. Ibid., p. 117.

70. Ibid., p. 99.

71. Cf. William J. Abraham, "Intentions and the Logic of Interpretation," *The Asbury Theological Journal* 43.1 (Spring 1988): 11-25.

72. *Essays on Biblical Interpretation,* p. 101.

73. Werner Heisenberg, *Physics and Philosophy: The Revolution in Modern Science* (London: George Allen and Unwin, 1959). Cf. especially chapter 3.

74. Cf. Stanley Fish, *Is There a Text in This Class? The Authority of Interpretive Communities* (Cambridge: Harvard University Press, 1980).

75. Hugh J. Silverman, "Introduction," *Derrida and Deconstruction,* ed. Hugh J. Silverman (New York: Routledge, 1989), pp. 2-3

76. Derrida, "Structure, Sign, and Play in the Discourse of the Human Sciences," *The Structuralist Controversy,* ed Richard Macksey and Eugenio Donato (Baltimore: Johns Hopkins University Press, 1970). Cf. Simon Critchley and Timothy Mooney, "Deconstruction and Derrida," *Twentieth-Century Continental Philosophy,* ed. Richard Kearney, p. 446. Cf. Yvonne Sherwood, "Derrida," *Handbook of Postmodern Biblical Interpretation,* ed. A. K. M. Adam (St Louis: Chalice Press, 2000), p. 70.

77. *Twentieth-Century Continental Philosophy,* p. 446. Yvonne Sherwood, "Derrida," *Handbook of Postmodern Biblical Interpretation,* p. 70.

78. Yvonne Sherwood, "Derrida," *Handbook of Postmodern Biblical Interpretation,* p. 70.

79. Cf. Derrida, *Aporias,* trans. Thomas Dutoit (Stanford, California: Stanford University Press, 1993), pp. 11-21

80. Stephen Hahn, *On Derrida* (Belmont, California: Wadsworth, 2002), pp. 1-13.

81.Derrida, "Structure, Sign, and Play in the Discourse of the Human Sciences," *The Structuralist Controversy*, pp. 247, 256, 267. Calvin O. Schrag, "Subjectivity and Praxis at The End of Philosophy," *Hermeneutics & Deconstruction*, ed. Hugh Silverman and Don Ihde (Abany, NY: State University Press of New York Press, 1985), pp. 25-32.

82. Derrida, "Structure, Sign, and Play in the Discourse of the Human Sciences," *The Structuralist Controversy*, p. 271.

83. Roberts, *Nothing but History*, p. 205

84. *Deconstruction in A Nutshell, A Conversation with Jacques Derrida*, ed. John D. Caputo (New York: Fordham University Press, 1997), pp. 20, 60.

85. Cf. Yvonne Sherwood, "Derrida," *Handbook of Postmodern Biblical Interpretation*, p. 70.

86. Ibid.

87. Hugh J. Silverman, *Textualities, Between Hermeneutics and Deconstruction* (New York: Routledge, 1994), p. 61.

88. Cf. Richard Rorty, *Philosophy and the Mirror of Nature*, pp. 322-356. G. B. Madison, "Hermeneutics, Gadamer and Ricoeur," *Twentieth-Century Continental Philosophy*, ed. Richard Kearney (New York: Routledge, 1994), pp. 296ff.

89. Richard J. Bernstein, *Beyond Objectivism and Relativism: Science, Hermeneutics, and Praxis*, pp. 52–71.

90. Rorty, *Philosophy and the Mirror of Nature*, pp. 315ff.

91. Paul Ricoeur, *Freud and Philosophy*, p. 27.

92. Dornisch, *Faith and Philosophy in the Writings of Paul Ricoeur*, p. 295.

93. *Interpretation Theory*, p. 36; cf. Dornisch, p. 320.

94. Cullmann, *Salvation in History*, p. 88.

95. Ibid., p. 89. Cf. Pannenberg, "Kerygma and History," *Basic Questions in Theology*, 1:81-95.

96. *Against Heresies*, iii.23.1.

97. *Against Heresies*, iv.23.1

98. Cullmann, *Salvation As History*, p. 294.

99. Roberts, *Nothing but History*, p. 301.

8

Postliberal Hermeneutics and Narrative Theology

Theology as Realistic Narrative

Before his death in 1988, Hans Frei taught at Yale University Divinity School for many years.[1] In 1975, he introduced the concept of "realistic narrative" in his book, *The Identity of Jesus Christ*. He based this concept on what he believed were "the hermeneutical bases of dogmatic theology." By realistic narrative, he meant that the New Testament is "history-like," and it should be read literally.

Frei maintained the literal meaning of the text is something different from whether or not it is "an accurate report of actual historical facts."[2] Realistic narrative is not concerned with what history is real and what is not. Stated simply, "realistic narrative" is retelling the story as literally presented in the text itself without subjecting it to critical examination based on modern historical methods.

It is not altogether clear that Frei's hermeneutical approach is consistent. For example, he presented the "story" of Jesus in the Gospels as a "story" and "not necessarily as history."[3] What the Gospel "story" presents is the picture of Jesus as one whose "identity is self-focused and unsubstitutably his own." He continued: "He is not the wandering stranger, but the one individual so completely himself that his inalienable identity not only points us to his own inescapable presence, but also is the focus toward which all of us orient our own identity—each one in his own person and place."[4] Rudolf Bultmann of course said as much in his own demythologizing exegesis. However, Frei seemed to think that his "realistic narrative" is faithfully reproducing the "story" of Jesus, as if this "story" is presented as something other than actual history. He wrote: "But do we actually know that much about Jesus? Certainly not, if we are asking about the 'actual' man apart from the story. But that is not our concern."[5] Frei further said "the resurrection is not, of course, an event subject to critical historical judgment; and even if it taken at face value, it, by itself, tells us little about the internal history of Jesus." In other words, Frei believed "we are, in fact, thrown back on the story simply as a story, regardless of whether or not it is well documented."[6]

The inconsistency of Frei's narrative theology is that he wants to allow that there can be a narrative without history, while at the same time maintaining that he was pursuing the "old-fashioned" hermeneutic of letting the text speak for itself.[7] He did not explicitly deny the story is history, but he said that he is not interested in that question. How then could he claim to develop a realistic narrative based on the actual exegesis of the biblical text when it is clear that the New Testament texts present the events in Jesus' life, death, and resurrection as a real story, a real history, and a real account of things as they were perceived?[8] Paul's defense of Jesus' resurrection in 1 Cor. 15 is based on eyewitness testimony of what happened. The story of the gospels is an affirmation that the tomb was empty. Is it hermeneutically appropriate to speak of "realistic narrative" unless that also means taking into consideration the actuality of the events as the intention of the gospel story? To set aside the historical question is to ignore the narrative.[9] Given his divorce between story and history, it is understandable that Frei specifically rejects Pannenberg's view of the resurrection as an event capable of being assessed as a historical actual event.[10] On the other hand, Frei waffled on the historical question.

In his criticism of Frei, Paul Ricoeur has noted that it is not enough to speak of the stories of the biblical texts as *"historylike,"* but rather "the question of the referential claims of these stories remains unavoidable."[11] He further notes that "to raise only questions of meaning and to drop questions about historical reality" fail to do justice to the biblical texts. Ricoeur particularly notes that the meaning of Jesus' resurrection necessarily entails the "vexing question" of the empty tomb.[12] Ricoeur says that no one should dismiss the question of what really is and try to separate it from the question of what is meaningful. "To give such elusive events the equally elusive status of the Kantian *Ding an sich* is a price that nobody wants to pay after Fichte's and Hegel's critique of the *Ding an sich*."[13] Ricoeur insists, over against Frei, that language is "fundamentally referential" or else it would not be "meaningful."[14] Having stated that he was not really interested in the historical question, Frei nonetheless permitted one to believe that Jesus' resurrection really happened, but the ground for that belief is "a matter of faith."[15] Perhaps it would be fair to say that Frei probably did believe in the historicity of the resurrection, although he was unprepared to argue for it. His emphasis upon "realistic narrative" has focused the need to listen to the Bible on its own terms, and this represents an important advance over modernist theology.

The Cultural-Linguistic Method

George A. Lindbeck, a colleague of Frei and professor emeritus of historical theology at Yale University Divinity School, further developed the concept of narrative theology in terms of "a cultural-linguistic approach." This method rejects the idea that theology is based on religious experience which is universally available to everyone; rather theology is an expression of faith that is embraced by a particular religious community. He distinguishes his approach from the cognitivist and the experiential-expressive approaches. The *cognitivist* believes that the subject matter of the biblical text can be formulated into a system of ideas. This was the method of orthodoxy until Kant "demolished" its "metaphysical and epistemological foundations" with his critical philosophy.[16] Following Kant's critique, Lindbeck says religion was left "intolerably impoverished" until Schleiermacher introduced the experiential-expressive method, which became the method of liberalism.[17] Religion represents "the pre-reflective experiential depths of the self," and religious language objectifies these inner religious feelings.[18] Hence the experiential-expressive method makes religious experience the primary basis of doing theology instead of the biblical text, and it assumes that religious language is aesthetically and symbolically expressive instead of literal.[19]

A third method is a combination of the cognitivist-propositional and the experiential-expressive approaches. Roman Catholicism, Pietism and Revivalism are cited as examples of this combined method.[20]

Lindbeck rejects these three methods on the grounds that the language of faith is more basic than doctrinal ideas or religious experience. Rather, religious language is the language of the biblical texts, which contains narratives derived from a specific culture. This language embodies the enduring and distinctive meaning of a religious tradition. In other words, "a religion can be viewed as a kind of cultural and/or linguistic framework or medium that shapes the entirety of life and thought."[21]

He says that the creeds and the liturgy of the Church are "neutral"[22] in reference to specific statements of fact. They allegedly have no cognitive-propositional intent in the primary sense; rather they intend to preserve the memory of the Christian narrative. This means church doctrine has a "regulative" and not a substantive function. This regulative view of doctrine means that the language of faith serves as general rules that govern the nature of Christian talk about the revelation of God in Christ. Lindbeck says: "This becomes the only job that doctrines do in their role as church teachings."[23]

This downsizing of church doctrine to a practical rule of faith rather than a definitive statement about what Christians believe is derived from Kant who specifically says that the language of faith has an "as if" status, which he called a "regulative" function rather than a substantive one. Lindbeck appeals directly to this idea of a regulative function of religious language,[24] but he also (mistakenly) cites the Early Church Fathers as proposing this same kind of *regulae fidei*.[25]

Lindbeck argues that this regulative role of Christian doctrine entails a new theological method. He asserts that it will resolve the problem of theological pluralism that has afflicted the ecumenical movement and kept it from moving forward in pursuit of Church unity.[26] The basic problem in ecumenical discussion is doctrinal conflict. He believes the cultural-linguistic method will allow for "doctrinal reconciliation without capitulation." Unlike the cognitivist method which assumes that if something is true at one point in time, it must be true forever, the cultural-linguistic method believes the Christian "story . . . is not primarily a set of propositions to be believed, but is rather the medium in which one moves, a set of skills that one employs in living one's life."[27]

For example, everyone in the Christian community affirms "Christ is Lord," but not everyone agrees on what this confession means doctrinally; hence the propositional content of this statement is secondary.[28] Until this confession is made from within a believing community, this phrase is not a statement of information at all. When it does become a cognitive meaningful statement, it is supposedly at best "modest cognitivism or propositionalism."[29] Likewise the claim that "Jesus was truly and objectively raised from the dead"[30] is not a statement of historical fact. The verbal confessions that "Christ is Lord" and that "Jesus is risen" are not assertions about what is historically true, rather they have a religious-ethical intention, namely, to enforce and to inspire a specific way of living.[31]

Lindbeck refers to his method as "postliberal" as opposed to the experiential-expressive method of liberalism, which he thinks failed to preserve the integrity of Christian speech. The idea of returning to a pre-liberal orthodoxy with its cognitivism was not a serious option.[32] A conspicuous similarity between Lindbeck's postliberalism and liberalism is their common moral-ethical interpretation of doctrine; for he argues that the purpose of doctrine is "to interiorize a set of skills by practice and training."[33] Another similarity is his minimizing the cognitive-informational meaning of the biblical narrative.

His postliberalism is an advance beyond liberalism with his focus on a realistic reading of the text. He joins Frei in asserting that theology should engage in a literal reading of the text. For example, "the story of Jesus" must be read like a "novel" or a "tale."[34] One simply and quite literally takes it as it is. The story of the Gospels intends to provide the reader with the *identity* of Jesus Christ, but whether or not his identity is real history is quite different from reading the text literally. Reading the biblical text is like reading a novel. Read it literally, but do not believe what you are reading is necessarily true. Lindbeck thus says that "the story of Jesus" is about "Jesus' identity" and "not his historicity."[35]

Here Lindbeck operates with a dualism of hermeneutics and history. One might call this a dualism between the *textuality of Jesus* and the *historicity of Jesus*. But this will not do. According to the basic principles of logic, the assertive function of a sentence involves three aspects. First, there is the person who makes a statement; second, the statement itself, and third, its objective frame of reference. This third component is essential, if it is making a factual statement at all. Yet this is the component that Lindbeck is eliminating in his concept of textuality. The text, like a novel, is the reality, not some factual and objective point of reference beyond itself.[36]

Lindbeck fails to point out the difference between the kind of literature that the biblical texts are and novels. Statements in a novel have no referential claims; these are fictitious statements and the reader understands them as fictitious. This is not the case with the biblical text. The reader is confronted with a narrative that is assumed to be truth. Its external frame of reference is an inherent meaning of the text. A literal reading thus means the reader must decide on the plausibility of the texts.

Lindbeck affirms the epistemological contributions of Michael Polanyi.[37] He particularly highlights Polanyi's concept of tacit knowledge. Lindbeck is right to insist on the intuitive embodiment of the story of Jesus that comes from the proclamation of the gospel,[38] and in this sense, the explicit and cognitive aspects are secondary. However, his cultural-linguistic method fails to incorporate adequately the cognitive dimension of Polanyi's continuum of the explicit and tacit dimensions of knowing.

A post-critical reading of the text should give primacy to the literal telling of the story, but it would also seek to give an explicit interpretation of it. This is similar to Pannenberg's view that faith does not have to wait for the results of historical criticism in order for one to believe. For Pannenberg, faith occurs in worship. He maintains that "faith in Christ" mediates salvation to the believer, yet the believer must at least accept that the historical foundation in order to have faith in the New Testament sense.[39] So the tacit and explicit poles of knowing exist in a continuum. To talk about "faith in Christ" that excludes the assumption that Jesus was really raised from the dead is eliminating the literal meaning of the biblical text. The New Testament narrative concerning Jesus' resurrection from the dead requires both questions be answered— "What does it mean?" and "Is it true?" A literal reading of the biblical texts offers an answer to both questions.

Surely Jesus did not die because of a fiction-like and history-like meaning, but because he believed that God had sent him into the world for a specific mission. A literal reading of the text makes this clear. Facing the cross was a reflection of his own self-identity as God's chosen means through whom the world would come to know God. The resurrection kerygma makes no sense without this implicit self-understanding of Jesus. The kind of persecution and martyrdom, which the church sustained in the first several centuries, cannot be explained on the basis of a fiction-like theory of biblical interpretation. To say that "Christ is Lord" was more than saying that they had embraced a specific way of behaving in the world;[40] rather, it meant that they really believed that the God of the universe had sent Jesus into the world as the savior of all people and that one's final destiny depended on one's relationship to him.

It may be that Lindbeck thinks that doctrine should be identified with a history-like, novel-like text rather than with real history, but he did not derive that definition from the biblical text itself, although Hans Frei sought (I believe unsuccessfully) to justify that definition based on exegetical considerations.[41] On the other hand, the priority of a realistic reading of the text can hardly be overemphasized, and in this respect the postliberal contributions of Frei and Lindbeck are significant in helping the larger Christian community to rediscover the biblical text.

Stanley Hauerwas and Narrative Theology

Stanley Hauerwas is the Gilbert T. Rowe Professor of Theological Ethics of Duke Divinity School. *Time* magazine named Hauerwas "America's

Best Theologian" in its issue of Sept. 17, 2001. He is probably the most prolific writer among theologians in America today.

Two of his best-known works are *A Community of Character* (1981) and *The Peaceable Kingdom* (1983). Methodologically, his premise is a simple one—theology is "relative to a particular community's convictions."[42] He maintains that Christian theology does not prove itself through rational apologetics, but rather the task of theology is to clarify what constitutes the biblical story culminating in Jesus Christ. Theology is not absolute knowledge because it is contingent: "It can only be passed on from one generation to another by memory. We test our memory with Scripture as we are rightly forced time after time to seek out new implications of that memory by the very process of passing it on."[43]

If Hauerwas' teacher, Hans Frei,[44] was unclear about his belief in the realism of salvation history, Hauerwas unequivocally affirms that the Christian narrative is based in the memory of the Scriptures and that this memory represents the real history of Jesus' self-identity. How does one know that the Christian story is real history? The only satisfying answer is that it is proven in the lives of those "exemplify its demands."[45] Does not the narrative itself need to be rationally verified? No, Hauerwas answers. The criterion of its truthfulness "is not so much like a principle as it is like a story that the saints' lives exhibit."[46] Does this mean that faith is anti-rational? No. Reason is integrated into the process of thinking by means of developing the consistent implications of the Christian narrative.[47] Although the Christian narrative contains principles and propositions that are believed to be true,[48] one does not begin with foundational principles[49] or with epistemology as a theoretical discipline. Rather the theologian begins with the specific knowledge of God contained in the narrative of revelation.[50] Barth's influence can be seen here in the way that Hauerwas interprets the Scriptures as a witness to God's self-revelation.[51]

Hauerwas wants to avoid being labeled a narrative theologian because theology does not create stories, but rather theology is a critical reflection on a tradition that has been shaped by the memory of its past, present, and its anticipated future. He specifically refers to himself as "an evangelical Methodist."[52] Yet, it is also fair to refer to Hauerwas as a narrative theologian because narrative forms the center of his thinking about the distinctive feature of Christian faith.

Is Hauerwas an "evangelical" as he professes? This would depend upon what is meant by this term. The term "evangelical" was used to describe the Wesleyan revival in the 18th century. The evangelicals were evangelists who went into the fields, homes, and makeshift buildings (not unlike the "tent meetings" which Hauerwas now resentfully used to attend as a child)[53] preaching the gospel and calling sinners to repentance and believers to be made perfect in love in an instantaneous moment of faith. Hauerwas is clearly not an "evangelical" in this sense.

If "evangelical" means neo-evangelical as originally used by Harold J. Ockenga and subsequently by Carl Henry who affirmed the inerrancy of Scripture, then clearly Hauerwas is not one of them. If by "evangelical" is meant one who affirms the Trinitarian faith of the Church and the authority of Scripture, then Hauerwas generally fits into this category. Hauerwas embraces "the authority of Scripture" because it is "the irreplaceable source of the stories that train us to be a faithful people."[54] The criterion, however, for determining what forms true Christian beliefs is not based on isolated texts of Scripture but on whether or not these beliefs "form a coherent narrative."[55] Hauerwas rightly rejects fundamentalist literalism.

Hauerwas' writings are a welcomed change from the way theology is often done among neo-evangelical theologians who set forth the "truth" of the Christian Scriptures in a rationalistic format as if faith were a matter of fixed propositions. He believes the way to do theology today is to follow the narrative thinking of the New Testament. He says this includes propositions, such as the doctrine of the virgin birth,[56] but these beliefs are accepted only because they form a coherent picture of truth implicit in the Christian story.

On the other hand, his one-sided emphasis on the coherent theory of truth exposes a serious weakness in his methodology. It may not be important for Hauerwas to ask the historical-critical question about the probabilities of faith being rooted in history, but I believe it is important for Christianity to ask this question. Certainly the apostles cited their eyewitness account as a reason for believing (I John 1:1; I Cor. 15:5-11). In spite of his dislike of Pietism, Hauerwas' methodology is pietistic in the general sense that the truth of the Christian faith is established and confirmed on the basis of the convincing qualitative life of those who profess to be followers of Christ.

Tillich has shown that the result of pietistic methodology weakened the Lutheran Orthodox method of rational apologetics in the 17th century and led to the overthrow both of Pietism and orthodoxy by the critical philosophy of Kant and Enlightenment deism.[57] Karl Barth's theology of the self-authenticating Word of God seemed to make it unnecessary to utilize historical criticism, and thus it was largely set aside in the 20th century in favor of Bultmann's existentialist theology, which took seriously the question of critical history for faith. In this sense, Pannenberg has rightly noted that Barth's methodology is pietistic in principle because he believed the truth of revelation is self-confirming.[58] It is likely that Hauerwas' experientially-based methodology will have the consequence of being abandoned because it does not see the need to use historical criticism and critical thought in general to assess the truth-claims of Christian belief.

Not only does Hauerwas' theological method have pietistic elements, it also has some of the more liberal additions as well. The hallmark of Schleiermacher's liberal theological method was a feeling of God in the human soul. By feeling, Schleiermacher extended the pietistic idea of the internal witness of the Spirit to an intuitive participation in God. This inner intuition permitted one to readjust Christian doctrine according to how one "feels" about it. That is, theology must be a coherent expression of one's own personal religious experiences and perceptions.

It is this point of deciding what is coherent that compromises the biblical narrative in Hauerwas' method. Subjectivism and relativism in general are a nagging problem of narrative theology. One gets to rewrite parts of the narrative that do not seem to be coherent with one's personal experiences. To be sure, Wesley believed that personal experience was an important part of understanding the Scripture, as he explained in his sermon on "The Witness of the Spirit." Hauerwas as a Methodist is on solid ground on this point. However, Wesley insisted that the text of Scripture is the basis of our beliefs, not experience.[59] We are not free to discard parts of the Scripture simply because we find them disagreeable. Wesley frankly said that he would be convinced that he had misunderstood the text if it did not prove itself in practical experience, but he also made it clear that one does not have the luxury of creating doctrine that is plainly contrary to the general sense of Scripture as a whole.[60] One of Wesley's criticisms of mysticism was "not being guided by the written word."[61] The result is that "you will find as many religions as books; and for this plain reason, each of them makes his own experience the standard of religion."[62] A similar problem exists for narrative theology.

This weakness can be seen in Hauerwas' recent work, *Sanctify Them in the Truth: Holiness Exemplified* (1998). His narrative theology allows him to embrace a view of homosexuality, which cannot be fitted into the Christian story. His reasoning for affirming a homosexual lifestyle shows that he retains remnants of the liberal-pietistic method in theology. Although Hauerwas is one of the most vocal critics of liberalism because it is controlled by culturally-conditioned, bourgeois values, he himself appeals to the cultural norm of friendship as basis for accepting the gay lifestyle. He reports that he discovered that "I had friends who are gay" and "they are among the most faithful Christians I know."[63] It is important to keep in mind that the methodologically decisive thing for Hauerwas is that the Christian narrative is true because it is exhibited in the lives of saints, and since these gay persons reflect faithful Christian lives according to Hauerwas' personal judgment, this shows that their gay lifestyle is Christian.

Hauerwas' develops the notion of friendship from Aristotle who argued that friendships are important for becoming persons of virtue and good character. If the gay lifestyle is wrong, then it is wrong to have gay friends, Hauerwas concludes, because their influence would be morally corrupting.[64] Since, in fact, their influence is positive and Christlike in Hauerwas' view, then one must conclude that their homosexual lifestyle is not inconsistent with their lives as Christians. Friendship with gays thus proves homosexuality is a viable alternative lifestyle.

This simple theological argument is not without its difficulties. First, Hauerwas could have cited many New Testament reference on friendship (*koinonia*), all of which assume that the believers are agreed on the meaning and practice of the Christian life (cf. 2 Cor 6:14; Gal. 2:9; I John 1, 3.), and this New Testament understanding of Christian practice excluded homosexuality (I Cor. 6:9). In a surprising way, Hauerwas does not discuss a single biblical text addressing the issue of homosexuality. This issue has been hotly debated in recent discussions, but it is impossible to avoid the consistent scriptural view of homosexual practice. This practice was obviously a widespread phenomenon in the ancient Near East, but it was strictly forbidden in the legal codes of Leviticus (18:22; 20:13) where it was condemned as an abomination. Rehoboam was condemned by God because he allowed homosexuality in Judah (I Kings 14:24; cf. I Kings 14:24; 15:12; 2 Kings 23:7).

It could be argued that the severity of the death penalty, as in the case of adultery (a penalty which was never carried out in practice), was intended to underscore the sanctity of marriage and the inherent meaning of human fulfillment in an appropriate relationship of husband and wife. In the beginning, God created human life as male and female as complements of each other. The family was the model of human relationships.

The biblical rejection of homosexual practice is not simply that sexual intercourse is for purposes of procreation, which is the only explanation that Hauerwas considered and which he found weak.[65] Paul plainly says that the desire for sexual intercourse is one reason for being married: "Because of the temptation to immorality, each man should have his own wife and each woman her own husband. The husband should give to his wife her conjugal rights, and likewise the wife to her husband" (1 Cor. 7:2-3). This implies a recreational view of sexuality as a fringe benefit of marriage that goes beyond mere procreational purposes.

There is an apparent depersonalizing and demeaning of human life that takes place in homosexual relationships, although these consequences may be well masked from view. This would explain why Jude spoke of "the unnatural lusts" of "Sodom and Gomorrah and the surrounding cities" as undergoing "a punishment of eternal fire" (Jude 7). Hence Paul said: "Do not be deceived; neither the immoral, nor idolaters, not adulterers, nor homosexuals . . . will inherit the kingdom of God" (1 Cor. 6:9-10). He condemned the practice of "sodomites" (1 Tim. 1:10). Paul also cites homosexual practices as engaging in "dishonorable passions" (Rom. 1:26). Paul noted that some of the Corinthians had been "homosexuals," but "you were washed, you were sanctified, you were justified in the name of the Lord Jesus and in the Spirit of our God" (1 Cor. 6:11). One of the marks of becoming a Christian believer was that these kinds of practices were discontinued.

To be sure, Hauerwas dislikes legalism and he specifically prefers to think of the larger problem of sin as a condition which distorts our relationship to God and others rather than to focus on specific sins.[66] His criticism of Pietism is that it focuses morally on the importance of living virtuously in terms of ceasing from individual sins through personal conversion. While it is easy to fall into a moralistic trap as if being a Christian means following a list of do's and don'ts, it is also possible to fall into antinomianism, particularly in reference to sins favored by cultural elites (as Wesley particularly warned against). It would be a mistake, thus, to conclude that one was a Christian believer because one abstains from sinful practices, such as sexual immorality, but it is also wrong to think that one is a faithful believer in spite of living in known sin, which the Christian narrative has designated as offensive to God.

Hauerwas also criticizes Pietism as being individualistic, but his critique is inadequate. It is also inconsistent with his Methodist heritage. The focus of the Wesleyan revival was on calling individuals to justifying and sanctifying faith through the preaching of the Word of God. To be sure, Wesley was a "catholic" Christian as Outler has shown and which Hauerwas highlights, but he was "an evangelical catholic" who emphasized the importance of personal, individual faith in Christ. Wesley certainly affirmed the importance of the sacramental means of grace and embraced high Anglican theology, but he adopted aspects of low Anglican theology. He also embraced aspects of Pietism. The primary focus of the revival movement of the 18th century was pietistic in the religious sense, which Hauerwas dislikes. Wesley experienced this personal faith at Aldersgate through the influence of Moravian Pietism, which Hauerwas also dislikes.[67] Hauerwas probably dislikes Paul's Damascus Road experience (Acts 9:3) as well. Hauerwas surprisingly considers the revivalist emphasis upon one's individual relationship with God as a "narcissistic fascination with my peculiar status."[68] I am not able to understand why and how Hauerwas can extract (sanitize?) these parts out of the Christian narrative, or minimize this part of his Methodist heritage. In fact, there would be no Methodist tradition today without these revivals, and the current Methodist institutions of higher learning would not even exist.

Perhaps it would be best to describe Hauerwas as an evangelical, postliberal Methodist employing a pietistic epistemology, while also utilizing the cultural-linguistic method proposed by Lindbeck. Hauerwas apparently assumes that the meanings of biblical texts can be neutralized and reinterpreted so that their purpose is to promote a way of life rather than morally prescribing certain practices as right or wrong. If the meaning of texts is "neutral" in regard to doctrine and specific ideas (as Lindbeck proposes), then these texts can be taken by different communities of faith to mean different things doctrinally. In a sense, Hauerwas espouses a theology of "cultural Christianity" in which the practice of the Christian community determines the nature of faith and its larger implications.[69]

To be sure, Hauerwas is evangelical in the sense that he affirms "Nicaea and Chalcedon as normative boundaries." However, he points out these guides to faith must undergo further corrections and transformations in the life of the Church as new issues surface on the horizon.[70] This is of course very true from any evangelical point of view, but what sort of limitation is placed on this development? It has been one of the convictions of the church as a confessing community of believers that the history of revelation has been finalized in the Scriptures, although the previously unnoticed implications of this history continue to be explicated for each new generation. In advocating a theology of "cultural Christianity," to what extent does Hauerwas permit contemporary practice to alter the narrative as well as to expand its inherent implications?[71]

This brings us back to the issue of homosexuality. Why should it now be legitimized in the church? Hauerwas thinks it should be because it is an extension of a theology of friendship. Now there is no doubt that what he says about friendship is highly significant. On a personal note, I was privileged that Hauerwas was invited to give a series of lectures in 1990 at the time of my installation into the Frank Paul Morris Chair of Theology, and his lectures were on the theme of "Happiness, the Life of Virtue and Friendship: Theological Reflections on Aristotelian Themes," which were published in *The Asbury Theological Journal.*[72]

However, I think there is a problem with his methodological use of friendship as a criterion of truth as a means of correcting and reinterpreting the Christian narrative. His argument is complex, but rather easy to understand. Virtue and friendship are inseparably related. There is no way to be virtuous without a community of friends who shape our lives. When we have friends who are positive influences in our lives and who inspire us and help us to be better Christians, we must assume that they are virtuous people. If it turns out that these people are homosexual partners, then we must conclude that homosexual practice is consistent with Christian values. If we must conclude that homosexual practice is not Christian, then we ought not have them as friends, Hauerwas maintains.[73] However, since they are friends who inspire us to be more like Christ, we must accept them and their homosexual practice.

In response to this argument, I would agree that it is not sinful for one to have a homosexual orientation. There are devout Christian believers who are chaste in spite of their homosexual orientation. Some have shared with me their personal dilemma of coping with it. I have encouraged and worked with seminary students who have suffered from depression over how to handle their homosexuality. Some seminary students have been denied ordination because they publicly admitted their homosexual orientation in spite of the fact they were model Christian believers and remained chaste. Although one has friends who are practicing homosexual, this is no basis for saying that, since they are fine persons, one should approve the gay lifestyle as acceptable Christian behavior. There is a limit to friendship with those whose lifestyle contradicts Christian ethics. There are men and women who live together outside the marriage bond, who are basically good people, but one would not be their friend if one encouraged them to think that their lifestyle was acceptable Christian behavior.

On a more pragmatic basis, there are some people who are not Christians whom I would rather have as friends than some Christian people. Let me tell you about a good friend who is an atheist, but he is one of the most gracious and best men you can ever want to meet. He is a nationally-known philosopher whose book on atheism is used as a text in universities across America. He has often lectured in my class on Christian ethics. He once contributed an article to the *Asbury Theological Journal* on a significant Methodist holiness leader of the 19th century. He gave the week-long holiness lectures at Asbury College several years ago. He once preached in chapel on the meaning of love, citing the lives of Jesus and Socrates as morally exemplary persons. Our families have often eaten together in each other's homes, and his family regularly attends church and participates in its activities, and on occasions he attends college and seminary chapels. My friend is a most inspiring person who is well liked and appreciated by all who know him—in spite of his atheism. He is a very sincere person, but he is atheist because he believes the idea of the goodness of God is incompatible with the incomprehensible suffering of human beings. It is as though he wants to protect the morality of God, as I once said to him. He is not bitter, but feels deeply the pain that others feel. One of his significant contributions in our Asbury community is that he models for us the meaning of friendship and social responsibility. After more than twenty years in our community, he and his wife recently moved back East to be near their son and his family, which is a loss for us.

It would be faulty reasoning to assume, however, that because he is a model of Christian behavior in so many ways he is a Christian. He does not profess to be one, and he would be offended if you called him one, although he would be gracious in response to such a judgment. Nor does his gracious and compassionate life prove that atheism is the truth. Yet some of the most conservative people in our Christian community consider him a friend even though they know he is an atheist.

The church is certainly a place where sinners should feel invited to come and to worship, including my atheist friend; otherwise none of us would be there. I also believe in the optimism of grace and that our lives can be redeemed from sins and from those specific behaviors that depersonalize us and deflect our attention from God and cause us to disrespect others. I also believe the church is a place where homosexuals can be encouraged to be chaste just as single, heterosexual persons need to be chaste. I also believe my atheist friend derived courage and strength for living through being in our Christian community and attending worship, although he remained an unbeliever. I also would not want to make any judgements about his real relationship to God because there is often a degree of dissonance between what we think and what we really are. I once said to him that I believe in his heart of hearts that he was believer, and he agreed this may be true. I am glad he came because his friendship "ministered" to our community.

The essence of the gospel is love, and love is inclusive, as Hauerwas emphasizes. Christian love also means that appropriate persons care enough to confront others concerning their misconduct. It also means willing to accept "outsiders" just as they are in order that through the living witness of believers they will be changed into the likeness of Christ as they too come to share in the Christian narrative. And as in the case of my atheist friend, "outsiders" can also be instruments of God's grace as well. Although it would be inappropriate to make ecclesiastical pronouncement about a nonbeliever's eternal destiny because God alone is the truly just and wise Judge, it seems clear enough that the standard of Christian ethics should be not be accommodated to suit individual opinions when the Scriptures have spoken clearly on an issue such as this. It is thus not legalistic and judgmental to point out that some practices are considered unChristian, whether it be adultery or homosexual practice. To be sure, there is grace and forgiveness, if we confess our sins.

More basically, it is not friendship itself that shapes who we are, but the grace of God mediated to us through others, specifically through the fellowship of the Church. It is even possible for the grace of God to be mediated through persons who are pretenders, as Paul noted and yet he rejoiced, "whether in pretense or in truth, Christ is proclaimed" (Phil 1:18). Aristotle was of course quite optimistic about the possibility of doing good and developing virtue if we have the right environment in which to live. Hence friendship with virtuous people was *sine qua non* of becoming virtuous. This is why Aristotle believed we should not be friends with non-virtuous people, because they will drag us down to their level. Christians are much more generous and can reach out as Jesus did who was known as "a friend to sinners." In this way, he was able to redeem lost people through befriending them.

Every congregation should befriend anyone who comes into their sanctuary, but this does not mean putting them into places of leadership until they have embraced Christian beliefs and become examples of acceptable Christian behavior. My atheist friend once asked me about the possibility of teaching philosophy of religion at Asbury Theological

Seminary. He noted that Asbury was involved in "the biggest business in the world" because it was training people who would change the world. He reassured me that he would do nothing to undermine students' faith in God. Although he often lectured on our campus, he understood and appreciated the confessional nature of the seminary, which expects its faculty to be in agreement with Wesleyan beliefs.

My purpose here is not to preach, but to address the issue of theological method. Hauerwas has allowed pastoral concerns unduly to influence theological method. To be sure, he is right to insist on the importance of lived theology as opposed to abstract notions and ideas, but pastoral theology should be rooted in a right understanding of the Christian narrative. It seems that the weakness of narrative theology in general, and with Hauerwas' theology in particular, is that one's own subjectivity too easily determines what is the core of the narrative. Hauerwas acknowledges there is an element of subjectivity that may lead to existentially contradictory views at times, but he notes that is part of the process of doing theology.[74] However, an issue such as chastity outside of marriage between a man and a woman which is an integral part of the Christian narrative should be respected, not because it is legalistically set forth in a religious book, but out of respect for the wisdom of the Scriptures which upholds the sanctity of marriage, the family, and the meaning of personhood.

Colin Williams showed that the founder of Methodism, John Wesley, cautioned against making experience the test of truth. Williams wrote:

> Experience is not the test of truth, but truth the test of experience. Wesley feared any approach to doctrine and worship which overlooked the necessity for personal experience, but he equally feared any reliance upon experience which left the question of truth to the vagaries of individual or collective feeling. He knew the danger of the Christian faith being torn from its historical moorings by being subject to the vagaries and limitations of human experience, and so he insisted upon the priority of the Word.[75]

The idea of the Scriptures as the basis of truth is not the same as turning them into a rational criterion of truth. The Scriptures are a means of grace and salvation. They are a witness to God's self-revelation. They are the sources of Christian belief. They reflect what the Christian community believes to be the wisdom of God. Hauerwas may wish to argue for the homosexual lifestyle using the criterion of friendship, but he has not shown how this rationally-based norm should transcend the canonical tradition of the Christian community. More specifically, the liberal-pietistic methodology assumed in such a criterion has become questionable in contemporary theology.

Notes

1. Cf. William C. Placher, "Hans Frei and the Meaning of Biblical Narrative." *Christian Century* 106 (May 24-31, 1989): 556-559.

2. Hans Frei, *The Identity of Jesus Christ* (Philadelphia: Fortress Press, 1975), p. xiv.

3. Ibid., p. 102.

4. Ibid., p. 102.

5. Ibid., p. 103.

6. Ibid., p. 103.

7. Ibid., p. xvi.

8. Ibid., pp. xv-xvi.

9. Cf. N. T. Wright, *The Resurrection of the Son of God*, pp. 21-22. who argues that the publicness of the claim concerning Jesus' resurrection shows that the historical question cannot be suspended without contradicting the apostolic claim.

10 Ibid., p. xiii.

11. Paul Ricoeur, *Essays on Biblical Interpretation*, edited with an introduction by Lewis S. Mudge (Philadelphia: Fortress Press, 1980), p. 44.

12. Ibid., pp. 44-45, 163.

13. Ibid.

14. *Interpretation Theory*, p. 21, cited by Dornisch, *Faith and Philosophy in the Writings of Paul Ricoeur*, p. 318.

15. Ibid., p. 152.

16. George A. Lindbeck, *The Nature of Doctrine, Religion and Theology in a Postliberal Age* (Philadelphia: Westminster Press, 1984), p. 20.

17. Ibid., p. 16.

18. Ibid., p. 21.

19. Ibid., p. 21.

20. Ibid., pp. 16, 22.

21. Ibid., p. 33.

22. Ibid., pp. 9, 18.

23. Ibid., p. 19.

24. Ibid., pp. 18-21.

25. Ibid., p. 18.

26. Ibid., pp. 7, 17.

27. Ibid., p. 35.

28. Ibid., p. 68.

29. Ibid., pp. 66-67.

30. Ibid., pp. 67.

31. Ibid., p. 34.

32. Ibid., p. 7.

33. Ibid., p. 35.

34. Ibid., p. 120.

35. Ibid., p. 120

36. Ibid., p. 114.

37. Ibid., p. 38.

38. Ibid., p. 36.

39. Pannenberg, "Response to the Discussion," *Theology As History*, pp. 268-269.

40. Lindbeck, *The Nature of Doctrine*, p. 68.

41. Frei, *The Identity of Jesus Christ*, p. xv.

42. Stanley Hauerwas, *A Community of Character* (Notre Dame, Indiana: University of Notre Dame Press, 1981), p. 2

43. Stanley Hauerwas, *The Peaceable Kingdom* (Notre Dame, Indiana: University of Notre Dame Press, 1983), p. 70.

44. Ibid., p. xxi.

45. Ibid., p. 70.

46. Ibid., p. 71.

47. Ibid., pp. 64-71.

48. Ibid., p. 66

49. Ibid., p. xxv.

50. Ibid.

51. Ibid., p. xxi.

52. Ibid., p. xxvi.

53. Stanley Hauerwas, *Sanctify Them in The Truth* (Nashville: Abingdon Press, 1998), pp. 9-10, 62.

54. Ibid., p. 70.

55. Ibid., p. 66.

56. Ibid., p. 105.

57. Tillich, *A History of Christian Thought*, pp. 311-315.

58. Pannenberg, "Kerygma and History," *Basic Questions in Theology* , 1:81-83.

59. Wesley, *Sermons*, ed. Albert C. Outler, "The Witness of the Spirit, II," 1:297.

60. Colin Williams, *John Wesley's Theology Today, A Study of the Wesleyan Tradition in the Light of Current Theological Dialogue* (Nashville: Abingdon Press, 1960), pp. 34-35.

61. *Works of John Wesley*, "Abridgements of Various Works," ed. Thomas Jackson (Grand Rapids, Michigan: Baker Book House, 1978) 14:277.

62. Ibid., "Letter to Mary Bishop," (September 19, 1773), 13:25.

63. Hauerwas, *Sanctify Them in The Truth*, p. 108.

64. Ibid., p. 116.

65. Ibid., pp.108-117

66. Ibid., p. 62.

67. Ibid., p. xi.

68. Ibid., p. 10.

69. Ibid., pp. 157-173.

70. Ibid., p. 5.

71. Ibid., pp. 157-173.

72. *The Asbury Theological Journal*, 45.2 (Spring 1990).

73. Hauerwas, *Sanctify Them in The Truth*, p. 108.

74.. Ibid., p. 7.

75. Collin Williams, *John Wesley's Theology Today, A Study of the Wesleyan Tradition in the Light of Current Theological Dialogue*, pp. 34-35.

76. Cf. William J. Abraham, *Canon and Criterion in Christian Theology* (New York: Oxford University Press, 1998).

9

Postmodern Hermeneutics, Ideological Criticism, and Liberation Theologies

Paul Ricoeur has given special attention to the way that ideology plays a role in postmodern hermeneutics.[1] Ideology is a term to describe how specific agendas and self-serving ideas are masked by special interest groups to promote their own cause. Ricoeur says Marx, Nietzsche, and Freud were the "masters of suspicion" who specifically highlighted the role of ideology in creating a false-consciousness in culture.[2]

Let me summarize their well-known arguments. Marx gave a critique of capitalism. He used ideological criticism to promote a theory of the historical development of society, particularly contending that the middle class (the bourgeoisie) used the working class of people (the proletariat) to further their financial gain through promising them "pie in the sky bye and bye." He generally interpreted religion as "the sigh of the oppressed"—poor working people looking to religion as solace from the oppression of life. In his view, the middle class used religion as an ideology or mask for retaining their privileged status in society.

Nietzsche showed how "will to power" was an underlying current in the structure of society, and he particularly argued that religious leaders compensated for their inherent weaknesses by controlling others and making them feel powerless and guilty. Religious virtues such as love and humility were interpreted as anger that had gone underground. Religious ideology was a mask to hide this weakness from the oppressed as well as the oppressor.

Freud argued that the underlying structure of cultural expression was an unconscious and anxious striving that obscures the distinction between illusion and reality. In particular, God was interpreted as a neurotic wish fulfillment as compensation for inadequate parents who are unable to protect one from the difficulties of life. Religion was thus an ideology to mask one's feelings of helplessness.

No one will deny that ideology plays a significant role in society. The

Marxist insight (despite its excessive interpretation) is a helpful tool for understanding how ideology intertwines itself with the governing elite in manipulating the purposes of society for its own advantage. Nietzsche has a good point in showing how religious virtues can be manipulated in an unconscious way to control others. And Freud is surely right to observe that many views of God are rooted in anxiety disorders.

Paul Ricoeur has further developed the concept of ideology to show how it can be used as a basis for being *skeptical* about the religious skepticism of Marx, Freud, and Nietzsche. He has shown how illusory it is to assume ideology is a point of view that one ascribes to another while assuming that oneself is free of it.[3] Hermeneutics can particularly use the concept of ideology to unmask the hidden agenda of exegetes who use the scriptures for their own personal and private prejudices.

Ricoeur's concept of the "surplus" of meaning in the text can be interpreted to mean that the reader is able to address a variety of situations and interpretations that transcend the particular agendas of self-serving individuals and communities.[4] No one group can rightfully dominate scriptural texts by imposing a meaning on other groups. Those who have been marginalized from the mainstream of the Christian tradition also have access to the text and can find meaning in that it addresses their particular social setting. This does not mean one has a license to abuse the text to make it say whatever one wants, but it is to acknowledge there is a larger horizon of the text that transcends the original historical setting and that even transcends what the author may have explicitly intended. Scripture took on an autonomous status once it was written, and it is able to speak beyond its immediate setting to distant social settings. This frees up the texts from the controlling interests of a self-protective community. Ricoeur shows how hermeneutics can overcome the modern split between subject-object in which the text as an object stands over against the exegete as subject who supposedly is able to control it and make it serve one's own ideological self-interests. Ricoeur's hermeneutical paradigm highlights the importance of a dialog between the reader and the text out of which comes a participatory understanding and which thus challenges the reader's own biases and ideologies.

Latin American Liberation Theology

The application of ideological criticism to Scripture is the method used in Latin American liberation theology.[5] In order to appreciate its concept of ideology, it will be important to identify several forces behind the rise of liberation theology. In the 1950's a theory of development was advocated by the United Nations in which Latin America was to be given the opportunity to develop economically and socially as other Northern Countries had. In the early part of the 1960's the Kennedy Administration put forward The Alliance for Progress in which social and economic provisions were to be made for reforming the Latin American economic situation. By the end of the 1960's hope for social, political, and economic changes had been greatly diminished. In spite of all reformist attempts to bring about change, there continued to be a wide gap between the rich and the poor, and democracy had been upstaged by military interventions preventing the larger poor population from participating in public policy making. Hence many Christian theologians and intellectuals were turning to Marxist categories as a hermeneutical means of challenging and critiquing the capitalist concept of development and reform.[6]

A second force behind the rise of liberation theology was the Second Vatican Council in 1965.[7] It had called upon Roman Catholics to give special consideration to the suffering and oppressed peoples of the world. Also some major social encyclicals (*Pacem in terries,*1963 and *Populorum progression,* 1967) by Pope John XXII and Pope Paul VI had cautiously suggested more socialist solutions as increased state planning, public ownership of key national resources, limitations on private property, more equitable distribution of the world's resources especially for the benefit of developing nations, and the right to violence under certain repressive situations.[8]

A third decisive force in the rise of liberation theology occurred at the Second General Conference of Latin American bishops held at Medellín, Colombia, in August 1968, when one hundred and fifty bishops from every country in Latin America met to discuss the lack of reform and the deteriorating economic and social situation. Based on the papal encyclicals issued in 1963 and 1967 (mentioned above) as well as Marxist categories which were currently being discussed in the literature generated by Latin American social scientists in the late 1960's, the bishops condemned "institutional violence" of the *status quo* and placed responsibility for injustice on those with a "greater share of wealth, culture, and power" who "jealously retain their privileges."[9]

Liberation theology incorporated a new strategy of evangelization, which intended to make Latin Americans aware and responsive to the need for doing something about injustice. Hence a theology of liberation emerged out of a desperate situation in which the social and economic processes were breaking down and the gap between the rich and poor was widening. However, the ecclesiastical hierarchy in Latin America was not happy about the direction of liberation theology. In 1974, it warned of a "superficial politicization of the faith," "easy enthusiasm for Marxist socialism," and "the temptation to violence" which was said to be a feature among the younger members of the Latin American Church.[10]

In September 1976, eight Protestant leaders in Latin America along with five others who would not reveal their identity out of fear of reprisals sent "An Open Letter to North American Christians" to the National Council of Churches' Division of Overseas Ministry. The letter was timed to be sent during the United States presidential election campaign. This letter blamed the United States in large measure for Latin America becoming "one gigantic prison" and "one vast cemetery" because of the United States' policy of fostering dependency, oppression, and exploitation. The letter continued: "If in the past you felt it to be your apostolic duty to send us missionaries and economic resources, today the frontier of your witness" now resides "within your own county" by political pressure being applied to bring about a change in the "colonialist and oppressive policy over our peoples."[11] This open letter particularly called attention to one of the major themes of liberation theology: capitalism as practiced in the United States is contrary to the gospel.

> Today we Latin Americans are discovering that apart from our own weaknesses and sins, not a few of our misfortunes, miseries and frustrations flow from and are perpetuated within a system that produces substantial benefits for your country but goes on swallowing us more and more in oppression, in impotence, in death. In a few words: Your precious "American Way of Life"—the opulence of your magnates, your economic and military dominion—feeds in no small proportion on the blood that gushes, according to one of our most brilliant essayist, "from the open veins of Latin America".[12]

This letter, in brief, said the United States is the symbol of capitalistic exploitation and Latin America is the exploited.

From this perspective, liberation theology found in Karl Marx the tools for analyzing their socio-economic world. In particular, Marx's critique of religion as an ideology to preserve the status quo of the wealthy and powerful became a theme of liberation theology. Marx showed that ideas are not innocent—they may be oppressive or liberating. Jose Miguez Bonino maintained that the Church "played the role of legitimizing and sacralizing the social and economic structure implanted in America" through Spanish colonization. The Church "served as an ideology to cover and justify existing conditions."[13]

In 1973, Gustavo Gutiérrez provided the definitive statement on liberation theology in his book, *The Theology of Liberation*, when he radically redefined the nature of the mission of the Church in terms of revolution. The gospel of love means engaging in violent combat against oppression on behalf of the oppressed.[14] Utilizing Marxist categories, such as utopia, class struggle, classless society, revolution, and historical materialism, Gutiérrez restructured the meaning of Christian doctrine accordingly.

In 1976, Juan Luis Segundo went beyond the idea of a theology of liberation to a liberation of theology. In his book, *The Liberation of Theology*, Segundo offered a radical new way of doing theology based on the Marxist principle of ideological criticism. He writes: "The one and only thing that can maintain the liberative character of any theology is not its content but its methodology. It is the latter that guarantees the continuing bite of theology."[15] What is this new methodology? It is a method of de-ideologizing Scripture by allowing the realities of the historical situation re-interpret the Bible. The text is the historical situation; the context is the Bible.

Segundo argues that Latin American liberation theology needs a liberation of theology from all forms of traditional authoritarianism. He called for a hermeneutical circle, which allows for a "continuing change in our interpretation of the Bible which is dictated by the continuing changes in our present-day reality, both individual and societal."[16] He finds Marx to be the inspiration for this new kind of methodology. The Marxist idea of a general theory about our perception of reality would "free academic theology" from the notion of "a simple eternal, impartial interpretation, or authorized translation, of the word of God."[17] Particularly, Segundo says the ruling class interprets Scripture in accordance with its socio-economic situation—to maintain their privileged position through exploitation. Contextualizing theology in this way means, for example, the eschatological future must be de-ideologized since the coming Kingdom of God is to be realized in and through the political-historical process. The idea of a future transcendent return of Jesus Christ into history is looked upon as an ideological device intended to perpetuate present abuses by offering to the oppressed the hope of "pie in the sky bye and bye."

Segundo explains his de-ideologizing exegesis by means of a commu-

nication theory, which distinguishes between proto-learning (the imparting of factual information) and deutero-learning (learning how to learn).
The specific content of Scripture is ideology. Deutero-learning is learning how to apply faith to a new situation through the ideologies in
Scripture.[18] Hence, faith is the ability to discern how to act, but this faith
is not bound to any ideology in Scripture. "That is why we hold a
Christian faith but a Marxist ideology"[19] This means the objective content in Holy Scripture is pedagogical in the sense that it teaches us how
to relate faith to the present. The Decalogue, as well as the Sermon on
the Mount, contains ideology that must be desacralized.[20] Only faith
activated by love revealed in Jesus Christ is our guide for life. Segundo
says there is no escape from epistemological relativism and "situation
ethics."[21]

It is not my purpose to ask how successful liberation theology has
been in bringing about a greater degree of social justice for Latin
America. In a minimal way, it should be acknowledged that liberation
theology has been successful in its conscientization intent, that is, it has
made the world more self-consciously aware of the economic-social
oppression in Latin America and that the Church has a biblical responsibility for being involved socially and politically in behalf of the poor and
marginalized people of Latin America. Neither is it my primary purpose
to ask how should liberation theology be critiqued. However, liberation
theology was too dependent upon Marxist socialism in its de-ideologizing of Scripture and restructuring of theology. The failure of Marxist
socialism and the fall of the Soviet Union in 1999 dealt a serious setback
to liberation theology, but it seems to be readjusting itself in the process
of rethinking its mission. A recent selection of the writings of Gustavo
Gutiérrez, *The Density of the Present* (1999) argues that the collapse of
socialism in the Soviet Union was a result of its totalitarianism, and not
the triumph of capitalism.[22] In a work on liberation theology in 1996,
Jon Sobrino argues that liberation theology has continuing relevance in
spite of the fall of socialism—"The origin, thrust, and direction of the theology of liberation is not in socialism, but in the experience of God in
the poor, an experience of grace, and exigency." He argues that " long as
is oppression exists, there must be a theology of liberation."[23]

Liberation theology has been put in the awkward position of having
to reconsider its concept of ideological criticism. Paul Ricoeur has shown
all hermeneutical theories need to be self-critical of their own ideologies.
Liberation theology originally made an ideological decision to focus
exclusively on the social and political needs of Latin America, but can

this "politicizing of evangelism" (as Gutierrez puts it) replace the primary focus of the gospel—the proclamation of the good news that only through justifying and sanctifying faith in Jesus Christ is there hope for the world. Even though the Church may have misused the central focus of the gospel as an ideological mask for preserving its privileged status in the world, this does not nullify the primitive apostolic kerygma. The gospel of redemption has very decisive social and political implications, but recent developments leading to the downfall of socialism in the Soviet Union imply that the categories of Marxism may not be applicable to the Latin American situation. Totalitarianism may not be separable from the Marxist concept of the dictatorship of the proletariat along with its concept of revolution. It could be interpreted that the developments in the former Soviet Union suggest that Marxism and Christianity are irreconcilable.

It may be that traditional Western theology failed to address the special situation of Latin America, as the liberation theologians have contended. However, Moltmann pointed out in the early days of liberation theology the ironic situation that liberation theologians turned to Marxism in the light of its rejection of Western thought. He writes: "We hear severe criticism of Western theology and of theology in general—and then we are told something about Karl Marx and Friedrich Engels, as if they were Latin American discoveries."[24] Moltmann goes on to say:

> They recommend that theologians in the whole world turn to a Marxist class analysis in order to stand in the concrete history of their people. But they do not carry through this class analysis with respect to the history of their own people; they only quote a few basic concepts of Marx …In them one reads more about the sociological theories of others, namely Western Socialists, than about the history or the life and suffering of the Latin American people.[25]

In the light of the collapse of Marxist socialism, perhaps liberation theology will now discover new ways of relating the gospel socially and politically that will be redeeming without compromising the essence of the gospel. This new challenge will require a new methodology that is more faithful to the history of salvation as opposed to Segundo's de-ideologizing hermeneutic that marginalized the primacy of Scripture and reinterpreted Jesus as a political revolutionary. There is no doubt that Jesus' life and teachings have radical political implications, but these should be put in the soteriological context of Jesus' self-identity.[26]

Black Liberation Hermeneutics

James H. Cone, the Charles A. Briggs Distinguished Professor of Systematic Theology at Union Theological Seminary, is the leading proponent of "Black theology" that developed in the late 1960s when black ministers began to reinterpret Christian theology from the perspective of the black struggle for freedom in the United States.[27] Cone is known as the "father of contemporary black theology."[28] Recognizing the role of religious ideology in Feuerbach's theory of projection, he offers a critique of traditional theology on the basis that it reflects a white racist ideology.[29] If he believes "white" theology has largely been driven by a racist ideology, he thinks Afro-American believers should interpret Scripture on the basis of being oppressed and victimized. Affirming that the Bible is a substantially reliable record of God's revelation in history,[30] he believes that its primary goal is to portray the liberation of oppressed people. He says this interpretation of Scripture as championing oppressed people is not religious projection;[31] rather, political and religious liberation combine to form the central hermeneutical key of Scripture.[32]

The hermeneutical principle of Cone's theology is that black people should interpret the Bible from the context of racism, which the white church and a white American society has subjected them to.[33] Because of the biblical emphasis on liberation from oppression, he believes it is theologically appropriate to construct a systematic interpretation of the Christian faith from the standpoint of the struggle of the black experience.[34] Cone says that black theology was the first to identify salvation with political liberation. God was the liberator of the oppressed Hebrew slaves and Jesus was the new liberator whom God anointed to preach the good news to the poor, to bring freedom to the captives, and to set at liberty those who are oppressed (Luke 4:18,19).[35] Cone notes that subsequent to the rise of black theology, this theme was adopted by feminist and Third World theologies.[36]

Cone is profoundly aware of the hermeneutical and theological assumptions, which have informed his decision to interpret the Scriptures from the standpoint of black oppression. Although he is aware that he cannot simply dispense with the meaning of the biblical texts in a self-serving manner, he intentionally highlights the political implications of the gospel. He agrees with Pannenberg that one cannot ignore the Christological implications of Jesus' identity, but he gives priority to the soteriological significance of Jesus as one who was concerned with political oppression.[37] More radically, Cone maintains that the saving significance of Jesus must be reinterpreted from the stand-point of contemporary black experience. The black community, he says, is discriminated against primarily because it is black. Unless Jesus suf-fered this bias against blackness in his death and resurrection and con-demned whiteness, then Jesus has no relevance. In prophetic-like, metaphorical language, Cone writes: "If he is not black as we are, then the resurrection has little significance for our times."[38]

More recently, Cone's methodological considerations have been influenced by feminist theology. In the revised preface (1997) to his ear-lier work, *God of the Oppressed* (1975), Cone assumes that Jesus Christ is one among other revelations of God, and he seems to deny the finality of Jesus as the ultimate revealer of God.[39] Considering that Cone's doc-toral dissertation was on the theology of Karl Barth who insisted that Jesus Christ is the one and only self- revelation of God, this represents a significant shift in Cone's theological orientation.

He now calls into question whether or not the death and sufferings of Jesus can be used as a means of promoting the black experience of discrimination and oppression. He believes feminist and womanist the-ologians have offered a compelling argument against any theory of the atonement. The idea that God's salvation was accomplished in Jesus' death serves as justification for child abuse and glorifies suffering and death. It further reinforces the idea that battered victims ought to accept their oppression. Instead of the cross being a symbol of love, it personi-fies disgrace that should never be passively accepted.[40]

Cone is right to say that the sufferings of Jesus and his death on the cross have been theologically used by religious leaders to encourage oppressed people to accept their plight with passivity,[41] but instead of dismissing the biblical images for the atonement, it would be more appropriate for Cone to argue against the ideological misuse of these images. In particular, Cone too easily agrees with the more radical fem-inist theology, which assumed that the biblical images of atonement reflect the image of "God as a Patriarch and Jesus as a passive surro-gate."[42] Moltmann, in particular, has shown that it is a serious misread-ing of the New Testament to interpret Jesus' concept of God as Father in a patriarchal manner. Instead, God is protective of his people, cares about the victims of suffering, and Jesus' death-resurrection and the out-pouring of His Spirit empowers believers to confront the forces of evil. The atonement does not mean a passive submission to the forces of evil (Matt. 26:53).

It is also serious misunderstanding of Christian theology to interpret the atoning death of Jesus as "child abuse." In response to Millicent Feske's feminist critique of Moltmann's theology of the cross, Moltmann noted there is nothing new about this criticism, and in the end this criticism entails the rejection of Christian faith. He writes:

> In her essay on my theology of the cross, Millicent Feske basically repeats a well-known argument that has been leveled against Christianity as a whole. While she claims that these opinions arise out of a liberationist/feminist perspective, in reality they arise out of the liberal, bourgeois, indeed masculinist theology (or anti-theology) of the Enlightenment. Whether God the Father is "sadistic," whether the sufferings of Christ is "child abuse," whether the cross of Christ can somehow take on the sufferings of the poor, the oppressed, and debased women, whether the sufferings of Christ support a religious and thus also militaristic/nationalist cult of sacrifice, was first raised by Lessing and Voltaire, and now two hundred years later these claims seem to me to be merely repeated again. It seems to me that such claims ultimately serve neither the emancipation of women nor the liberation of slaves, but ultimately lead only to an abandonment (as with Voltaire) of Christianity. Such perspectives do not seem to get to the heart of the problem of suffering in any critical sense.[43]

Jesus' relationship to his Father is not based on patriarchy. Jesus revealed a new dimension about the nature of God, showing that the fatherliness of God is not connected with masculinity. The sonship of Jesus was not based on the concept of masculinity. Rather, Jesus was the Son as one who fully embraced the image of his Father, and he redeemed humanity through the power of the Spirit through his life, death, and resurrection. Mutuality and fellowship are the determining characteristics of the Trinity, not dependency. The notion that the Son was sacrificed for the sake of his Father as if he was an immature son serving the needs of his domineering father is a grotesque distortion of the New Testament. Rather, Jesus' death was atoning precisely because God the Father fully identified with fallen humanity, and because His Son suffered for us, God can be touched with the feelings of our infirmities as finite human beings. And because he experienced the utter consequences of rejection and alienation, God is able to identify with sinners and all victims of oppression. In the final sense, only a wounded healer can really heal. That is to say, God must fully understand us to save us, and that is the essence of Jesus' atoning death—as Charles Wesley's hymn puts it, "My God is reconciled." It is not so much that we are reconciled to God, but God is reconciled to us. He is the offended party in the breach; humanity is guilty of insulting the Almighty God and Lord of the universe. In Jesus Christ, God the Father takes the initiative and sends his Son who humbled himself, even to the point of the death on the cross, in order that God might bring us back into the life of the divine Trinity. The essence of this gospel is grace, not a paternalistic instinct to rescue us from our misdeeds. We could not restore ourselves through our own works-righteousness, nor could God simply wipe away our offenses with a patriarchal decision to forgive us by killing his Son. Rather, grace was very costly for the Father who suffered the loss of his Son. Jesus revealed by his life, his teachings, and his death that the Lord God Almighty is not a patriarchal monarch who self-indulgently controls the world, but a loving Father whose Son reflects his eternal love and whose Spirit restores us to fellowship in the kingdom of God. The theme of the New Testament revelation is that through Jesus' death we have become brothers and sisters of Jesus Christ and we are children of God (Hebrews 2:10-13). How this redemptive action on the part of God could be interpreted to be "child abuse" or patriarchy is unimaginable.

If Cone in his *Theology of Black Liberation* (1990) argued that his hermeneutics avoided ideological illusion because it was based on the historical revelation of God in Jesus of Nazareth, in 1997 he can be charged with falling prey to the Freudian projection theory because his view of God is constructed out of his own social and personal need. He is willing to set aside methodologically the biblical history of salvation in favor of his own ideology. He says the Bible is still "an important source of my theological reflections, but not the starting point." [44] He writes: "I am *black* first—and everything else comes after that."[45] It may not be clear what Cone means by denying the Bible is "the objective Word of God," [46] but most likely his point is that the Bible is to be read and inter-preted by each new generation, but he comes close to downsizing the importance of the central events of salvation history, particularly Jesus' death.

Cone's writings have shown how the gospel of Jesus Christ has spe-cial relevance for the black experience, but his latest shift away from making the cross and resurrection of Jesus Christ the essence of the gospel deprives his theology of the one hope that inspires the black com-munity to believe in the possibility of a more loving and just world. Cone failed to see Jesus' death was not a passive submission and acquiesce to political forces. Jesus' death-resurrection means we have "authority" to renounce evil and confront wickedness in high places because Jesus has overcome tyranny and oppression. In the name of Christ who suffered and conquered sin and oppression on behalf of all people, we are indeed free—spiritually, emotionally, and politically regardless of what the institutions of government prescribe otherwise. Do the sufferings of Christ entail a life of pacifism for Christians? Considerable debate in the history of the Church has focused on this question, and no attempt to answer it will be made here. However, it is clear that the death of Jesus was not a pacifist response to Roman authority; it was God's full identification with fallen humanity in order that God might fully "atone" for our sin and set us free. It was a divine liberation from oppression.

If Cone sees in the black experience a special relevance of the Exodus event, he ought also to see the special significance of Jesus death-resurrection, for as biblical scholarship has shown the Exodus event is to the Old Testament as the Resurrection event is for the New Testament. The Exodus event was preparatory for the Easter Event. Both events involve liberation, first politically and then in terms of personal salvation and readiness for eternal glory. The history of Jesus is the fulfillment of the history of Israel, and today all are invited to share in this history. The uniqueness of the black experience thus fits into the openness of this history. Cone is surely right to highlight this point and to interpret the history of Jesus in ways that have special relevance to the black community. However, he seems now to be misled by the patriarchal ideology of radical feminist criticism.

Feminist Liberation Theology

In 1973 Mary Daly, now retired professor of Boston College, pioneered a feminist hermeneutics in her book, *Beyond God the Father.* Her primary concern was to offer a critique of the Father-image of God that she believed served as patriarchal ideology to dominate women. Her proposal was to replace all concepts of God with non-personal images, such as "Be-ing."[47]

Sandra M. Schneiders, an associate professor of New Testament studies and spirituality at the Jesuit School of Theology at Berkeley, agrees that patriarchy is the primary problem with the image of God as Father. She defines patriarchy as a social, political, and economic system in which the male head wields absolute power and ownership over the social unit by divine right. This male-centeredness (androcentrism) has condemned women to powerlessness, poverty, and subjection, enabling men to dominate and exploit them.[48]

Schneiders believes patriarchy is deeply embedded in the specific *content* of the Bible and thus the Bible has been used to oppress women.[49] She is an advocate for "reclaiming the Bible for women,"[50] but without some hope for resolving the problem of patriarchy, she admits that she "would have long ago abandoned the field of biblical scholarship."[51] Her method for doing this is a reader-response method of showing how the New Testament implicitly moved beyond patriarchy.[52] One instance of this is her "feminist critical hermeneutical approach" in interpreting Jesus' encounter with the Samaritan woman (John 4:1-42). This pericope represents Jesus' message as one of inclusiveness as opposed to sexism, racism, and classism. The full social implications of this revelatory moment were not immediately appreciated in the history of the Church, but readers today are coming to understand the true liberating character of Jesus' ministry for the poor, the marginalized, and oppressed.[53]

Jürgen Moltmann agrees the feminist critique has rightly called attention to the need "to seek a non-patriarchal way of talking of God the 'Father' which is in accord with the gospel and which liberates men and women."[54] Moltmann proposes a Trinitarian solution to the problem. It begins with the realization that the fundamental issue is not gender language for God. He notes that the feminist critique is primarily concerned with the patriarchal concept of fatherhood, not the differences between the sexes, and not fatherhood as such, but the claim of male domination based on the belief that maleness is the true humanity.[55] He believes the solution to patriarchy is found in Jesus' messianic concept of Fatherhood. The God of the Bible is not a continuation of the age-old deity of religious patriarchy, but rather the identity of God comes to full expression in the "the Father of Jesus Christ" who "leads men and women into the shared freedom of the messianic time in which there will no longer be matriarchy and patriarchy."[56]

Moltmann points out that God is rarely called "Father" in the Old Testament, and he notes that the concept of Father had no gender-specific reference, especially because God had no female consort. However, Moltmann acknowledges patriarchal practices were prevalent in ancient Israel,[57] and yet the image of God included both sexes (Gen. 1.27). As Father, God is the Lord of creation and of history and as the covenant God who chooses Israel (Dt. 32.6; Isa. 63.16; Jer. 31.9). The mother image is used to express God's mercy (Isaiah 66:13). As Lord, God acts in a fatherly and motherly fashion toward Israel as the "firstborn son" (Ex. 4.22).[58]

Moltmann points out that God is called "Father" eleven times in the Old Testament, but 170 times by Jesus.[59] Moltmann argues that Jesus' use of Father entailed a more explicit non-patriarchal connotation. His reliance upon Jeremias' interpretation of *Abba* as denoting childlike familiarity with one's father is a controversial point of view in biblical studies,[60] but it is clear the New Testament presents God as a Father enjoying the intimacy and "family" togetherness with his Son Jesus Christ through the power of the Spirit. Inclusion and mutuality are inherent in the divine relationship of Father, Son, and Holy Spirit.

Moltmann believes the patriarchal concept of fatherhood was decisively introduced into the Church during the Constantinian period when "Roman ideas about father were transferred to the Christian God through a work by Lactantius, entitled *On the Wrath of God.*" Moltmann notes that "this fusion of the Christian and the Roman concept of God gave Christian history in Europe a fundamentally patriarchalist stamp." This patriarchal intrusion "goes against belief in the fatherly nearness of God."[61] Because there are texts from Qumran that address God in personal terms of "my Father," it would be claiming too much to say that the New Testament view of Jesus addressing God as "my Father" was without parallel.[62] Nevertheless, it is clear that the New Testament presents Jesus as possessing a unique relationship of God that shows him to be "one" with the Father, possessing intimacy and partnership with his Father (John 17:11, 21).

What emerges out of the New Testament picture of Jesus, as God's Son, is that God is not simply one divine person (monarchical patriarchy), but rather, the Father is in relationship with the Son who through the Spirit forms a community of persons (a divine Trinity). Moltmann says patriarchy stands in contradiction to the Trinitarian interpretation of God.[63] He has particularly called attention to the social relevance of Trinitarian thinking, noting that fellowship, mutuality and community of divine persons serve as a model of inclusiveness within the human community.

Moltmann believes the notion of *perichoresis* as developed by John of Damascus in the eighth century as a refinement for explaining the relationship of the Persons of the Trinity is free of domination language because it entails the view of togetherness, equality, and mutuality.[64] Each of the three Persons is there for one another and with one another. They interact with each other with equal mutuality.[65] Moltmann believes this social understanding of the Trinity resolves the primary concern of the feminist critique because the concept of God as Father is inclusive of motherly kindness, thus eliminating the patriarchal implications of male domination.

Moltmann believes this non-patriarchal view of "Father" is just as important for men as women because there is a "growing irresponsibility of men towards their families and children and masculine regression into childish games of narcissistic self-concern." This "irresponsibility" and "regression" is because of the "sorry side-effects of the depatriarchalization of modern society." It is important that men "adopt a masculinity which does not lay claim to domination and a fatherhood without loss of power and feelings of powerlessness."[66] Moltmann believes, in this regard, that Freud demonstrated the importance of the Father's unique role in a child's developing sense of identity, and hence the importance of the Trinitarian concept of Fatherhood.[67]

In 1983, Patricia Wilson-Kastner developed a feminist interpretation of Moltmann's Trinitarian theology in her book, *Faith, Feminism, and the Christ*. She is Trinity Church Professor of Preaching at United Theological Seminary and considers herself a "reformist feminist" who seeks to take a "constructive approach."[68] She notes that at the heart of the Christian faith is Jesus Christ, a male. Though God may be re-imaged, the maleness of Jesus cannot be explained away.[69] Nonetheless, she disagrees with feminists who think that Jesus Christ must be left behind as the self-revelation of God.[70] She also disagrees with feminists who prefer to speak of God as a Goddess because this places the emphasis on gender rather than on the operations of God.[71] She further thinks that attempts to neutralize God-language by speaking of God as Creator, Redeemer, and Sanctifier may be helpful, but this manner of speaking only talks about the way God relates to us and it does not speak of God's inner Trinitarian relationship.[72]

She agrees with Moltmann that the offensive issue is fundamentally patriarchal domination rather than gender language. She notes that there probably never has been a truly matriarchal society and women throughout the history of humanity have taken a lesser role and have been considered less important than men, but why have men in the Christian traditional been condescending toward women? She believes that Jesus' view toward women was not patriarchal,[73] and yet the Christian tradition has often marginalized women as second-class citizens. She believes this is so in part because men have struggled with sexual purity and hence the rights of women were suppressed because they were perceived as a temptation and threat to men's personal and spiritual well being.[74]

Wilson-Kastner shows that the classical Christological creeds do not say that God assumed "maleness," but rather that Christ assumed "human nature."[75] This is because sexuality itself is not radically constitutive of personhood. The biblical assumption is a unified humanity and human wholeness.[76] She believes that though Jesus was a man, God was revealed through the humanity of Jesus, not through his maleness. Hence, women as well as men fully identify with Jesus' saving history.

She believes that the doctrine of the Trinity offers "the best option for feminists within a Christian context."[77] She believes "the Trinity is at the heart of the Christian faith" because God has been revealed as "Father, Son/Word, and Holy Spirit."[78] Because the Trinity highlights inclusiveness, community, and freedom, this means that notions of patriarchy, classism, and racism are contrary to the self-revelation of God. She draws from Moltmann's emphasis on *perichoresis* to show love rather than sovereignty is the most basic attribute of God.[79] Hence patriarchy is excluded.

Does the exclusion of patriarchy from the concept of God as Father mean that it is appropriate to speak of God as "Mother"? Moltmann points out that the Holy Spirit has often been called "Mother" in the earliest traditions of Christian devotional literature. He points out that the idea of "the motherly office of the Holy Spirit" was introduced into the mystical piety of East and West through the fifty homilies of Pseudo-Macarius.[80] Count Zinzendorf was particularly inspired by this concept derived from Pseudo-Macarius. In 1741 when he established his first American religious community in Pennsylvania, he declared that they were brothers and sisters because of the concept of family implicit in the doctrine of the Trinity. He said that "the Father of our Lord Jesus is our true Father and the Spirit of Jesus Christ is our true Mother." [81]

Moltmann does not take this speculation literally about the family concept of the Trinity (Father, Mother, and Child), but he believes the feminine characteristics of the Spirit (such as the "birth of the Spirit," John 3:5, and the feminine symbol of the dove, Luke 3:22) rightly point out that being created in the image of God includes femininity as well as masculinity.[82]

If one does call God "Mother," does the specter of pantheism emerge? Elizabeth R. Achtemeier, a well-known Presbyterian preacher and biblical scholar, thinks it does. She argues that giving birth from the womb suggests an identification of God with the world.[83] Andrew Dell'Olio, a philosophy professor of Hope College, disagrees. He maintains that mothers are no more identical with their children than fathers.[84] Dell'Olio thinks that it is important to affirm that God is "Mother" because it helps to make it clear that the biblical view of God does not entail a gender-specific orientation.[85]

Dell'Olio probably dismisses the issue of pantheism too readily, though he has a good point about overdoing this issue. There are biblical references that could be interpreted pantheistically, if the larger context were ignored. For example, Paul cites with apparent approval that we are God's "offspring" and that "in him we live and move and have our being" (Acts 18:28). Peter says that we are "participants of the divine nature." (2 Peter 1:4). No one would interpret these biblical references as pantheistic, and likewise it could be argued that with proper qualification God may be called "Mother" without implying pantheism.

Dell'Olio also has a good point in showing that overdoing the issue of the transcendence of God may contribute to the social problem of "absent or aloof fathers."[86] Moltmann has shown that monarchical monotheism with its emphasis upon the transcendent oneness of God is the religion of patriarchy. He shows that it is derived from the Greek and Roman view of the gods in which ultimately authority resides in Zeus, "the father of all." On the other hand, Moltmann notes that the religion of matriarchy has "a pantheistic character, and the divine was understood as eternally-fertile: the individual phenomena of life arise from the great motherly stream of life and return to it, to be born from it anew."[87] Moltmann's point is that patriarchy or matriarchy emerges when the abstract oneness of God is emphasized over against the three Persons of the Trinity. Wilson-Kastner also says: "If one images God as three persons, it encourages one to focus on interrelationship as the core of divine reality, rather than on a single personal reality, almost always imaged as male. In monotheism [as opposed to Trinitarianism] God has historically been imaged as a male, patriarchal and dominating."[88]

Dell'Olio probably too easily assumed that it is perfectly proper to refer to God as "Mother" because he focuses on God as "a single personal reality" rather than as a Trinity of Persons. Moltmann has shown that to call God "Father and Mother," as Pope John-Paul I did, implies both patriarchy and matriarchy. Moltmann and Wilson-Kastner have cautioned against this practice. Wilson-Kastner writes: "One might substitute a unitarianism of the Mother Goddess for that of God the Father in heaven. Unhappily the same sorts of limitations are present as in patriarchy, but with a woman's face."[89] Moltmann has pointed out that human freedom is effectively eliminated in both patriarchy and matriarchy. If one simply changes the name of the first Person of the Trinity from "Father" to "Mother," one simply exchanges patriarchy for matriarchy, and in both cases personal freedom is eliminated.[90]

Why did the image of "Father" become the image of God rather than "Mother" in the history of salvation? Pannenberg believes it was conditioned by the contingencies of God's self-revelation even as it was one of the contingencies of history that Jesus was a Jew rather than a Chinese or a German. This is a form of the so-called "scandal of particularity." Just as the Nazi's were disturbed by Jesus' Jewishness, so some today are bothered by Jesus' Sonship and by his language of Father as a reference to God.[91] Does this mean that the image of "Mother" can be substituted for "Father"? Pannenberg says no because we participate in God through the history of Jesus who proclaimed God as "my Father." Pannenberg writes:

> We have to realize that the word *father* in Jesus' own language functioned not as an exchangeable image, but as the name he used in addressing the God he proclaimed. Therefore, in the Christian church the name father, and its use as Jesus used it, belongs to the identity of the Christian faith. It cannot be changed without abandoning that identity, because it is by entering into Jesus' relationship to God as father that we share in his sonship and—because of our communion with him— obtain the hope of eternal life.[92]

This means the concept of "Father" belongs to the essence of God. In Exodus 3:14, the name of God is revealed as "I Am Who I Am." Nowhere in the Old Testament is the essence of God defined in terms of "Father." Rather, the concept of Father was used to show that God was Creator and the Protector of Israel (Dt 32:6). However, Jesus defined his relationship to God primarily as "my Father" (Matt. 11:27). Drawing from Exodus 3:14, Jesus spoke of himself as "I Am the bread of life," "I Am the water of life," "I Am the way, truth, the life," "I Am the good shepherd," etc. He also spoke of his essential relationship to God as: "I and the Father are one" (John 10:30).

In this regard, Moltmann shows that this revelation of God as "the Father of Jesus Christ" goes beyond the Old Testament notion that God is the Father-Creator of the universe. The idea of Father-Creator describes one of God's many functions, but the idea of God as the "Father of Jesus Christ" defines God's inner life. God is identified as the Father who eternally begets a Son.[93] Thus, the identity of God as the "Father of Jesus Christ" is the basis of our salvation, as Paul put it: "And because you are children, God has sent the Spirit of his Son into our hearts, crying, "Abba! Father!" Paul also wrote: "You have received a spirit of sonship. When we cry, "Abba! Father!" it is that very Spirit bearing witness with our spirit that we are children of God" (Rom. 3:15-16).

Pannenberg points out that the language of the "Father of Jesus Christ" is the language we must use today because we know God through the history of Jesus. We are not free simply to rewrite his history with our own cultural concerns. To do so is to embrace a "Feuerbachian type of conceiving of religious language" and "this assumption endangers the truth claims of religious language by reducing it to human projection."[94]

There is one caveat, however, in speaking about Jesus' Sonship. The pre-existent Son of God was not a male. Of course Jesus was the male son of Mary, but as the eternal Christ, the Sonship of Jesus was not an expression of maleness just as the Fatherhood of God is not an expression of maleness. Just as the motherly qualities of mercy and kindness were incorporated into Jesus' concept of God as "Abba," so Jesus' Sonship reflected the motherly qualities of sacrificial love.

Jesus' humanity was of course inseparably connected with his deity, and his humanity was specifically linked to being male, but as Wilson-Kastner has noted, the fact of Jesus' maleness was only incidental to the more basic fact that he was human, and humanity belongs equally to male and female.[95] Hence women and men are equally included in the redemptive life of Jesus. This is particularly highlighted in the concept of Jesus' Sonship, which includes sisterly and as well as brotherly characteristics. Jesus thus raised the meaning of sonship to a new level by excluding patriarchal connotations.

Pannenberg made a humorous comment on the implication of the God-language debate. A questioner once asked if women would not be marginalized by the concept of God as Father. Pannenberg observed that it was not so unusual for a woman to relate to a father and even if God were wrongly imaged as a male, Pannenberg pointed out that women do have healthy relationships to men. Besides, he noted that daughters and fathers often have a better relationship than fathers and sons. He further noted that if we were able to choose the gender of God, men might prefer the image of a beautiful woman whom they could adore rather than a father. A female deity might be more predisposed to favor her son, as it sometimes known to be the case.[96]

It could also be argued that one of the reasons why women are often more attracted to faith in Jesus than men is because men find it difficult to talk about loving another man. The notion of loving two "men"

(Father and Son) is often less attractive to men than to women. However, Christians are not given this option of choosing the gender of their God, because God has none, and consequently, devotional bonding to the Father and Son through the Holy Spirit has no heterosexual or homosexual connotations.

An additional question needs to be asked that feminists raise, namely, why have women played a minor role in the history of salvation? The answer seems clear enough. Patriarchy has been normative throughout the history of humankind and it too has played a part in the history of salvation. Significantly enough, the history of salvation concludes with Jesus' self-revelation of God, and his messianic ministry challenged the institution of patriarchy and put an end to its legitimacy. Patriarchy has been so embedded in human society that only today are we beginning to understand the full liberation of the gospel and that patriarchy, racism, and classism have no place in the kingdom of God.

Inclusive language is an important means of implementing the right of women to be free from male domination. However, the non-patriarchal concept of God as "the Father of Jesus Christ" is inclusive of women as well as men in a way that the concept of God as "Mother" is not. Jesus revealed that his "Father" is protective and powerful and yet merciful, gracious, and loving.

Perhaps a fatherly concept of God as Mother could have been developed in lieu of a motherly concept of Father in the history of salvation, but, as Pannenberg has noted, it is a contingency of history, a "scandal of particularity," that we come to know God as Father through sharing in Jesus' Sonship. We are not free to reshape Jesus' history to fit our own social and cultural norms. To be sure, we must interpret his history in a way that is intelligible to every new generation (which is what is being attempted here), but it would be anachronistic to reconfigure his history to fit our own times. However, we should not have to do so because the messianic concept of God as "Father" and of Jesus' Sonship destroyed the basis of patriarchy and matriarchy. If one engages in sex discrimination one is rejecting the "Father of Jesus Christ."

What if one believes that it is still important for them to call God "Mother"? There is no explicit prohibition against it. One can cite examples in Church history where mystics have prayed to God as "Mother."[97] Feminist Wilson-Kastner points out that the concept of God as Mother has emerged in the Christian tradition "to express the nurturing aspect of Christ's work among humanity—Jesus as a mother who seeks to find and heal all of her children."[98] Julian of Norwich in the late Medieval period particularly linked the motherly aspect of Jesus' Sonship with the crucifixion.[99] Mark McIntosh notes that the mystics used the "dialectical play of gender language *in order to* convey the transgressive, excessive reality of God."[100] Although it may be appropriate to speak of God as "Mother" in some situations, it should be remembered that Jesus taught us that the normative way of praying to God is: "Our Father who is in heaven."

1. Don Ihde, *Hermeneutic Phenomenology, The Philosophy of Paul Ricoeur*, pp. 213ff.

2. Paul Ricoeur, *Freud and Philosophy*, p. 33. Loretta Dornisch, *Faith and Philosophy in the Writings of Paul Ricoeur*(Lampeter, Dyfed, Wales: Edwin Mellen Press, Ltd, 1990), pp. 109ff.

3. Cf. Dornisch, *Faith and Philosophy in the Writings of Paul Ricoeur*, pp. 16ff.

4. *Essays on Biblical Interpretation*, p. 101.

5. Cf. Deane William Ferm, *Third World Liberation Theologies, An Introductory Survey* (Maryknoll, New York: Orbis Books, 1986), p. 26. Cf. Juan Luis Segundo, *The Liberation of Theology*, trans. John Durry (Maryknoll, New York: Orbis Books, 1976), pp. 13-19.

6. Ferm, *Third World Liberation Theologies*, pp. 9ff.

7. T. Howland Sanks and Brian H. Smith, "Liberation Ecclesiology: Praxis, Theory, Praxis," *Theological Studies*, 38.1 (March 1977): p. 6. Cf. Ferm, *Third World Liberation Theologies*, p. 60

8. T. Howland Sanks and Brian H. Smith, "Liberation Ecclesiology: Praxis, Theory, Praxis," *Theological Studies*, 38.1 (March 1977): pp. 1-6.

9. Ibid., p. 6.

10. Ibid., p. 4.

11. "An Open Letter to North American Christians," *Christianity and Crisis*, 36.16 (October 18, 1976): 231.

12. Ibid., p. 230.

13. J. Miguez Bonino, *Doing Theology in a Revolutionary Situation* (Philadelphia: Fortress Press, 1975), p. 7.

14. Gustavo Gutiérrez, *A Theology of Liberation*, trans. Caridad Inda and John Eagleson (Maryknoll, N.Y.: Orbis Books, 1973), p. 276.

15. Juan Luis Segundo, *The Liberation of Theology*, pp. 39,40.

16. Ibid., p. 8.

17. Ibid., p. 19.

18. Ibid., p. 179.

19. Ibid., p. 103.

20. Ibid., p. 167.

21. Ibid., p. 167.

22. Gustavo Gutiérrez, *The Density of the Present, Selected Writings* (Maryknoll, NY: Orbix Books, 1999), pp. 48-50.

23. *Systematic Theology, Perspectives from Liberation Theology*, ed. Jon Sobrino and Ignacio Ellacuría (Maryknoll, NY: Orbis Books, 1996), p. ix.

24. Quoted in *Third World Theologies*, ed. Gerald H. Anderson and Thomas F. Stransky (New York: Paulist Press, 1976), p. 59.

25. Quoted in *Third World Theologies*, ed. Gerald H. Anderson and Thomas F. Stransky, p. 63.

26. Cf. John Yoder, *The Politics of Jesus* (Grand Rapids: Wm. B. Eerdmans, 1972).

27. James H. Cone, *For My People. Black Theology and the Black Church* (Maryknoll, NY: Orbis Books, 1984), p. 1.

28. Rufus Burrow, "James H. Cone: Father of Contemporary Black Theology," *The Asbury Theological Journal* 48.2 (Fall 1993): 59-75. For a helpful introduction and summary of black theology, cf. Dwight N. Hopkins, *Introducing Black Theology of Liberation* (Maryknoll, NY: Orbis Books, 1999).

29. James H. Cone, *God of the Oppressed* (Maryknoll, NY: Orbis Books, 1997), p. 77.

30. Ibid., p. 102.

31. Ibid., p. 91.

32. Ibid., p. 91.

33. Ibid., p. 40.

34. Ibid., p. 53.

35. Ibid., p. 80

36. Ibid., pp. 80-81. Cf. Cone, *For My People. Black Theology and the Black Church*, p. 172.

37. Cone, *A Black Theology of Liberation*, p. 1.

38. Ibid., p. 120.

39. *God of the Oppressed.*, p. xxiv.

40. Ibid., p. xv.

41. Ibid.

42. Ibid.

43. Moltmann, "Response to the Essays," *The Asbury Theological Journal* 55.1 (Spring 2000): 131.

44. Ibid., p. xi.

45. Ibid.

46. Ibid.

47. Mary Daly, *Beyond God the Father* (Boston: Beacon Press, 1973), pp. 34ff.

48. Sandra M. Schneiders, "Does the Bible Have a Postmodern Message?" *Postmodern Theology, Christian Faith in a Pluralist World*, ed. Frederic B. Burnham (New York: Harper and Row, Publishers, 1989), p. 66.

49. Ibid., p. 65.

50. Ibid., p. 70.

51. Ibid., p. 71.

52. Cf. Sandra M. Schneiders, *Women and the Word: The Gender of God in the New Testament and the Spirituality of Women* (New York: Paulist, 1986), 42-49;

Sandra M. Schneiders, *The Revelatory Text,* second edition (Collegeville, MN: The Liturgical Press, 1999), pp. 180-197.

53. *The Revelatory Text,* pp. 296f.

54. Moltmann, *History And The Triune God,* trans. John Bowden (New York: Crossroad, 1992), p. 1.

55. Ibid., p. xv

56. Ibid., p. 1.

57. Ibid., p. 21.

58. Ibid.

59. Ibid., p.10.

60. Cf. James Barr, "'Abba, Father' and the Familiarity of Jesus' Speech," *Theology* 91.741 (May 1988): 173-179; James Barr, "Abba Isn't 'Daddy'," *The Journal of Theological Studies,* 39.1 (April 1988): 28-47.

61. Ibid., pp. 11-12.

62. May Rose D'Angelo, "*Abba* and 'Father': Imperial Theology and the Jesus Traditions," *Journal of Biblical Literature,* 111.4 (Winter 1992): 618.

63. Moltmann thinks that Paul's concept of the husband as "head" can be interpreted in a patriarchal way, but even so it is significantly altered in terms of servanthood. Moltmann thinks that Paul was under the influence of a more monotheistic as opposed to a Trinitarian view of God when he spoke in this patriarchal way. *History And The Triune God,* p. 21. As opposed to Moltmann's interpretation, it can be argued that Paul's concept of headship transcends the idea of patriarchy. Significantly, Paul prefaces his remarks about "headship" with the exhortation that husbands and wives should submit themselves to each other with mutuality (Eph. 5:21), and he qualified "headship" in a Christological way by saying that husbands are to love their wives as Christ loves the Church. This Christological concept of headship can hardly be called patriarchal. It could be argued that the implication of Paul's comment about husbands loving their wives unconditionally was far more revolutionary and liberating for women than perhaps he even realized. In effect, it undermined any notion of patriarchal domination.

64. *History And The Triune God,* p. xv.

65. Ibid., pp. xv-xvi.

66. Ibid., pp. 3-4.

67. Ibid., p. 4.

68. Patricia Wilson-Kastner, *Faith, Feminism, and the Christ* (Philadelphia: Fortress Press, 1983), p. 64.

69. Ibid., p. 4.

70. Ibid., p. 5.

71. Ibid., p. 33.

72. Ibid., p. 133.

73. Ibid., p. 72.

74. Ibid., p. 74.

75. Ibid., p. 78.

76. Ibid., pp. 65ff.

77 Ibid., p. 123.

78. Ibid., p. 121.

79. Ibid., p. 127.

80. Moltmann, *History and the Triune God*, p. xiv.

81. Cited by Moltmann, *History and the Triune God*, p. 64.

82. Ibid., p. xiii.

83. Elizabeth R. Achtemeier, "Exchanging God for "No Gods": A Discussion of Female Language for God," *Speaking the Christian God*, ed. Alvin F. Kimel, Jr. (Grand Rapids: Wm. B. Eerdmans, 1992), p. 8. Cf. "Why God is Not Mother," *Christianity Today* 16 (August 1993): 16-23.

84. Andrew Dell'Olio, "Why Not God the Mother?" *Faith and Philosophy*, 15.2 (April 1998): 203.

85. Ibid., p. 205.

86. Ibid., p. 203.

87. Moltmann, *History and The Triune God*, p. 5.

88. Wilson-Kastner, *Faith, Feminism, and the Christ* (P. 122-123.

89. Ibid., p. 123.

90. Moltmann, *History and the Triune God,* p. xiv.

91. Wolfhart Pannenberg, "Feminine Language About God," *The Asbury Theological Journal* 48.2 (Fall 1993): 29.

92. Ibid.

93. Cf. Moltmann, *The Kingdom and The Trinity*, trans. Margaret Kohl (New York: Harper & Row, 1981), pp. 166f.

94. Wolfhart Pannenberg, "Feminine Language About God," *The Asbury Theological Journal* 48.2 (Fall 1993): 28.

95. Wilson-Kastner, *Faith, Feminism, and the Christ,* p. 115.

96. Pannenberg, "Feminine Language About God," *The Asbury Theological Journal* 48.2 (Fall 1993): 28-29.

10

Moltmann's Concept of
The Trinitarian History of God

Karl Barth called for a new theological paradigm of the Holy Spirit shortly before his death in 1968. He suggested that this task might be done
by one of his own students. He confessed that his Trinitarian doctrine of
God had neglected the doctrine of the Holy Spirit because he wanted
to avoid falling into the subjectivism of Pietism and liberalism as represented by Schleiermacher and Harnack. As the father of modern theology, Schleiermacher represented both Pietism and liberalism in the early
part of the nineteenth century, making experience the primary basis for
establishing the beliefs of Christian faith instead of the Bible. Barth perceived that Schleiermacher's methodology was a serious threat to
authentic faith because he had subordinated the biblical witness to personal experience. Modernism (as Barth called it) threatened the church's
self-understanding of God as triune.[1] Hence Barth's theology was constructed largely as an antidote to Schleiermacher's liberalism.

It is well known that Barth introduced into contemporary theology
the significance of the Trinity as the key to a Christian understanding of
God. Barth was aware that the prominence he was giving to the doctrine of the Trinity was "very isolated" in the history of doctrine, but he
insisted that it must be the starting point of Christian doctrine because
God is revealed as triune in the history of salvation.[2]

In his *Church Dogmatics*, Barth rejected his earlier espousal of liberal
Protestantism. He protested vigorously against its compromise with secular thinking and its watered-down version of biblical faith, especially its
negative view of the Trinity as if it were an unnecessary appendage to
Christian belief. Barth reinstated in a radical way the priority of a supernaturalistic concept of the triune God who has spoken "from above." All
human efforts to prove or disprove God's reality are ineffective. God
alone is the absolute Subject of God's own revelation to humanity. Jesus
Christ is the absolute focal point of the self-revealing God, and every-

thing in Scripture is a witness either by anticipation in the Old Testament or by recollection in the New Testament to Jesus Christ. God as Father and God as Holy Spirit are interpreted in the light of this christomonism.

One of Barth's last acts before his death was to criticize this christological Trinitarianism of his *Church Dogmatics* because he had not adequately integrated the doctrine of the Holy Spirit into theology.[3] Barth admitted his "perplexity" on how this task might be done. He recognized that the subjectivistic concept of experience in Enlightenment rationalism and in Schleiermacher's liberalism was concerned implicitly with the doctrine of the Holy Spirit, but Barth recognized that a fear of subjectivism could not serve as an excuse for his failure to develop a theology of the Spirit.[4]

Enlightenment thinkers like Lessing and Kant, and Hegel among the Romantics, were influenced by the Trinitarian theology of Joachim of Fiore (a 12th Century Cistercian abbot) who proclaimed that the "age of the Spirit" had now come.[5] Hence Barth had good reasons for saying that the rationalists with their philosophy of subjectivity were expressing the same concern implicit in a doctrine of the Holy Spirit. This perception that there is a link between the subjectivity of modern philosophy and the subjectivity implied in a doctrine of the Holy Spirit is reinforced when one recalls the pietistic influence in the Enlightenment thinkers. Pietism developed a compelling theology of feeling over against the sterile doctrinal thinking of Protestant Orthodoxy. Its focus was upon the sanctification of the inner life through the Holy Spirit. This theological subjectivity inadvertently brought down Protestant Orthodoxy in the seventeenth century and opened the door to Enlightenment thought in the German universities. Protestant Orthodoxy had been strongly in place in the universities of Germany in the seventeenth century and acted as a fortress against Enlightenment rationalism. But Pietism so stressed the subjective, individualistic dimension of truth and downplayed the importance of objective intellectual precision that it weakened the doctrinal stronghold of Protestant Orthodoxy and formed part of the vanguard of Enlightenment thinking.[6] Protestant Orthodoxy never recovered its equilibrium. Consequently, Enlightenment rationalism overthrew Protestant Orthodoxy as the dominant intellectual force in German universities.

The Enlightenment concept of rationality and the Pietistic concept of the immediacy of the Spirit are like two sides of the same coin because they appeal to the autonomous nature of thought and feeling respectively.[7] It can be argued that modern subjectivity is a secularized version of

"the age of the Spirit" envisioned by Joachim of Fiore in the twelfth century[8] and further catapulted to significance in the doctrine of the sanctification of the Spirit among the Pietists. Kant was reared in a Pietist
home, in addition to being influenced by Joachim's concept of the "Age
of the Spirit." He considered his critical philosophy to be an enlightened
version of Pietism.[9] This is not to say that the subjectivism of the modern world can only be accounted for in terms of Joachim's concept of
"the Age of the Spirit," or the subjectivism of Pietism, but it is to recognize that these were strong winds blowing, along with other theological
movements which stressed "the inner light" of the Spirit.

Hegel specifically said, however, that the rise of modern thought and
its emphasis on subjectivity and self-consciousness was a direct and
explicit translation of the doctrine of the Spirit into secular terms.[10] He
rejected what he called the rationalism and intellectualism of
Enlightenment thought because it negated the actual personal experience of the Spirit in history. He rejected Pietism (especially
Schleiermacher) because it restricted knowledge of God to religious feelings. Hegel believed the significance of modern philosophy as it had
developed in his own dialectical system was that the truth of the
Christian religion had become fully developed as a self-consciousness of
the Spirit. Hence for Hegel the modern concept of subjectivity was the
fullest expression of the Christian faith, especially Lutheranism.[11]

To this extent, Barth is a "modern theologian" in spite of the fact that
he attacked theological modernism—because his starting point was an
exclusively subjectivistic focus on the self-authenticating Word of God.
His definition of God as *a self-revealing Subject* was a corollary concept
to the modern notion of the human self as *a thinking subject.* Ironically,
Barth attacked the subjectivism of modernism with his own neo-orthodox form of subjectivism; for the categories that he used to theologize
his biblical exegesis were borrowed largely from the philosophy of subjectivity developed by Hegel and incorporated into theology by Richard
Rothe and I. A. Dorner.[12] It is especially significant that Barth's concept
of revelation as the moment of the *self*-revelation of God's very self
comes from Hegel's concept of Spirit.[13] Indeed it is appropriate to call
Barth a "modern theologian" (as Moltmann does).[14]

Since Barth suggested that the modern concept of subjectivity is a
secularized version of the subjectivity implied in a doctrine of the Holy
Spirit, it is understandable that he would follow up his call for the development of a new paradigm of the Holy Spirit with an energetic warning
not to fall back into the trap of equating pneumatology with anthropol-

ogy.[15] This subjectivizing tendency is what Barth meant by his "perplexity" over the doctrine of the Holy Spirit—namely how to avoid the built-in tendency of any doctrine of the Spirit to be subjectivistic.

Moltmann's Multidimensional Model of Experience

Jürgen Moltmann was a student of Barth who responded to his call for a new paradigm of the Holy Spirit. Instead of beginning with the subjectivistic notion of God as revealing Subject, Moltmann begins with the idea of God in relational categories of the Trinitarian Persons. His Trinitarian doctrine of God is largely free of the subjectivism which plagued Barth's theology because it highlights a relational and historical understanding of theology unlike Barth's christological Trinitarianism, which was authoritarian-based in a concept of revelation "from above" without any rational or affective basis other than mere faith in God's self-disclosure. Barth's autocratic concept of revelation created the sense that theology after all was an irrational affair and that God was nothing more than a projection of our human ego as Feuerbach had charged. But with Moltmann, the revelation of God is not a private affair, subjectively imagined to happen in a non-historical moment of self-disclosure. Rather, the revelation of God is a real historical happening in the concrete world and can be affirmed with rational integrity.

Barth had suggested that Moltmann might be the specific person who would promote and even independently "revise" *Church Dogmatics*. Reading *Theology of Hope* encouraged Barth to think Moltmann could possibly be his intellectual and theological heir. Barth had one major problem with this expectation. Moltmann had made eschatology the dominating principle of his theology. Barth rightly perceived this new orientation to be a radical departure from his *Church Dogmatics*. He hoped that Moltmann's subsequent writings would bring about realignment with Barth's supernaturalistic model, which sharply distinguished between the immanent and economic Trinity.[16] This would not be forthcoming because Moltmann developed an eschatological model of reality, which disallowed Barthian dualism. Moltmann replied in a letter to Barth that his doctrine of the immanent Trinity set over against the economic Trinity was a point in *Church Dogmatics* where "I always lost my breath."[17] As we shall point out below, Moltmann was not denying the self-existence of God, but he was rejecting the idea of an artificial distinction between God and the world. Eschatology emphasizes the actual presence of God in the world, and Moltmann believes this divine presence is more than a chronologically future event. Rather, this real future event is happening now. Eschatology includes real history.

The title of one of his recent books, *History and The Triune God*, says it well. Moltmann believes that the history of salvation is rationally and existentially defensible, personally transforming, and socially revolutionary. Without this historical/objective perspective, any doctrine of the Holy Spirit would easily bog down in the quagmire of subjectivism. Hence it would have been difficult for Barth to develop a new paradigm of the Holy Spirit since his christological Trinitarianism was already heavily enmeshed within a subjectivism, which ironically he had fought so hard and so long against. Moltmann's *Theology of Hope* (1964) pointed the way out of the entanglements of subjectivism by critiquing positivism which had become the working assumptions of modern historical criticism. He also exposed existentialism and neo-orthodoxy as inadequate solutions.

Moltmann has sought to reinstate the role of personal experience as a basis for doing theology without succumbing to the liberalism of Schleiermacher and the subjectivistic tendencies of Pietism.[18] Moltmann's focus is that through the third person of the Trinity believers enjoy a shared and personal experience with God. Moltmann writes: "By experience of the Spirit I mean an awareness of God in, with and beneath the experience of life, which gives us assurance of God's fellowship, friendship, and love."[19] This experience of the Spirit includes the remembrance of Christ and the expectation of God's future. Hence in Moltmann's doctrine of God, pneumatology presupposes christology and prepares the way for eschatology.[20]

Ever since the rise of modern philosophy and the development of modern science, the concept of experience has been restricted to denote the way facts can be controlled and interpreted clearly and distinctly through rational reflection. Truth claims are always the result of one's own empirical experience. To paraphrase Kant, we create reality by our own active thinking because there is nothing we know through experience, which is not first put there by our creative minds.[21] This reduction of all truth and reality to the active determinations of the human mind is the hallmark of modern scientific methodology. With the elimination of any passive elements entering into our consideration of what is real, the experimental method elevates the concepts of domination, self-consciousness, and rational demonstrability. This modern rationalistic concept of experience means the rejection of the primal dimensions of experience and the consequent "desolate erosion of life."[22] And quite obviously a personal experience of God is impossible, as Kant maintained.

Moltmann, however, attacks this one-sided modern definition of experience as inadequate on the grounds that self-experience is not nearly so absolute as modern thought would have us believe. An analysis of the social pattern of inter-subjectivity demonstrates that the consciousness of the self is mediated to us through other selves as well. It is not entirely self-constituted. Likewise, Moltmann points out that social experience is not in itself totally self-constituted; rather, there is a relationship, which exists between human beings and their world. More specifically, we as human beings have a body within the larger framework of nature, which provides the basis for our primal and tacit experiences of ourselves and our understanding of our world, which the modern concept of experience ignores.[23]

Moltmann proposes a multidimensional concept of experience. He does not simply reject modern scientific methodology, rather he calls for broadening this base to allow for potential experiences beyond consciousness and the self-determination of things. This larger meaning of experience, while incorporating the element of critical analysis, assumes a fundamental attitude of trust about our capacity to experience reality. The one-sided hermeneutic of doubt and skepticism assumed in the modern concept of experience destroys human community as well as diminishes the personal meaning of human life. The knowledge of God is a meaningful concept only if human experience is truly open to a dimension of reality beyond its own self-determination.

This is not to suggest that human experience has a natural capacity for grasping the reality of God, rather to point out the *passive* capacity of human experience to receive what lies beyond itself. This means that transcendence is not to be limited to *self*-transcendence as modern thought assumes. Rather, we experience God as transcendent in, with, and beneath each experience of the larger world. Even so, we not only experience God, but God experiences us. Unless we can talk about God objectively in terms of his own experience, then any talk about our experience of God evaporates into sheer subjectivism. Moltmann further points out that only if we understand the world as existing within the life of God can we once again talk about those special experiences of God in the history of salvation, which form the basis of the Christian narrative.[24]

Moltmann is a true student of Barth because he takes seriously Barth's warning not to turn pneumotology into anthropology. This is evident in the way that Moltmann has emphasized the distinctive person-hood of the Holy Spirit. The Holy Spirit is not an extension of the human spirit. The Holy Spirit is not just a point of union between God the Father and the Son. The Holy Spirit is not just the Father and Son work-ing together and relating together as a "we." Rather, the Holy Spirit is also just as distinctive in his personal specificity as the Father and Son.[25] This personal specificity of the Holy Spirit had not received adequate theo-logical recognition in modern and contemporary theology—until Moltmann brought it into center stage.

The Perichoretic Unity of the Trinity

Moltmann asserts that Western Christianity has developed a defective soteriology because it has a defective pneumatology. The root cause of this problem is a fundamental misunderstanding of the nature of God. Ever since the development of the concept of the Trinity in the Western tradition, beginning with Tertullian's coining of the word *trinitas* and Augustine's more systematic development of *una substantia, tres personae*, the unity of God has usurped the role which rightly belongs to the three persons of the Godhead. Consequently, Western Christianity has implic-itly been monarchical in its view of God; it has focused more on the Father of the Son, giving rise more to a duality rather than a Trinity. And the Holy Spirit, for all practical purposes, has taken on the role of a force or power rather than a distinct person of his own.[26]

Moltmann believes that this monarchical tendency was exacerbated further by the "unofficial" introduction of the so-called *filioque* clause into the Nicene Creed in the West, which finally led to the schism between the Eastern Orthodox Church and the Roman Catholic Church in 1054. The Nicene Creed affirmed that the Holy Spirit proceeded from the Father, but the Western church added that the Holy Spirit proceeded from Father *and Son*. The Eastern theologians argued that this downgrad-ed the distinct personhood of the Holy Spirit by subordinating the Holy Spirit to the Son, as if the Spirit was a mere power or effect of Christ. To say that the Son is the origin of the Spirit thus confuses the Trinitarian relationships and makes the Holy Spirit less than divine in comparison with the Son. To say that the Son is also the origin of the Spirit is unin-tentionally turning the Son into a second Father.[27] The Father alone is the source of all reality; the Son is the mediator of reality; and the Holy Spirit is the agent of God in reality. So the Father creates through his Son by the power of the Holy Spirit. In terms of *constitution*, Moltmann insists of course that the Father is the eternal origin of the Son and the Spirit. So Moltmann acknowledges the "monarchy" of the Father in the eternal sense of the *constitution* of the Trinitarian Persons, but in terms of the actual movement of the divine persons they are totally equal without any degree of subordination. Moltmann calls this movement "the circulation of the divine life,"[28]

Beginning with the Cappadocian Fathers, the Trinitarian relationships were defined in terms of reciprocity and mutual interpenetration. In particular, John of Damascus in the eighth century gave a summary of the Eastern church's position on the Trinity in terms of *perichoresis*.[29] The Father exists in the Son, the Son in the Father, and both of them in the Spirit, just as the Spirit exists in both the Father and the Son. The Trinitarian Persons possess their own unique characteristics, which distinguishes them from each other and at the same it is their personal differences which bind them together in love and mutual reciprocity. Intimate friendship is the defining quality of their oneness and unity. The threeness of God is what determines the oneness of God, and the oneness of God is defined in terms of God's threeness.

This "circulation" of the divine persons in not a tritheism. For God is not composed of three separate, independent beings who come together at some time later to form a fellowship. Nor is this a modalism. For the three persons are not three modes of being without eternal personal differentiations. Rather, it is the eternal "circulation" of the divine persons in perfect love for each other and in fellowship with each other, which constitutes their experience of eternal life. This inner-Trinitarian relationship is what constitutes their oneness. This stands over against Augustine's model of God as one substance, three persons.

Moltmann argues in favor of the Eastern church's understanding because the Western idea of divine substance minimizes the personal differences which exists among the three persons of the Trinity. Likewise Moltmann rejects the modalism of Barth who defines God as Absolute Subject with three eternal modes of being. What constitutes the unity of God is not substance or modes of being, but the relational, perichoretic indwelling of the three persons. This divine process is what constitutes their fellowship and perfects them in a unity of love. In this way, the pitfall of subordinationism is eliminated, and a monarchical model is avoided. The significance of Moltmann's work in pneumatology is that he takes this perichoretic model and deepens its meaning and application for our contemporary world. He shows that we must think of the Trinitarian Persons as equals; each possesses will and understanding;

each speaks to each other; each turns to each other in love and communion.[30]

How is this perichoretic unity of the Trinity to be arrived at theologically? Moltmann's answer is that through salvation history we come to see that God is revealed in this fashion. What this history of salvation reveals is that God is not a distant monarch who stands over against the world and above the world in a dominating and threatening way. Rather, what is perceived through the history, which God has with Israel and finally in Jesus of Nazareth, is a God who is Father, Son, and Holy Spirit. This triune God is the Father of our Lord Jesus Christ through the power of the Holy Spirit. God is Father, not only because he is the source of all reality, but because he is the Father of Jesus Christ. It is his relationship with his Son, which bestows upon him his sense of Fatherhood. Likewise, the Son's relationship to the Father is what bestows upon him his sense of sonship. And it is the power of the Holy Spirit who enables the Father and the Son to be so related and at the same time for the Father and Son to be in the Holy Spirit and the Holy Spirit to be in the Father and Son. The point of creation, reconciliation, and glorification is that men and women and all of creation might become a part of the "circulation" of the triune God.[31]

One of the social implications of the perichoretic concept of the Trinity is that just as there is mutuality, reciprocity, and equality among the persons of the Trinity, likewise this is a model for the world. Wolfhart Pannenberg raises the issue whether Moltmann's distinction between the divine "constitution" and divine "circulation" can be used to minimize the concept of the monarchy of the Father. Pannenberg insists on the unity of the Trinitarian Persons as grounded in the monarchy of the Father. This issue represents a sharp difference between Pannenberg and Moltmann.[32] What has to be considered in this debate between Pannenberg and Moltmann is the practical issue that the term, monarch, has a negative connotation for many people because it implies a tyrannical notion of domination rather than a loving father whose desires the affection of his children. Yet, the "monarchy" of the Father which Moltmann allows with qualifications to be a part of the divine constitution cannot be bypassed because it is an implication of the Trinitarian revelation.

The Modern Concept of Person

The concept of person emerged as a result of the church's attempt to define how Jesus could be called God and man at the same time in the fourth and fifth centuries. Gerhard Von Rad has pointed out that the biblical concept of God who is revealed in history as personal is the original source of the concept of person. "Here alone, in his encounter with God, does mankind become great and interesting, breaking through the enigma of his humanity to discover all the inherent potentialities of his self-conscious existence." [33] Interestingly enough, the late neo-Marxist atheist and Czech philosopher Vitézslav Gardavsky (a personal friend of Moltmann) has also shown that the Old Testament revelation of God to Abraham as a self-conscious, transcendent being who stands outside of nature is the original source for the emergence of the concept of person in the modern world. [34]

The Greek word for person (*prosopon*) meant "mask" which actors in the ancient Greek theater wore on their face as they confronted the audience representing a particular character. The word literally means "face, visage, countenance." It had strictly an objective meaning without any reference to subjective self-consciousness or permanent duration. In Latin theology, the term person was first used in reference to Sabellian modalism—one God with three masks or roles (*prosopon*). In Greek theology, the Greek term *hypostasis* (a parallel term to *prosopon*) was used in developing the doctrine of the Trinity. The term *hypostasis* did not carry the meaning of mask or mere appearance, but was used to denote the individual existence of a particular nature. Whereas *hypostasis* was eventually the word Greek theology chose for the Trinity, the Latin term *persona* was developed in Western theology and was deepened in its meaning to describe one's particular, unique, individual, permanent existence. [35] By the sixth century Boethius formulated the definitive, classical definition of personhood: "A person is an individual substance of a rational nature."[36] In other words, a person is one who possesses unique individual existence with intelligence and thus is non-interchangeable with others.[37]

Using Boethius' definition of personhood, Moltmann shows that the three persons of the Trinity are not mere modes of being. They are not simply three masks which God wears in his revelation to humanity, nor are they mere roles or expressions of the one God. Rather, the three persons of the Trinity "are individual, unique, non-interchangeable subjects of the one, common divine substance, with consciousness and will. Each of the persons possesses the divine nature in a non-interchangeable way; each presents it in his own way."[38] Accordingly, there is both the divine nature which the three persons have in common, but there is also the natures that the three persons uniquely possess for themselves each in his own way.

The particular nature of each divine person is shaped by their relationship to one another. The decisive characteristic of each person is not simply an abstract oneness which binds them together; rather, what gives each person a own unique nature as Father, Son, or Holy Spirit is the relationship which they share together in their common bond. Being a person thus involves more than just being a unique individual possessing rationality, but it also includes the social element of being in relationship with others.[39]

Moltmann shows that "relations" and "substantial individuality" are essential ingredients for understanding the Trinity today. Unfortunately, the Western understanding of Trinity defined "person" largely in terms of "relation" as if a person *is* relation. But God as Father means more than just God is related as Father. It means that the Father has concrete existence as a person with being, not just a mode of being. The Father has his fatherhood by relation to the Son, but this relation is not the concrete existence of the Father, rather this relationship presupposes his actual, distinct existence. Person and relation are reciprocal in their meaning, for to be a person presupposes relations, and relations presuppose persons. To restrict the meaning of "persons" to "relations" is modalistic because it eliminates the enduring concrete subjective existence of the person. We have Augustine largely to thank for introducing the concept of relation into the meaning of personhood. Even so, his explanation for describing the Holy Spirit as the relational unity of the Father and Son implies that the Holy Spirit has no genuine personal identity of his own. This implies that the Holy Spirit is more like an impersonal force than a real person who is intimately related to the Father and Son as an equal partner. The need to recognize the distinct person of the Holy Spirit as an equal partner in the triunity of God is why the Eastern Church preferred the use of *hypostasis* instead of *prosopon*.[40] Unless "relation" also includes "substantial individuality," then the Holy Spirit is not really thought of as a divine subject along with the Father and Son.[41]

On the other hand, Moltmann finds the Orthodox tradition to be weak because it only assumes that the relations "manifest" the three persons, as if the relations are not essential aspects of the distinctive nature of the three persons. Moltmann argues that the "relations" of the three persons must be taken seriously in the sense that they are mutually and reciprocally bonded together in fellowship and love. Personality and relationships are inextricably connected.[42]

This mutual reciprocity and interdependence of the triune God is the social model for understanding the meaning of the whole of human life and creation. Moltmann finds in this personal model for God as Trinity the basis for social reconstruction and change in the world. Hence his concern for human liberation, ecological concerns, and the many troublesome aspects of social life. Particularly he finds consolation and hope in spite of the experience of widespread suffering in the world today because the God of Jesus is revealed as one who suffers with us. Without God's capacity for pathos and emotional involvement with us, God would not be the God of hope. And only in Trinitarian thinking does it make sense to talk about the love of God and God's emotional capacity to feel with us.

In the Enlightenment period, the subjective concept of autonomy led to a focus on the absolute, substantial idea of personhood as in Kant's concept of the transcendental ego. But even the concept of autonomy as used by Kant did not mean the sheer irrelevance of feeling nor the idea of mere individualism. For Kant the autonomy of reason meant that a mature individual was one who was properly in touch with one's own potentiality and inner resources for living responsibly in the world. Autonomy meant having the courage to think for oneself as opposed to living in an immature relationship of dependency upon others. For Kant the concept of autonomy clearly included a sense of moral responsibility to treat others with dignity and respect. This relational aspect shows that he did not have in mind an individualistic experience of arbitrariness when he spoke of the autonomous individual.[43]

With Fichte and Hegel, God came to be defined as Absolute Subject as opposed to Augustine's concept of God as Substance. Karl Barth picked up this Hegelian concept of God as Absolute Subject to define the nature of God's oneness, and he consequently substituted "modes of being" for the Trinitarian Persons.[44] Barth's concern was that the meaning of persons carries with it today the absolute concept of sheer autonomous individuality and self-consciousness without reference to being-in-relationship with other persons[45] Barth thus thinks that the modern concept of personality was not included previously in the pre-modern world.[46] Hence he called for a new way of framing the doctrine of the Trinity, which would not be in conflict with the meaning of personhood as it is used today.

Barth featured the oneness of God who in a threefold manner repeats itself in the mode of Father, Son, and Holy Spirit. God's oneness is defined as a person with self-consciousness, which is reflected from within itself as a threefold "divine repetition."[47] In fact, Barth's fear of tritheism is so great that he studiously avoids any possibility of ascribing personality to the Trinity distinctions. For Barth any idea of individual conscious existence given to the three distinctions within God "is scarcely possible without tritheism."[48]

Is Barth right that the term, person, can no longer be used in reference to the Trinitarian distinctions because the modern usage is allegedly different? And is it true that only in the modern period has the concept of self-consciousness been applied to the concept of personhood?[49] Moltmann disputes the claim that the word person has undergone such a radical difference in meaning in the modern period. He also disputes the claim that self-consciousness is a modern addition to its meaning as well.[50] Moltmann surely seems right in his assessment over against Barth. While it is true that Augustine's concept of the relational concept of person minimized the element of substantial individuality (*hypostasis*) and hence his tendency toward modalism, Boethius' definition of personhood as a *rational* individual carried with it the twin ideas of individual existence and self-consciousness.

Trinitarianism as Panentheism

Some suggest that Moltmann identifies God with the natural process.[51] This is erroneous because Moltmann certainly does not identify God with the finite world. No one writing in the area of theology has developed more clearly the nature of God as Creator *ex nihilo*. Quite literally for Moltmann, God spoke the temporal world into being through the divine Word in the power of the Spirit. God in no way is to be identified ontologically with the world in a pantheistic sense. But neither is God's relationship to be defined in terms of deism, as if God stands above the world in another realm separate from this realm. Moltmann defines God's transcendence in terms of the future, a concept first suggested by Johannes Metz.[52] God stands ahead of us and is certainly different in essence from the world.

Moltmann's use of "panentheism" is only a terminological substitution for monotheism because he still preserves the unity of God who transcends the world. Literally, panentheism means "everything is in God" and is to be distinguished from pantheism, which means "everything is God." Pantheism simply equates God with the world, whereas panentheism distinguishes between God and the world though they are intimately interrelated. In agreement with pantheism, panentheism normally implies that God includes the natural order of the world as part of the divine being. The major difference between them is that pantheism entails a strictly fatalistic and deterministic view of the world, whereas panentheism allows for a measure of freedom and openness for decision. Another distinguishing features is that pantheism makes static being the essence of God, while panentheism says God is in process of becoming. Moltmann is not a pantheist or panentheist in the sense of confusing the essence of God with the world

Pannenberg disagrees with Moltmann's decision not to use the term, monotheism, but he defends Moltmann against the misunderstanding of his critics who accuse him of abandoning the historic Christian view of God. Pannenberg in particular defends Moltmann against the charge of tritheism.[53] Moltmann and Pannenberg are in essential agreement concerning the new focus and deepened understanding of the significance of the Holy Spirit. Moltmann's choice of panentheism[54] is related, however, to his concern to show that God is the source of all reality, the agent in all reality, and the power active in all reality. He decides against the term monotheism because it fails to convey the dynamic involvement of God in Creation and it specifically obscures the Trinitarian nature of God's essence. Some, having given only a cursory reading of Moltmann's writings, think that his "panentheism" identifies God's essence with the world.[55]

Roger Olson reflects this misunderstanding of Moltmann's view of God's relationship to the world.[56] He thinks Moltmann's denies God's eternal triune existence because Moltmann says that the immanent Trinity is the economic Trinity. He failed to see that Moltmann is only taking seriously the revelation of God in history and that what God is, is really revealed in history and what the Son of God experiences in our history also is incorporated into God's own experience. Of course only the Son of God, for example, suffered on the Cross (Moltmann is not a patripassionist), but his sufferings were experienced by the Father as the loss of his Son. In other words, Jesus' death was felt by the Father who loves His Son and who enters affectionately into the life of the Son through the Spirit. Moltmann frankly recognizes that his statement that the immanent Trinity is also the economic Trinity is open to misunderstanding "because it then sounds like the dissolution of the one in the other,"[57] but he clearly explains his meaning that there is no artificial distinction between what God is in God's very self and what God is in history. We can speak of the three persons of the Trinity (the immanent Trinity) because we can speak of their concrete actions in history (the economic Trinity). We worship God for what God is in God's very self (the immanent Trinity), but we come to know the immanent Trinity through what God is revealed to be in history (the economic Trinity). This means "the triune God can only appear in history as he is in himself, and in no other way."[58] This distinction between the immanent and economic Trinity thus does not mean that there are two different Trinities.[59]

The decisive thing about God is "the coming God," not "an unmoved Mover."[60] God is not a timeless being who exists above the world. God does not exist only as the depth or soul of the world. God is the future who comes and is present in history. The "future" as the essence of God's nature is what is revealed through the economic Trinity, but God as the future and creator of all things is not first known through theological discovery on our part. We come to know God as the future of all things through salvation history. More specifically, God's transcendence (the immanent Trinity) as the future of all things is a paradigm derived through our reflection on the resurrected Lord and the outpouring of the Holy Spirit upon the Church. The difficulty with a dualistic view of the world as seen in a supernaturalistic monotheism is its tendency to artificially divide up the immanent and economic Trinity into two independent compartments. This makes it impossible to emphasize the personal character of God who truly identifies with the emotional depths of humanity. The advantage of defining the immanent Trinity in terms of the future of all things (as opposed to a monarch who stands outside the world) is that God is revealed in the context of real history and real people. Thus the pain of Jesus' death on the cross expresses an emotional truth about the immanent Trinity. We cannot simply identify Jesus' pain with the economic Trinity; for it expresses the deep pain of loss which the Father felt as well. God's transcendence means that God has reality in God's own self (the immanent Trinity), but his reality as the future of all things means that all things inhere in God who comes (the economic Trinity). God is "ahead of us," not "above us."[61] This futurist model for locating God's transcendence as opposed to a spatial dualism of God above the world shows how indeed God is truly personal. God feels with his creatures because the immanent Trinity coincides with the economic Trinity. God as the future (the immanent Trinity) is the one who comes to us in the present (the economic Trinity). God is not separated from us in a world above (as a spatial metaphor suggests).[62] "Advent" is the nature of the God of history. God's coming also means something for the immanent Trinity as well as for us[63]

Olson questions whether Moltmann is an "Evangelical ally" because of "hints of panentheism."[64] If any theologian has ever consistently maintained God's divine otherness from the created order, it is Moltmann. He explicitly rejects the process theology of Schubert Ogden and John Cobb with their identification of God with the world and its rejection of a traditional doctrine of the Trinity based on revelation.[65] Moltmann's critique of Tillich's "panentheism" strikes at the root concern of Olson. Moltmann rejects Tillich's inclusion of God's essence within the created world.[66] Moltmann clearly affirms God's involvement with the world, but it is an involvement based on God's decision of love. It is not an ontologically pantheistic involvement![67] Moltmann is no more pantheistically inclined than Peter who speaks of our being made "partakers of divine nature" (2 Peter 1:4) or Paul who speaks of everything existing in Christ (Col. 1:17). Moltmann clearly distinguishes between an emphasis on the nearness of God to his creation and a pantheistic identification of God with the world.[68] He rejects Whitehead's identification of God with "a unified, world process" because this means "God is turned into the comprehensive ordering factor in the flux of happening."[69] Over against all other forms of panentheism, Moltmann insists on "the fundamental distinction between creation and Creator."[70] Over against the one-sided "monotheistic" divorce between God and the world, he insists on a Trinitarian view of Creation.[71] The panentheism of Cobb, Ogden, and Whitehead resulted in a "divinization of the world,"[72] whereas traditional "monotheism" is monarchical in tendency, and its extreme de-divinization of the world has resulted in a godless view of nature. Trinitarian theology preserves God's essential distinction from the world, while at the same time the world God has created exists in him.[73] Moltmann's theology of creation *ex nihilo* is clearly expressed in his own words: "The World was created neither out of pre-existent matter, nor out of the divine Being itself. It was called into existence by the free will of God."[74] Moltmann's shows that the free will of God does not mean arbitrariness, rather God's freedom is rooted in God's love.[75] Hence the divine love of the Trinitarian Persons is the panentheistic basis for a theology of creation.

The choice of the term, "panentheism," was based on its ability to express the close proximity of the Creator with his creation—"everything is in God and God is in everything." The term monotheism is disadvantaged by its inability to be so comprehensive in its designation of God's relationship to the world. There is not the slightest trace of pantheism to be found in Moltmann's panentheism. Barth has shown that the safest protection against atheism and pantheism is the doctrine of the Trinity.[76] Surely Moltmann's unequivocal affirmation of the Trinity, along with the doctrine of *creatio ex nihilo*, leaves no room for misunderstanding his theology as a pantheism or humanism.[77]

The Panentheism of American Process Thought

Alfred North Whitehead (1861-1947) and Charles Hartshorne (1897-2000) developed a philosophy of panentheism in the 20th century, which is to be distinguished from Moltmann's concept of panentheism. Whitehead and Hartshorne were sons of clergymen. They rejected Christian faith and attempted to develop an alternative natural religion. Whitehead was a British mathematician, logician, and philosopher of science until he went to Harvard University in 1924 as a professor of general issues in philosophy, where he developed a comprehensive metaphysical system known as process philosophy. Charles Hartshorne further developed the process thought of Whitehead, contributing his own unique analytical approach. Hartshorne taught at the Universities of Chicago, Emory University, and finally at the University of Texas at Austin, retiring in 1976.

Their basic religious premise was that God should be defined as God-and-the-world rather than as the transcendent creator of the world.[78] Creativity belongs to the inherent nature of the world rather than just to God.[79] God is an ongoing changing reality with no stable identity and is always in the process of development by being shaped by the changing events of the world. God is not a personal, Triune being, but the emerging synthesis of the world. [80]

United Methodist theologians, Schubert Ogden (Professor Emeritus, Perkins School of Theology) and John B. Cobb, Jr. (Professor Emeritus, Claremont School of Theology), have sought to theologize the process thought of Hartshorne and Whitehead. Cobb's student and successor at Claremont is David Ray Griffin who has now become the primary spokesperson for process theology. Griffin says that process theology is the best reinterpretation of Christian faith in the postmodern world.[81]

However, there are serious problems with process thought, philosophically, scientifically, and theologically, which make it doubtful that process theology is a viable option in Christian theology. *Philosophically*, process philosophy is still enmeshed in foundationalism. Whitehead and Hartshorne contributed significantly to the downfall of modernist epistemology with a devastating critique of its dualism, but inverted the modernist philosophy of being into a philosophy of *process*. Process theology ignores that postmodern thought has subverted foundationalism and deconstructed philosophy by showing that there are no stable meanings that can be sustained rationally. Process and flux mean everything is decentered. Postmodern thought has offered a fairly convincing critique of the pretensions of reason to discover universal principles and foundations of truth. Yet process theology has disregarded this postmodern critique of reason. Having deconstructed the modernist "religion within the limits of reason alone," process philosophy has reconstructed another natural religion based on the pretensions of reason to develop coherent and universal principles of reality independent of biblical revelation.

Intelligibility, coherence, and a correspondence with scientific data, integrated into a self-consistent theory through moral-religious intuitions are the criteria for Whitehead's philosophy.[82] Though he praised "the Galilean origin of Christianity" with its view of God as love, Whitehead did not incorporate the history of Jesus as a criterion for his philosophy, setting it aside in favor of a strictly scientific, philosophically abstract theory. He assumed that ultimate truth about God and the world is derived from the ability of reason "to frame a coherent, logical, necessary system of general ideas in terms of which every element of our experience can be interpreted."[83] He argued against the traditional view of supernaturalism on the ground that it was influenced by a feudalistic idea of an absolute king in Medieval culture. [84] However, is not his view of God as an actual, conscious "occasion" who synthesizes all the various aspect of the world into a single whole just as much influenced by modern culture? [85] Is not this democratic concept of God vulnerable to the same criticism of the projection hypothesis of Feuerbach?[86] Picturing God as the chief exemplification of all metaphysical principles is perhaps nothing but a projection of the image of a democratically elected president. If so, Whitehead's concept of God is just as much culturally conditioned by modern Western society as the Medieval concept was by a feudalistic society.

Postmodernism has shown that reason alone can only pretend to construct a view of reality based on what it imagines is a universal foundation for truth. This postmodern critique of reason is less an attack on reason and more of an attack on the claim of reason to offer a grand view of things. Process philosophy can be viewed as just another attempt to have religion within the limits of reason alone, similar to Kant's futile attempt, but it succumbs to the same negative judgment of the postmodern critique, namely, that foundationalism is an illusion of reason.

Scientifically, the basic premise of process philosophy is not compatible with contemporary science. It assumes that the building blocks of the universe are a series of disconnected "actual occasions," or "events," which are like a series of islands discontinuous with each other. There is no inherent connection among these island-like entities, although there is the built-in possibility that these discrete entities may create a unity with each other.[87]

John Polkinghorne, a British quantum physicist, has pointed out that Whitehead's idea of "punctuated discrete events" is not in agreement with the data of science. To be sure, an electron wave packet in an atom, for example, will change and even collapse, but this is not the same thing as a discrete event. Rather, it is only a discrete moment of identifying the collapsing wave packet. Otherwise, the quantum world develops in a continuous manner without any absolute breaks or gaps.[88]

Theologically, American process philosophy contradicts Christian belief in a Creator God.[89] Although Whitehead rightly pointed out that the monarchical tendencies of supernaturalism was a mistranslation of the biblical idea of God as love, his idea of God as a correlate of the world falls short of the biblical concept of God as Creator.[90] The idea of God and the world as existing together as co-partners and collaborators has more in common with Plato's demiurge of the *Timaeus* than the Old Testament. Such an ontological dualism is absent in the Scriptures and entails the idea that God is finite. It is one thing to say that God intentionally chose to limit the exercise of unilateral power when God created the world and granted humans with finite freedom, but it is remarkably unbiblical to think that God's limitation of power was superimposed by recalcitrant, eternal matter. Without an adequate view of God, then the rest of Christian doctrine is also eroded. The attempt to theologize the process thought of Whitehead and Hartshorne has been mostly unsuccessful, primarily because it remained committed to the modernist method of foundationalism and to the adequacy of reason to construct an understanding of God in self-conscious opposition to the real history of salvation.

Its views of creation and redemption reflect this inadequacy. Its foundational premise is that God could not be the creator of space-time, rather God and the world exist as co-partners in the formation of reality, and the power of God is only persuasive rather than omnipotent.[91] It rejects the idea that God redeemed humanity through the life, death, and resurrection of Jesus of Nazareth. One of the foundational principles of process thought is that dead men do not rise again. The significance of Jesus is not derived from the events of history; rather the universal principles of reason must be used to reinterpret his significance. His significance is "his outlook on reality"—not his teachings about God, not his incarnation, not his atoning death on the cross, and not his resurrection from the dead, all of which are denied.[92] Nor do we have any sure hope there is such a thing as everlasting life.[93] Neither do we have any "absolute" or "provisional" assurance that good shall ultimately prevail over evil.[94] What about prayer? Polkinghorne has noted that process theology "presents too weak an account to be adequate to accommodate the Christian experience of prayer or the Christian intuition of God's providence at work in history."[95]

Over against American process thought, Moltmann's panentheism shows that the unity of God and the world can be affirmed without resorting to a confusion of God with the world. He shows that Christian theology can avoid the pretensions of reason and foundationalism through embracing a historical understanding of human life, which leads to belief in Jesus of Nazareth whose life, death, and resurrection have significance for all people. Human thought may not be able to construct a view of reality on its own that is coherent, adequate to the facts, and illuminating, although Griffin thinks it can,[96] but Moltmann has shown that reason can respond in a responsible theological way to the disclosure of truth in the real history of salvation.

The History of God

Critics have suggested that Moltmann reduces God to the finite historical process.[97] This is a miscontrual of Moltmann's concept of history. He believes that history needs to be redefined and enlarged in its meaning from the positivistic view of history which has dominated contemporary thought. History is not simply the realm of the finite, as if God stands above history and his revelation has to be inserted vertically from above. Rather, reality *is* history. This is so because history is the sphere of the personal and the history of salvation reveals that the ultimate reality of God is personal. Hence it is appropriate to speak of the history of humanity, but it is also appropriate to speak of the history of God. God is not a lifeless, static, monarch devoid of movement and relationship. To be sure, God has one "essential nature."[98] However, it is best to speak of this unity of God as an "at-oneness" or "unitedness"[99] of three distinct, interrelated subjects who possess will, feeling, and understanding. These three *hypostases* are beings-in-relationship. Their reality is also historical because of their personal involvement in the life of each other. Their Trinitarian history is not a finite process. It does include the concept of process in terms of the divine *procession* of the Spirit from the Father of the Son, as Origen maintained.[100] As critics of Moltmann realize this enlarged and more biblically derived meaning of history, their objections to his speaking of the history of God will be alleviated. Interestingly enough, Moltmann defends Joachim of Fiore against the heretical charge that he reduced the Trinity to world history.[101]

This historical understanding of reality has its origin in Hegel's philosophy of history. Just as Aristotle had defined reality as substance, so Hegel defined the comprehensive whole of reality as history. Just as for Aristotle substance was not a category among other categories of reality but was reality itself, so history is not a category of reality among other categories but is reality itself. Hegel's emphasis upon history as reality is rooted in the biblical emphasis that the decisive meaning of revelation is the personal disclosure of God in history. History is the sphere of the personal and hence the very essence of reality itself. To be sure, Hegel's philosophy of history and his articulation of the nature of God seemed to get lost in his use of dialectical abstractions. Moltmann also believes that Hegel's concept of the Trinity is modalistic. Nevertheless, Hegel's highlighting the nature of reality as historical constitutes his greatest contribution. Any theology that is going to address the contemporary mind in a persuasive manner cannot avoid acknowledging the rise of the modern historical consciousness. Moltmann and Pannenberg are the influential thinkers in the contemporary world largely because of the effectiveness of presenting a historical understanding of reality in contrast to the nonhistorical, substantialist thinking of classical thought derived from Aristotle. To be sure, the category of substance is not simply dropped out of their vocabulary, but it is re-conceptualized in historical terms.

This understanding of history as reality also explains why for Moltmann history does not come to an end in the eschaton, although time as we know it will come to a sudden halt at the coming of Christ in the eschaton and then the kingdoms of this world will be delivered to the Father by the Son. Time will cease and eternity will begin for redeemed humanity and the whole of creation in its past, present, and future as it is embraced by the kingdom of God, but reality as history will not come to an end.[102] This meaning of history is larger than a positivistic view which assumes that history is merely a record of finite happenings, just as the concepts of process and becoming have a larger meaning than is assumed in American process thought. Eberhard Jungel shows Barth interprets the Trinity to mean that God's being is in process of becoming, but the concept of becoming does not imply finite development; rather, it implies life and movement.[103] Likewise the concept of process does not imply finite change as the classical doctrine of the *procession* of the Trinity illustrates. Also, the concept of history as reality does not imply finitude, but most fundamentally implies that reality is an engagement of persons in relationship with each other. Thus history as reality will never cease even though world history and time will come to an end in the eschaton, and the divine process of becoming in eternity does not entail the notion that God will undergo personal growth and finite development, but rather it suggests the fullness of life and love.

Moltmann emphasizes that this coming of Christ is something that is a real happening in time. Unlike some theologians who want to demythologize the advent of Christ or reinterpret it in a supra-temporal and nonhistorical manner, Moltmann preserves the biblical focus on a real, temporal eschatological happening. He says: "But if Christ's parousia is equated with God's eternity, then there is no moment at which it can enter time. There is then no future end of time - nothing but the limitation of all the times of human history through God's eternal moment. But this puts an end to all the real and futurist expectation of the parousia which echoes in the early Christian 'maranatha - come soon!', and transforms eschatology into mysticism."[104] Moltmann criticizes Barth because he interprets the advent of Christ as if it were only the final presentation of the salvation perfected in Christ's death on the cross. But if the real future time of Christ's coming "can do no more than disclose the perfect tense of salvation," Moltmann argues that "the New Testament's futurist assertions about salvation are meaningless."[105]

No theologian in recent times has had a stronger emphasis on the real, temporal, future happening of the coming of Christ to bring about the end of time and the beginning of eternity for creation than Moltmann. He seeks to protect the understanding of the parousia of Christ from being interpreted either as merely temporized or merely eternalized. He complains that the "Christian expectation of the parousia was also stifled by the theologians who declared that the so-called delay of the parousia was a fictitious problem which had nothing to do with true faith, since faith experiences and expects God's grace every moment."[106] This minimizing of the future expectation of the coming of Christ due to the supposed embarrassment of Christ's delay was the price the church paid for its integration into the Roman Empire, which had the effect of turning Christianity into a civil religion.[107] Moltmann notes the development of an eschatologically-oriented theology in recent years helped the church to restore the parousia of Christ to its rightful position within the framework of Christian faith.[108]

The main reason Moltmann has been able to speak more biblically, forthrightly, and convincingly about the transcendent realities of the parousia, heaven, the Trinity, the bodily resurrection of Jesus from the dead, his deity, and the personal ministry of the Holy Spirit in human life and in creation is because he has taken seriously the modern historicization of reality.[109] The extreme supranaturalistic ontology of Barth which radicalized God's being above the world in a dualistic fashion leaves one with the feeling that Christian belief is dogmatically handed down from God above in an irrationalist and authoritarian manner. To be sure, Barth's theology presupposed a real (as opposed to a demythologized) history of salvation, but his dualistic view of God and the world worked against his evangelical exegesis and actually moves in the direction of thinking of this world in secularistic terms. It is significant that the "Death of God" theologians of the 1960's were largely Barth's students who specifically said that their secular interpretation of the gospel was "initiated with Barth."[110] Other students of Barth such as Moltmann and Pannenberg embraced his biblically-based theology and its focus on the history of salvation while rejecting his dualistic, supranaturalistic bifurcation of God and the world. Moltmann's *Theology of Hope* addressed the same concern of secularism reflected in "Death of God" theologians who had taken seriously Barth's idea of God's absence and total otherness from the world. The main difference between Moltmann and secular theologians was that Moltmann appropriated Barth's style of evangelical exegesis of Scripture and his corresponding theology of salvation history, but Moltmann developed a Trinitarian view of history that preserved God's transcendence for the world instead of a dualism of God over against the world. In this way, he was able to take the central theological distinctives of Barth and develop them in a more consistent fashion—both logically and biblically. Hence Moltmann's Trinitarian pneumatology is fundamentally a theological refinement and further development of Barth's Trinitarian christology.

Barth's irrationalist understanding of faith creates a skeptical feeling that faith really does not have a basis beyond its own imagination after all. His dualistic image of God occupying space above the world as a divine monarch makes it practically impossible to affirm the history of salvation in the Bible in which God is intimately related to his people as

Father, Son, and Holy Spirit. As opposed to the deistic tendencies of a supranaturalistic ontology, Moltmann's Trinitarian history of salvation and his eschatologically-oriented theology with its focus on the immediacy of God's Holy Spirit in the world today, have contributed to a revitalization of the biblical understanding of God which serves as the basis for bringing about social change, ecological responsibility, and personal transformation in the lives of human beings starving spiritually, emotionally and physically from deprivation, abuse, domination, and discrimination. For Moltmann, only as human beings are brought into a saving relationship with the Father of Jesus Christ through the fellowship of the Holy Spirit is there salvation for individuals as well as the world as a whole. Moltmann's focus on the social implications of a Trinitarian doctrine of God and a corresponding belief that a relationship with God commits the believer to take an attitude of moral responsibility for the whole of creation is a fitting reminder to the Christian community that we do not take the gospel seriously if we try to privatize the meaning of faith in a mystical retreat from the world. For the biblical revelation is most adequately understood in terms of reality as history, not in a dualistic split between God and the world, as if theology could be compartmentalized into a religious ghetto isolated from the whole body of knowledge.

The Postmodern Relevance of Moltmann's Doctrine of the Trinity

This essay began with a comparison between Barth's and Moltmann's Trinitarianism. Moltmann begins with Barth's basic insight concerning the centrality of the Trinity. Moltmann moved beyond Barth's christological focus on the Trinity to a pneumatological Trinitarianism. This shift is more than a slight readjustment or "refining" of Barth's theology. It represents the difference between "modern" and "postmodern." Barth's extreme supernaturalism was an attempt to make room for God in a modern world where the secular realm was devoid of God. The godless natural world and the supernatural world of revelation "coexisted." Moltmann's "panentheism" moves us into the postmodern world beyond the dualism of God and the world. It takes us beyond the rational criteria of modernism to the Trinitarian history of salvation.

Notes

1. Karl Barth, *The Theology of Schleiermacher*, ed. Dietrich Ritschl, trans.

Geoffrey W. Bromiley (Grand Rapids: Wm. B. Eerdmans, 1982), pp. 276-279.

2. Barth, *Church Dogmatics,* 1.1.345-346.

3. Barth, *The Theology of Schleiermacher,* p. 278.

4..Ibid., p. 279.

5. Jürgen Moltmann, *The Spirit of Life,* tran. Margaret Kohl (Minneapolis: Fortress Press, 1992), pp. 2, 203-209]

6. Theodore M. Greene, "The Historical Context and Religious Significance of Kant's *Religion,"* in Kant, *Religion Within the Limits of Reason Alone* (New York: Harper, 1960), p. xiv.

7. Paul Tillich, *A History of Christian Thought,* p. 286;

8. *The Spirit of Life,* pp. 295-296.

9. Kant, *Religion within the Limits of Reason Alone,* p. xxx.

10. Hegel, *Reason in History,* trans. Robert S. Hartman (New York: The Bobbs-Merrill Co., Inc., 1953), p. 25.

11. Ibid., pp. 23,24.

12. Moltmann, *History and the Triune God,* trans. John Bowden (New York: Crossroad, 1992, p. 140.

13. Cf. Pannenberg, "Introduction," *Revelation as History,* p. 5

14. *History and the Triune God,* pp. 140-142.

15. Barth, *The Theology of Schleiermacher,* p. 279.

16. *Karl Barth Letters 1961-1968,* ed. Jürgen Fangmeier and Hinrich Stoevesandt, trans. and edited by Geoffrey W. Bromiley (Grand Rapids, MI: Wm. B. Eerdmans Publishing Company, 1981), pp. 174-176.

17. Ibid., p. 348.

18. *The Spirit of Life,* pp. 17-31.

19. Ibid., p. 17.

20. Ibid., p. 18.

21. Kant, *Prolegomena to Any Future Metaphysics* (New York: The Bobbs-Merrill Co., Inc., 1950), pp. 66-69.

22. *Spirit of Life,* p. 30.

23. Ibid., pp. 33-34.

24. Ibid., pp. 31ff.

25. Ibid., pp. 58-77.

26. *The Trinity and Kingdom,* trans. Margaret Kohl (New York: Harper & Row, Publishers, 1981), p. 140.

27. *History and the Triune God,* p. 38.

28. *Theology and the Kingdom of God,* p. 176.

29. *The Spirit of Life,* p. 59; Barth, *Church Dogmatics,* I, 1, p. 425.

30. *History and the Triune God,* pp. 84-85.

31. *Theology and the Kingdom,* p. 178.

32. Pannenberg, *Systematic Theology,* I, 324-325; Moltmann, *History and the Triune God,* p. xix.

33. Von Rad, *The Problem of the Hexateuch,* trans. E. Dickens (New York: McGraw Hill, 1966), 153.

34. Vitezslav Gardavsky, *God is Not Yet Dead,* trans. Vivenne Menkes (Baltimore: Penguin, 1973), p. 28.

35. Barth, *Church Dogmatics,* I, 1, 408-409; Moltmann, *The Trinity And the Kingdom,* p. 171.

36. Cf. Frederick Copleston, *A History of Philosophy* (New York: Doubleday, 1962), Volume 2, Part I, p. 118 for a discussion of this concept and its subsequent impact on Western thought through Aquinas.

37. *Trinity And The Kingdom,* p. 171.

38. Ibid.

39. Barth, *Church Dogmatics,* I, 1, 419; Moltmann, *Trinity And the Kingdom,* p. 171.

40. Barth, *Church Dogmatics,* I, 1, 408.

41. *Trinity And The Kingdom.* p. 168-169.

42. Ibid., pp.172-173.

43. Tillich, *A History of Christian Thought,* p. 321.

44. *Church Dogmatics,* I, 1, 407.

45. Ibid., p. 410.

46. Ibid.

47. Ibid., p. 412.

48. Ibid., p. 411.

49. Ibid., p. 420.

50. *Trinity And The Kingdom,* p.141, 145-146.

51. David P. Scaer, "Theology of Hope," *Tensions in Contemporary Theology,* p. 218.

52. *Trinity And The Kingdom,* p. 92.

53. *Systematic Theology,* 1:336n.

54. *Trinity And The Kingdom,* pp. 19,129-132.

55. I once mentioned to Moltmann that some of his American critics accuse him of being a humanist or possibly a pantheist to which he replied with an expression of surprise and disbelief.

56. Stanley J. Grenz and Roger E. Olson, *20th Century Theology, God and the World in a Transitional Age* (Downers Grove, Illinois: InterVarsity Press, 1992), pp. 182-183.

57. *Trinity and the Kingdom,* p. 160.

58. Ibid., p. 153.

59. Ibid.

60. *History and the Triune God,* p. 95.

61. *The Spirit of Life,* p. 111; *The Theology of Hope,* p. 16.

62. *The Way of Jesus Christ,* trans. Margaret Kohl (New York: HarperCollins, Publishers, 1990), p. 331.

63. *History and the Triune God,* p. 95.

64. Roger E. Olson, "Is Moltmann An Evangelical's Ally?" *Christianity Today* (January 11, 1993): 32.

65. *History and the Triune God,* p. xviii.

66. *God in Creation,* ed. Margaret Kohl (San Francisco: Harper and Row, 1985), p. 83ff.

67. Ibid., p. 85.

68. *The Spirit of Life,* p. 35.

69. *God in Creation,* p. 78.

70. Ibid., p. 79.

71. Ibid., p. 98.

72. Ibid., p. 78.

73. Ibid., p. 98.

74. Ibid., p. 75. Gerhard May, *Creation Ex Nihilo, The Doctrine of "Creation out of Nothing" in Early Christian Thought* (Edinburgh: T. & T. Clark, 1994), is the definitive study on the historical development of this topic. He shows there was no systematic reflection on the creation process until the second century (Ibid., pp. 1ff, 35). Much like the Trinitarian and christological doctrines which were not formulated until the 3rd and 4th centuries, so other doctrines as well, including *creatio ex nihilo,* were only developed later as Christianity was forced to defend itself against "heresies" when it became necessary to employ philosophical categories to clarify Christian belief. May shows that with Irenaeus the doctrine of *creatio ex nihilo* settled and fixed the position for subsequent orthodox thinking about creation. Irenaeus' view of creation was linked to his view of salvation history, that the purpose of creation out of nothing was the framework for the history of salvation (ibid., p. 176).

75. Ibid., p. 75.

76. *Church Dogmatics,* I, 1, 347.

77. David P. Scaer, Theology of Hope," *Tensions in Contemporary Theology,* ed. Stanley N. Gundry and Alan F. Johnson (Grand Rapids, Michigan: Baker Book House, 1976), 218.

78. Charles Hartshorne, *A Natural Theology for our Time* (La Salle, Illinois: Open Court, 1967), pp. 80ff; *Divine Relativity* (New Haven: Connecticut: Yale University Press, 1948), p. 135.

79. Hartshorne, *A Natural Theology for our Time,* p. 82.

80. Whitehead, *Religion in the Making* (New York: The Macmillan Co., 1927), pp. 98, 99.

81. David R. Griffin, *A Process Christology* (Philadelphia: Westminster Press, 1973), p. 10.

82. Cf. A. N. Whitehead, *Process and Reality* (New York: The Free Press, 1929).

83. Ibid., p. v.

84. Ibid., p. 404.

85. Whitehead, *Religion in the Making,* pp. 98, 99.

86. Whitehead writes: "The consciousness which is individual in us, is universal in him." *Religion in the Making,* p. 158.

87. Whitehead, *Process and Reality,* p. 73; cf. Pannenberg, *Metaphysics and the Idea of God* (Grand Rapids, Michigan: Wm. B. Eerdmans, 1988), p. 114.

88. Cf. John Polkinghorne, *Faith, Science, and Understanding* (New Haven, Connecticut: Yale Nota Bene, 2001), p. 151. Pannenberg has also shown that Whitehead's philosophy of atomism failed to address the philosophical problem of the one and the many and that his concept of discrete events of reality is unintelligible, succumbing to his own criticism of others who commit "the fallacy of misplaced concreteness." *God and the Idea of Metaphysics*, pp. 117-129.

89. Pannenberg, *Systematic Theology*, 1:

90. *Process and Reality*, p. 403; cf. Pannenberg, *ST,* 1:367.

91. Ibid., p. 404. *Religion in the Making*, pp. 72-73. Cobb, *God and the World* (Philadelphia: Westminster Press, 1969), pp. 90f.

92. David R. Griffin, *A Process Christology* (Philadelphia: Westminster Press, 1973), pp. 15, 17, 24156.

93. John B. Cobb, Jr., *God and the World*, pp. 101, 112.

94. Ibid., pp. 99f.

95. Polkinghorne, *Faith, Science, and Understanding*, p. 152.

96. Griffin, *A Process Christology*, p. 157.

97. Olson, *20th Century Theology*, pp. 183, 186.

98. *Trinity And The Kingdom*, p. 92.

99. Ibid., p. 150.

100. The mistake of American process theology is that it does not make the theological distinction between the eternal procession of God as Father, Son, and Holy Spirit and the temporal, natural processes of nature and finite time.

101. *Trinity And The Kingdom*, p. 204.

102. *The Way of Jesus Christ*, p. 319.

103. Eberhard Jungel, *The Doctrine of the Trinity.*, translated by Horton Harris. (Grand Rapids: Wm. B. Eerdmans, 1976), p. 1.

104. *The Way of Jesus Christ*, p. 318.

105. Ibid., p. 318.

106. Ibid., p. 317.

107. Ibid., p. 312.

108. Ibid., p. 316.

109. Ibid., p. 331.

110. Thomas J. J. Altizer and William Hamilton, *The Death of God* (New York: The Bobbs-Merrill Co., Inc., 1966), p. xii.

11

A Hermeneutical Validation of Faith

Paul Ricoeur raises the question of the criterion of truth when he asks: "Do we have the right to invest a moment of history with an absolute character?"[1] Ricoeur maintains that the answer to this question could not be provided by modern epistemology because it pre-established rational criteria that precluded the possibility of hearing the summons of the biblical text to trust in Jesus as the Christ.

We noted in Chapter 7 that Ricoeur turned away from modern epistemology to hermeneutical philosophy as the method of understanding God, the self, and the world. He in particular highlighted a "philosophy of testimony" to show that one today can believe in Jesus as the Christ, not in the pre-critical sense that simply fused the Jesus of history with the Christ of faith, but in a post-critical sense that focuses on the act of understanding historically why this confession came to be affirmed in the text.[2] Ricoeur used post-critical categories of hermeneutical theory to show that the modernist epistemology of objectivism needed to be replaced with a philosophy of testimony and that the modernist notion of verification and universal rational criteria needed to be replaced with the categories of validation and existential significance.

This final chapter will examine whether or not faith can responsibly confess that Jesus is the Christ. A key consideration will be the distinction between epistemology as criteria and hermeneutics as interpretation. As opposed to modernist notions of verification and objectivism, it will be argued that this claim can be validated through the divine summons issued through the proclamation of the gospel and through a historical understanding of the text as testimony of what was seen and heard.

Canon and Criterion

The distinction between *epistemology* as *criteria* and *hermeneutics* as *interpretation* of the biblical text has been developed in a similar way in the writings of William Abraham, the Albert C. Outler Professor of Historical Theology at the Perkins School of Theology. His book, *Canon and Criterion*, argues that there is a difference between canon and criterion. The word canon means the list of books, which were included in the Scriptures because they were recognized by the Church.[3] Canon also came to be used in reference to entities such as the liturgy, creeds, and sacraments. The Christian community has set apart these canons as means of grace and salvation.

Abraham says that the idea of criterion implies epistemology and critical norms of justifying beliefs. He shows that canon and criteria have been regularly confused. He argues that it is a mistake to think of scripture, tradition, experience, creeds, etc., as criteria of truth. For example, the scriptures are authoritative, not because they function as rational criteria of truth, but because they have a soteriological intent in "mediating divine revelation and in bringing salvation."[4] The Scriptures provide knowledge of God's revelation, but the "epistemizing of the concept of Scripture" entails the idea that Scripture intends to be like a textbook or handbook on truth. Abraham recognizes that "the Scriptures and the Creed were indeed a kind of standard or norm" because their purpose was to establish "a standard of teaching and instruction for the Church in its worship, its catechesis, and the direction of its spiritual life."[5] One might refer to this standard as a soteriological norm, not an epistemological norm. Abraham writes: "The Scriptures and other canonical material can contain genuine knowledge of and about God without also containing a theory of religious knowledge. It is simply mistaken to confuse knowledge of God with a theory of knowledge of God."[6] It should be noted that Abraham is not arguing against the possibility of developing norms and criteria, which may serve as a basis for developing knowledge of God independent of the canonical tradition of the church.[7] He is only saying that it is important to see that this is not the function of the Scriptures and other canons of beliefs that have been developed in the life of the church.

He argues that the canonical heritage of the Church was illegitimately shifted into the arena of becoming a criterion of truth, resulting in it being held in "epistemological captivity"[8] with disastrous consequences. He wants to free up the canonical heritage of the Church to become once again the means of grace and salvation that it intends to be. This liberation would mean the canonical tradition would no longer be compromised by putting it into competition with rational criteria. This epistemological captivity particularly created a break in the heritage of the

Church in the modern period as criteria competed for primacy over canon. The result has been that the contemporary church has forgotten who it is as the story-line has shifted. Abraham examines "the great experiments in modern theology represented by John Locke, Friedrich Schleiermacher, John Henry Newman, the great Princeton theologians of the nineteenth and early twentieth centuries, Karl Barth, Schubert Ogden, and representative feminist theologians." He demonstrates that each of these theologies "denote one failed attempt after another to rescue Christian theology from the epistemological captivity to which it has been subject since it lost its moorings in the canonical heritage of the early Church."[9]

As an example of this confusion, Abraham shows that while the early English reformers valued the canonical tradition and appealed to the Scriptures, tradition, and reason as means of grace and salvation, the later English reformers as Richard Hooker (1554-1600) turned these into criteria and warrant for making theological claims.[10] This shift away from treating the Scriptures, tradition, and reason as soteriological norms to thinking of them in terms of epistemological criteria was occasioned by the need to combat the foundationalist ideas of the Puritan reformers. These reformers had originally fled to the European Continent because of the persecutions of "Bloody Mary," and they studied in reformation centers like Geneva where their ideas of reformation were radicalized. They returned to England following the death of "Bloody Mary," and they became known as Puritans because they wanted to further purify the Church of the residual influences of Roman Catholicism. These 16th and 17th century reformers had come to see the Bible in terms of the criterion of the *sola scriptura* principle, which they had learned from their Continental counterparts. The Continental reformers had thus turned the Bible into a foundationalist, intellectualist criterion of truth instead of it being primarily a witness to God's saving activity in history.

These returning radical reformers rejected the *Book of Common Prayer* with its liturgy and episcopacy, claiming that the early English reformers had not gone far enough in reforming the church because practices and beliefs not explicitly allowed in Scripture had been retained. In opposing the Puritan reformers, Hooker defended the *Book of Common Prayer* and the Edwardian homilies (which summarized the essential beliefs of the English reformation) by using scripture, tradition, and reason as epistemological criteria.[11]

As an Anglican priest, John Wesley used scripture, tradition, reason, along with experience, but Abraham shows that he used these as means of grace for furthering the cause of the Methodist revival, but Wesley was not interested in developing epistemological criteria.[12] Interestingly enough, Wesley criticized the Continental reformers along the same line that Abraham has done. Wesley noted that the reformers brought about a reformation in doctrine, not a revival of vital piety and holiness.[13] Their interest was thus in objective criteria of truth rather than in holiness. Wesley followed the lead of the early Greek Fathers in emphasizing sanctification because he was primarily interested in spiritual formation. He was not interesting primarily in the justification of belief, nor in setting up the Scriptures as a criteria of truth. He accepted the doctrinal heritage of the Church, believing them to be consistent with the Bible and relevant as means of saving grace.

Scripture, reason, tradition, and experience were turned into formal criteria for establishing doctrines when the United Methodist Church was organized as a denomination out of the merger of the Methodist Church and the Evangelical United Brethren Church in 1968. Under the guidance of Albert C. Outler, *The Book of Discipline* highlighted these four criteria for the basis of theological pluralism.[14]

Abraham believes that we have reached the end of this epistemizing process.[15] This corresponds with Paul Ricoeur's view that we have reached the end of traditional concerns with epistemology. That is why Ricoeur proposes that hermeneutics replace epistemology. Although Ricoeur focuses on the interpretation of the biblical text as opposed to epistemological criteria, he believes that the critical epistemological issues have prepared the believer to have a greater appreciation for interpreting the Bible. It may be that the epistemizing of the canonical tradition will have had a beneficial effect in the long run, if we move beyond Enlightenment rationalism without abandoning its gains in making us critically aware of what is involved in "believing again" and embracing a "second naïveté." We are not expected to believe things that are logical nonsense and irresponsible assertions. But "to believe again" beyond the "desert of criticism" means that epistemological criteria will not be allowed to prejudge the canonical tradition of the church. Paul was very much aware of the epistemological criteria of the Jews and the Greeks who prejudged the "scandal of particularity" as "offensive" and "foolish," but Paul asserted the priority of preaching as testimony to the saving grace of God (1 Cor. 1:23).

Scripture as Canon or Criterion?

The Scriptures are the primary source of the canonical tradition of the church because they contain the original witnesses in the history of salvation. More specifically, F. F. Bruce (1910-1990), the late Rylands Professor of Biblical Criticism and Exegesis at the University of Manchester, England, has shown that the criteria of canonicity for the New Testament included: (1) apostolic authority even though a book was not necessarily written by one of the apostles, (2) antiquity; (3) orthodoxy, (4) catholicity, (5) traditional use, and (6) inspiration.[16]

Abraham has noted that the inspiration of Scripture was reinterpreted as an objective criterion of truth in the period following the Early Church Fathers. Abraham affirms that the Scriptures were "inspired of God" and "uniquely related to God."[17] In his earlier work on *The Divine Inspiration of the Holy Scriptures,* he shows that inspiration entails the idea of "unity within the biblical literature" as well as "a reliable and trustworthy account of God's revelatory and saving act."[18] Abraham noted that one should expect God to be interested in preserving a faithful record of his revelatory acts in history.[19]

This view corresponds with the use of inspiration in the early Church period. Irenaeus speaks of the Scriptures are "perfect" because they are "inspired."[20] Inspiration is not a *rational criterion* of truth, but a *recognition* that the Scriptures faithfully preserved the history of salvation. His dispute with the heresies of Valentinus and Marcion was that they misinterpreted the Scriptures because they embraced the criteria of Gnosticism and did not acknowledge the canonical heritage of the Church.

The apostles and the primitive Christian community initially had only the Old Testament as its Scripture, while the teachings and life of Jesus circulated as standardized oral traditions. These oral traditions were eventually put into writing and called the four gospels. The writings of the apostles also began to circulate, and they immediately assumed the status of Scripture, as 2 Peter 3:16 confirms by linking Paul's writings with "other scriptures."

This emphasis on the *written* story of Jesus in the four gospels as inspired Scripture is assumed in the writings of the apostolic fathers, that is, those in the 2nd century who were close in time to the apostles. The most significant of these early fathers was Irenaeus (120-202), who was born approximately fifteen years after the death of John the Apostle. He was a student of Polycarp, a close friend of John. Polycarp and those influenced so heavily by John were "distinguished by a firm grasp of Scripture," as Otto W. Heick has pointed out.[21]

Irenaeus was well informed of the philosophies of his day, but his interest was not in formal theories of truth but in soteriology, and his focus on the inspiration of the Scriptures was to show that we have a reliable record of God's saving activity in history.[22] Thus when Irenaeus talks about the apostolic tradition, he is not merely speaking about oral traditions; rather, he means the written tradition.[23] Irenaeus writes: "We have learned from none others the plan of our salvation, than from those through whom the Gospel has come down to us, which they did at one time proclaim in public [oral tradition], and, at a later period, by the will of God, handed down us in the Scriptures, to be the ground and pillar of our faith."[24] Here Irenaeus shows his interest in the apostolic tradition as Scripture because it contains "the plan of salvation," and it is the Scriptures which are "the ground and pillar of our faith." Significantly, Irenaeus quotes from every New Testament book that was later canonized, with the exception of Philemon, and none from the Old Testament apocrypha.[25] Irenaeus also considers these writings as Scripture "equal in significance to the Old Testament," as Bruce Metzger points out.[26]

Irenaeus defends the apostolic teaching on the grounds that it is "the canon of truth" because it is inspired of God. He writes: "The Scriptures are indeed perfect, since they were spoken by the Word of God and His Spirit."[27] He refers to the four gospels as "true and reliable."[28] He writes: "But as we follow for our teacher the one and only true God, and possess His words as the rule [canon, *kanon*] of truth (*aletheia*), we do all speak alike with regard to the same things, knowing but one God, the Creator of this universe, who sent the prophets, who led forth the people from the land of Egypt, who in these last times manifested His own Son, that He might put the unbelievers to confusion, and search out the fruit of righteousness."[29] Here it is again seen that Irenaeus' interest in the Scriptures is salvific, for their purpose is to encourage unbelievers to "search out the fruit of righteousness."

This salvific function of Scripture is often repeated throughout his writings, showing that the Scriptures are a rule of faith because they are the means of grace. Irenaeus writes:

> The disciple [John] of the Lord therefore desiring to put an end to all such doctrines, and to establish the rule [*kanon*] of truth (*aletheia*) in the Church, that there is one Almighty God, who made all things by His Word, both visible and invisible; showing at the same time, that by the Word, through whom God made the creation, He also bestowed salvation on the men included in the creation; thus commenced His teaching in the Gospel: "In the Beginning was the Word, and the Word was with God, and the Word was God."[30]

Irenaeus shows that revelation is found in the testimony of Scripture: "Having therefore the truth itself as our rule (canon), and the [written] testimony concerning God set clearly before us, we ought not, by running after numerous and diverse answers to questions, to cast away the firm and true knowledge of God."[31]

Irenaeus everywhere considers the writings of the apostles as Scripture, and he makes no distinction between the Old Testament as inspired and the New Testament as inspired. Their inspiration is one and the same.[32] Metzger writes:

> According to Irenaeus, the same gospel which was first orally preached and transmitted was subsequently committed to writing and faithfully preserved in all the apostolic churches through the regular succession of bishops and elders. Over against the ever-shifting and contradictory opinions of the heretics, Irenaeus places the unchanging faith of the catholic Church based on Scripture and tradition, and compacted together by the episcopal organization (*Adv. Haer.* III.i.1).[33]

For these apostolic fathers, belief in the canon of Scripture as the rule of faith and practice is not a criterion that competes in the arena of epistemologies; it is a recognition that the Scriptures contain the history of salvation, which is the means of God's saving grace.

A common notion in the history of theology is the idea of a "canon within the canon." For example, the doctrine of justification by faith served as a "canon within the canon" for Martin Luther. Irenaeus assumed the canon within the canon was "the economy of salvation," including the recapitulation of the history of salvation in Jesus of Nazareth, which ties together all the various parts of Scripture and brings them to their fulfillment. A contemporary restatement of Irenaeus' theology is found in Oscar Cullmann who has argued that the idea of salvation history serves as a canon within the canon. He writes: "Through the *collection together* of the various books of the Bible, the whole history of salvation must be taken into account in understanding any one of the books of the Bible."[34] F. F. Bruce remarks that Cullmann "presents a very attractive account of the coherence of the canon of scripture. This coherence is specially to be found in the witness borne to the author of salvation, the way of salvation, and the heirs of salvation. Even those parts of the Bible in which salvation is not so central as it is in others make their contribution to the context in which the history of salvation can be traced"[35]

The authority of the Scriptures cannot be compromised without the loss of the history of salvation, but this authority is not something that we ascribe to it on the basis of epistemological criteria. This authority is not something that was once ascribed to it by any church council, although the Third Council of Carthage in 397 formally acknowledged the sixty six books of the Bible as canonical because they were already universally received and recognized as apostolic.[36]

One reason why it took so long to recognize the final list of sixty-six books was related to the problem of communication within the larger Christian community, which was spread out across the East and West from Constantinople to Rome. Although only a few books were contested for a period of time, there was a need to verify that these books were apostolic. F. F. Bruce explains this process of individual books gaining universal acceptance: "Each individual document that was ultimately acknowledged as canonical started off with local acceptance . . . . But their attainment of canonical status was the result of their gaining more widespread recognition than they initially enjoyed."[37]

Significantly, after the Council of Nicea in 325 when Christian leaders from all parts of the church from East and West were brought together, the controversy over which books were truly apostolic ceased. Undoubtedly these leaders compared manuscripts and shared pertinent information about their authenticity as they assembled together for a period of three months in intimate discussion about the core meaning of the apostolic tradition. The fact that these representatives of the universal church produced the Nicene Creed, comparing manuscripts and debating all aspects of the apostolic tradition, indirectly contributed to the unanimity of opinion about the canon in the immediate years following.[38]

Although there is no document that indicates any discussion took place regarding a list of books which should be included in a formal canon, the primacy of Scripture was affirmed at the Council of Nicea as the foundation of doctrine and life.[39] This was the most significant assembly of Christians leaders ever to meet. If an agreement on *the nature of Jesus' relationship to God* was at stake at this council, an agreement on *the nature of the Scriptures* was not. They were simply accepted as the given of faith. To be sure, there were a few disputed books in some sections of the church at the time of this great assembly. These contested books were defined as those books which were not received by everyone, though they were received by the majority. These books included 2 Peter, James, Jude, and the last two letters of John.[40] But there was no disagreement about the authority and primacy of the Scriptures. An elevated throne was set up in the assembly on that great occasion and on that throne was placed a copy of the Gospels to signify that the Scriptures were the supreme rule of faith to answer all controversies.[41] Constantine, in his address, reminded the delegates that they possessed "the doctrine of the Holy Spirit written." He said: "The books of the evangelists and of the apostles, and the oracles of the prophets teach us clearly and certainly what we must believe, concerning the things of God, so that all differences must be determined by reference to the divinely inspired words."[42] The primacy of the Scriptures as the foundation of the Creeds was thus recognized from the very beginning of the Council of Nicea, and it affirmed that doctrine must be faithful to the Scriptures.

After the Council of Nicea concluded, Louis Gaussen has shown that "there was an immediate and marked change in the dispositions of those who had before manifested some uncertainty about this or that of the contested books. Hesitations immediately began to disappear, until, at last, the whole body of the Christian church reached . . . unanimity."[43] This unanimity was later expressed by Athanasius. He was the prominent leader at Nicea who assumed the leadership role in the church in the subsequent years. In his "Easter Letter" in 367 which was addressed to the universal church, he apparently was the first person to use the word canon directly in reference to a list of books, and his list corresponded to our present canon.[44]

Athanasius explained the need to identify the specific list of Christian books in this way, self-consciously adapting the words of Luke's prologue to Theophilus:

'Forasmuch as many have taken in hand to set forth in order' a list of the apocryphal books, and to mingle them with the inspired Scriptures which is 'most surely believed among us, even as they delivered them unto' the fathers, 'which from the beginning were eye-witnesses, and ministers of the word; it seemed good to me also,' urged by true brethren, to set in order the books held as canonical, and transmitted and believed to be divine books, that whosoever may have been led into error may condemn his false guides.[45]

Then follows a list of books in his letter, which correspond with our present canon. He allows that some other books may be read with profit, such as the Old Testament apocrypha, although they are not inspired. He writes:

But, for greater exactness, we must necessarily add that besides these books there are others which are not canonized, it is true, but which have been marked by the fathers to be read by those who, recently come among us, are desirous of being instructed in the word of piety: the Wisdom of Solomon and the Wisdom of Sirach, and Esther [that is, the seven apocryphal chapters added to the book of Esther after chapter 10], Judith, and Tobit, the Institutions called Apostolical, and the Shepherd.[46]

Athanasius explains why it was important to identify the proper list of Christian books: "These [books] are fountains of salvation, that he who thirsts may be satisfied with the living words they contain. In these alone the teaching of godliness is proclaimed. Let no one add to these; let nothing be taken away from them."[47] Here it is clear that Athanasius does not appeal to Scripture as an epistemological criterion, but as the means of saving grace. The first council to accept the canon as defined by Athanasius was the Council of Hippo Regius in North Africa in 393. Its documents are lost, but its decisions were read at the Council of Carthage in 397 A. D. and approved. The books of the Bible were considered authoritative, not because Athanasius or a council defined the canon. Rather, as Athanasius affirms, they teach godliness and are "the fountains of salvation."

In addition to the canon of Scripture, the Church also canonized credal statements, such as the Nicene Creed and the Chalcedonian Creed, to make the message of the New Testament, dominated by a Jewish worldview, intelligible to largely Greek-speaking believers. Other traditions were also canonized, such as Church liturgy. Significantly, aspects of this liturgical canon have only been recently rediscovered and reinstated in most Protestant churches.[48] However, as Abraham has noted, "the canonical tradition as a whole is itself relatively stable." He further observed that "new canonical tradition can only be added and absorbed if it is perceived to be substantially in keeping with the core canonical material."[49]

One question that is often asked is whether or not other literature might just as well be considered inspired as the canon of scripture.[50] F. F. Bruce answers: "This betrays a failure to appreciate what the canon actually is. It is not an anthology of inspired or inspiring literature." Rather its "chief concern is to get as close as possible to the source of the Christian faith." Bruce notes that the canon of scripture is "the foundation documents of Christianity, the charter of the church, title-deeds of faith. For no other literature can such a claim be made." The scriptures are uniquely inspired because here unlike any other canonical document "the voice of the Spirit of God continues to be heard."[51]

The Impasse between Canon and Criterion

Although this explanation of the development of Scripture as canonical is too simplified, it points out that the canon of Scripture has primarily a soteriological intent, as Abraham has argued. If it is a rule of faith, it is so because it is a means of grace, not because it serves as an epistemological criterion of truth as such. One highly informed resource which has been used for discussing this issue has been Louis Gaussen (1790-1863), a French Reformed professor at the theological college in Geneva in the 19th century. His research is amazingly thorough. Metzger calls him "a vigorous proponent of Reformed orthodoxy."[52] One of his concerns was to develop the authority of Scripture as a criterion of truth in opposition to the authority of the Roman Catholic Church. However, his attempt to provide a foundationalist basis for doing theology confused the soteriological intent of the Scripture with rational apologetics. As previously noted, Irenaeus showed that the canon of truth is the Scriptures because they are the testimony of God offering salvation in Jesus Christ. In spite of Gaussen's insightful and scholarly discussion of the canon of Scripture, his interest was primarily in a criterion of truth, not soteriology and Pneumatology

As Abraham has noted, it is naturally easy to slide from canon to criterion.[53] I may not be able to follow consistently his distinction between canon and criterion, but I think his point is well made and this distinction has great merit. The intent of *Canon and Criterion in Christian Theology* was not to discuss the doctrine of inspiration, previously offered in his *The Divine Inspiration of Holy Scripture*, nor to grade the varying degrees of importance of the various canons of the Church. His one overriding thesis was that canon and criteria need to be distinguished if the integrity of the Christian tradition was to be maintained. He has shown that the failure to preserve this distinction has led to disastrous consequences for the church theologically and pastorally.

William Abraham or Kierkegaard?

The impasse between the canonical tradition and epistemological criteria was recognized by Lessing in the 18th century when he complained of the "ugly, broad ditch" between faith and history because his epistemological criteria could not be reconciled with belief in Jesus' resurrection. Hence he saw the history of salvation as the progressive education of humanity becoming aware of God instead of the story of God becoming incarnate in humanity.[58] In accordance with his criteria, he redefined faith as rational insight that the idea of God is the larger whole of reality, giving meaning to the world, rather than faith as trusting in the redeeming history of Jesus Christ. This sort of theological deformation of the canonical tradition is the obvious consequence of subordinating Scripture to epistemological criteria. The "wide ugly ditch" was not really between faith and history, but between Lessing's rational criteria and the canonical tradition of the Church.

The philosophy of Kierkegaard in the early 19th century was in part a response to Lessing's "ugly, broad ditch."[59] *A Concluding Unscientific Postscript* was an extended footnote to his earlier work, *Philosophical Fragments*, which addressed the specific issue—can one's eternal happiness have a historical point of departure? In both works, Kierkegaard argued that it was impossible to do theology from the standpoint of any kind of rational criteria, including Holy Scripture, the Church, and the "proof of the centuries" as objective criteria.[60] Although he affirmed the real history of salvation, the full inspiration of the Scriptures, and the Church as the Body of Christ, he derided the idea that these could serve methodologically as criteria. He writes: "Anyone who posits inspiration, as a believer does, must consistently consider every critical deliberation, whether for or against, as a misdirection, a temptation for the spirit."[61] He observed that with the idea of inspiration under attack in the Enlightenment period the "Danish idea" was a "letting go of the Bible and laying hold of the Church"[62] as a criterion of truthfulness, but he also showed that the idea of the Church could not "serve as the certain objective recourse."[63] The only basis for doing theology was the acceptance of God's revelation that comes in the moment of faith. This is not a blind faith, but a faith that has its sole condition in the initiative of God who creates the condition of faith through the testimony of the Scriptures.

Kierkegaard's critique of epistemology intended to show its inadequacy. His method showed there is no human method for verifying the existence of God or divine revelation. He did not explicitly appeal to the canonical heritage of the Church as a basis for faith, although his separation of theology and philosophy bears some points of similarity to Abraham's distinction between canon and criteria. He appealed to God alone as the basis of faith. If a believer accepts the Bible as inspired, it is because God alone is the source of this belief. On the other hand, I suspect that Kierkegaard would have been critical of making the canonical heritage a basis for faith because it too could be seen as a criterion and as attempting to over-compensate for the lack of objective criteria. It can also be argued that Kierkegaard's emphasis on faith became a substitute criterion for reason and hence an over-compensation for the lack of objective criteria.

Clearly Kierkegaard's reaction to the objectivism of modern theology was overdone because the subjective and objective distinctions cannot be bifurcated without distorting the doctrinal heritage of the Church. It should be said Kierkegaard himself was aware that this methodology was extreme because he called his philosophy a "pinch of spice,"[60] something which does not make for a very good diet. He also said that "an existentialist system" was a contradiction in terms[61] and that the idea of logical contradictions was unacceptable, although some of his critics have misunderstood him at this point.[62] Kierkegaard had a noble cause with a good point—the faith of the Church should not enter into competition with rational criteria, though it should not disclaim reason, a point which Kierkegaard made clear through his paradoxical use of reason to show the inadequacy of reason.

Abraham's distinction between canon and criterion is a helpful way for understanding how the church has been theologically sidetracked in the past by allowing rational criteria to replace the Church's canonical heritage. The purpose of the Scriptures, for example, is to be a witness to faith in Jesus-Christ and not to enter the arena of philosophical epistemology. Yet a canonical approach to theologizing cannot practically dispense with criteria because a canonical approach is actually using the criterion of the canon to establish its own autonomy. That is why I prefer to speak of the hermeneutical validation of faith, which includes both the act of interpreting the witness of the Scriptures for today and a critical awareness of the historical process through which Jesus became the Christ. The distinction between validating and verifying needs to be carefully made. Abraham allows for the process of validation by showing that the concept of the canonical tradition implicitly raises questions of criteria that cannot be ignored.[62] Interestingly enough, Abraham finishes off his critique of criteria much like Kierkegaard's critique of reason, suggesting that being "epistemologically agnostic" might be the most responsible attitude about criteria serving the needs of theology.[64] But if Abraham is agnostic about criteria, he is confident about the oversight of the Holy Spirit to lead the people of God into the future in continuity with, and through the testimony of, its canonical heritage.

This brings us back to the central confession of Jesus-Christ as the risen Lord. Faith entails the acceptance of the testimony of the apostles, but this testimony is not demonstrable according to the rational criteria of foundationalist and objectivist thinking, although it is validated as a reasonable faith because men and women saw the risen Lord and witnessed the empty tomb. Faith is also validated and reasonable because the resurrection of Jesus was given an *interpretation* by the apostles; it meant he was Jesus-Christ, Jesus the Son of God (Roman 1:4). The distinction between the *event* of Jesus of Nazareth and his *meaning* as the Christ requires a type of reader-response interpretation today. To call this a "reader-response" interpretation is to say that the canonical heritage must be incorporated with fresh insight and meaning for today. However, unless this interpretation is consistent with its canonical heritage, the Church no longer exists because a denial of Jesus' resurrection from the dead constitutes an absolute break with the past. And without the resurrection there is no Pentecost and no Holy Spirit. This means there would be no divine Trinity, and without the life of the Trinity there would be no community of the Church and no participation in the divine life. There would no creeds, no liturgy, or other canonical means of grace. This is why, in the final analysis, a distinction between canon and criterion is vital to the life of the Church. The canonical traditions testify to the saving history of God ultimately in Jesus Christ, whereas criteria is a human attempt to ascertain what is true and what is false. The two methods cannot be divorced but they should be carefully distinguished.

Heinz W. Cassirer—A Personal Testimony

The Christian witness of Heinz W. Cassirer illustrates the transforming power of the apostolic testimony and how he overcame the impasse between the canonical heritage of the Church and epistemological criteria. His father was the eminent Kantian scholar, Ernst Cassirer. Heinz Cassirer went to Britain in 1934 and taught at Glasgow University. At the age of thirty, even before going to Britain, he was recognized as an authority on Aristotle. When he became a permanent faculty member at Glasgow University in 1946, he became an authority on Kant's philosophy in his own right. At the age of 50, he says he had "no knowledge whatever of religious problems nor any interest in them. My sole preoccupation was with philosophical questions."[65] For unknown reasons, Cassirer began to read the writings of the Apostle Paul when he was fifty years old. He was immediately impressed with Paul's moral insights and understanding of the relationship between law and grace. Cassirer admits that he had grown dissatisfied with the pretensions of reason, which he thinks typically characterize the writings of philosophers. He writes:

While philosophy is supposed on all sides to be a purely rational activity, relying upon the intellect and the intellect alone, without ever allowing itself to be swayed by any personal or emotional bias, there remains this disturbing fact: Utterly different conclusions are reached by various thinkers, each philosopher arguing with great vehemence and ingenuity in favor of the position he wishes to uphold, while yet the possibility is wholly excluded that agreement might be reached between him and his opponents. This, of course, raises the crucial problem whether any such thing as a reliable criterion of truth is available within the compass of philosophical thinking at all. So far as I could see, no satisfactory solution had ever been offered.[66]

In the light of the impasse that reason was locked into, he wondered whether the intellect was a suitable instrument for dealing with the fundamental problems of existence."[67]

At the age of 56, Cassirer was baptized and wrote a treatise on Paul, Kant and the Hebrew prophets, which he called *Grace and Law.* At the conclusion of his book, he explains his reasons for coming to accept the Christian faith. It was because of the moral, life-changing message of the grace of God of which Paul was a powerful witness. "As for myself, I may explain here that, if I have come to embrace the Christian religion, this has been almost wholly due to the impression made upon me not only by St. Paul's teaching but by his personality as it reveals itself in his epistles."[68] He goes on to say that "there is only one way a human being can become his or her true self, and that is by making a complete surrender to Christ."[69]

Is it really possible to conclusively prove that the Christian faith is true? Cassirer says:

I am, of course, fully aware that nothing that has been said may serve to establish either that Jesus Christ is the Son of God or that he appeared to St. Paul on the road to Damascus. Yet, as I have remarked before, I myself have no doubt that St. Paul is right on both counts. This is largely because the impression I have formed of St. Paul is that he was the very last man to fall victim to self-deception and because, in consequence, I find it impossible to entertain seriously the idea that his spiritual pilgrimage had a hallucinatory experience for its starting point.[70]

Heinz Cassirer's testimony smacks of sheer subjectivity for modernists. But he gave the biblical documents a serious study, and the overall body of evidence validated for him the moral, spiritual, and intellectual truth that faith in Christ offers salvation and hope. Our choices about the meaning of life are never purely rationalistic and intellectualistic, as he points out and as post-critical hermeneutical theory shows as well. The personal and religious issues of life are not finally resolved by rational criteria, as important as reason is. The decisive factor in the life of faith is attending to the canonical heritage of the church and hearing the divine summons through the proclamation of Jesus-Christ. Cassirer was summoned to the reality of faith by listening to the testimony of Paul. He did not look for rational verification, but found there was sufficient and compelling evidence to believe. In setting aside the modernist pretensions of reason, he heard the word of God that came through the testimony of Paul. Perhaps this is what Paul meant when he said: "It pleased God through the folly of what we preach to save those who believe" (1 Cor. 1:21).

Notes

1. Ricoeur, *Essays in Biblical Interpretation,* p. 142.

2. Ibid., p. 143.

3. Cf. F. F. Bruce, *The Canon of Scripture* (Downers Grove, Illinois: InterVarsity Press, 1988), pp. 18, 150, 179.

4. William J. Abraham, *Canon and Criterion in Christian Theology,* p. 202.

5. Ibid., p. 141.

6. Ibid., p. 48.

7. Ibid., p. 478f.

8. Ibid., p. 21.

9. Ibid.

10. Ibid., p. 194

11. Ibid., pp. 194ff.

12. Ibid., p. 240. Abraham also believes the Anglican distinction among scripture, tradition, and reason are "a most valuable pedagogical device in theology (ibid., p. 212).

13. Wesley, *Sermons,* ed. Albert C. Outler, 2:465, "The Mystery of Iniquity."

14. *Canon and Criterion in Christian Theology.,* p. 188.

15. Ibid., p. 21.

16. Bruce, *Canon of Scripture in Christian Theology,* pp. 255-269.

17. *Canon and Criterion in Christian Theology,* p. 42. A helpful book for students is F. F. Bruce, *The New Testament Documents: Are They Reliable?* (Grand Rapids: Wm. B. Eerdmans, 1959) which is now online at http://www.worldinvisible.com/library/ffbruce/ntdocrli/ntdocont.htm (23 April 2004).

18. William J. Abraham, *The Divine Inspiration of Holy Scripture* (New York: Oxford University Press, 1981), p. 68.

19. Ibid.

20. *Against Heresies,* ii. 28.2. Cf. *The Apostolic Fathers,* 1:399.

21. Otto W. Heick, *A History of Christian Thought* (Philadelphia: Fortress

Press, 1965), 1:107.

22. Heick, *A History of Christian Thought*, 1:108.

23. Gaussen, *The Canon of Holy Scriptures* (Boston: American Tract Society, 1862; reprinted Grand Rapids, 1980), pp. 181-182

24. *Against Heresies*, iii.1. Cf. *The Apostolic Fathers with Justin Martyr and Irenaeus*, American edition, ed. A. Cleveland Coxe (Grand Rapids: Wm. B. Eerdmans, 1981, reprint), 1: 414. Cited hereafter as *The Apostolic Fathers*.

25. Bruce M. Metzger, *The Canon of the New Testament, Its Origin, Development, and Significance* (Oxford: Clarendon Press, 1997), pp. 154-155. Cf. Gaussen, *The Canon of Holy Scriptures*, pp. 179-184. Irenaeus does not have a single quotation from any of the apocryphal writings. Gaussen, *The Canon of Holy Scriptures*, p. 184. These writings were later placed in the Roman Catholic Bible. These early Fathers considered the Old Testament apocrypha as containing valuable information and wisdom, but they were not recognized as inspired until the Council of Trent in 1546. Jerome had listed sixteen of these books which he rejected as canonical, but the Council of Trent in 1546 included eleven of them as "sacred and canonical." Gaussen, p. 454.

36. Metzger, *The Canon of the New Testament*, p. 156.

27. *Against Heresies*, ii. 28.2. Cf. *The Apostolic Fathers*, 1:399.

28. *Against Heresies*, iii. 428.9.

29. *Against Heresies*, iv. 35.4. Cf. *The Apostolic Fathers* , 1:514.

30. *Against Heresies*, iii.11.1. Cf.*The Apostolic Fathers*, 1:426.

31. *Against Heresies*, ii.28.1. Cf. *The Apostolic Fathers*, 1:399

32. Metzger, pp. 154-156

33. Ibid., p. 154.

34. *Salvation in History*, pp 294, 297..

35. Bruce, *The Canon of Scripture*, p. 280

36. Ibid, p. 97. Cf. Abraham, *Canon and Criteria in Christian Theology*, pp. 31-35.

37. Bruce, *The Canon of Scripture*, p. 262.

38. Gaussen, p. 57.

39. Gaussen, p. 54.

40. Ibid., pp. 47-48; Metzger, *The Canon of the New Testament*, p. 309.

41. Gaussen, p. 54.

42. Cited by Gaussen, p. 54.

43. Gaussen, p. 56.

44. Bruce, *The Canon of Scripture*, pp. 77, 208.

45. Cited by Gaussen, p. 67.

46. Ibid..

47. Athanasius' Thirty-Ninth Festal Epistle (367 A.D.), cited in Metzger, *The Canon of the New Testament*, pp.. 312-313.

48. Cf. Laurence W. Wood, *The Meaning of Pentecost in Early Methodism, Rediscovering John Fletcher As John Wesley's Vindicator and Designated Successor* (Lanham, MD: Scarecrow Press, 2002).

49. *Canon and Criterion in Christian Theology*, p. 60.

50. Bruce, *The Canon of Scripture*, p. 282.

51. Ibid., p. 283.

52. Metzger, *The Canon of the New Testament*, p. 21.

53. *Canon and Criterion in Christian Theology*, p. 14.

54. *Lessing's Theological Writings*, translated with an introductory essay by Henry Chadwick (London: Adam and Charles Black, 1956), pp. 51-55.

55. Kierkegaard, *A Concluding Unscientific Postscript*, trans. David F. Swenson and Walter Lowrie (Princeton: Princeton University Press, 1941), pp. 59-113.

56. Ibid., pp. 23-55.

57. Ibid., p. 27.

58. Ibid., p. 36

59. Ib.d, p. 37.

60. Cf. Karl Barth, "A Thank You and a Bow: Kierkegaard's Reveille," *Christian Journal of Theology*, trans. H. Martin Rumscheidt, 11 (January, 1965): 7.

61. *A Concluding Unscientific Postscript*, p. 107.

62. Kierkegaard wrote: "Nonsense therefore he cannot believe against the understanding, for precisely the understanding will discern that it is nonsense and will prevent him from believing it." He further said faith believes "against the understanding," that is, it recognizes that the things of faith are ultimately incomprehensible, but they are not nonsense. Ibid., p. 504.

63. *Canon and Criterion in Christian Theology*, pp. 478-480.

64. Ibid., p. 480.

65. Heinz Cassirer, *Grace and Law* (Grand Rapids: Wm. B. Eerdmans Publishing Co., 1988), p.xiii.

66. Ibid., pp. xiii-xiv.

67. Ibid., p. xiv

68. Ibid., p. 167

69. Ibid.

70. Ibid., p. 168

Select Bibliography

"An Open Letter to North American Christians," *Christianity and Crisis* 36 no. 16 (October 18, 1976): 231.

Abraham, William J. *Canon and Criterion in Christian Theology.* New York: Oxford University Press, 1998.

———. "Intentions and the Logic of Interpretation," *The Asbury Theological Journal* 43.1 (Spring 1988): 11-25.

———. *The Divine Inspiration of Holy Scripture.* New York: Oxford University Press, 1981.

Achtemeier, Elizabeth R. "Why God is Not Mother," *Christianity Today* 16 (August 1993): 16-23.

Althaus, Paul. *The So-called Kergyma and the Historical Jesus.* Translated by David Cairns. Edinburgh: Oliver and Boyd, 1959.

Altizer Thomas J. J. and William Hamilton, *The Death of God.* New York: The Bobbs-Merrill Co., Inc., 1966.

Anderson, Gerald H. and Thomas F. Stransky, eds. *Third World Theologies.* New York: Paulist Press, 1976.

Anderson, Walter Truett, ed. *The Truth about The Truth.* New York: G. P. Putnam's Sons, 1995.

Bauckham, Richard, ed. *God Will Be All in All. The Eschatology of Jürgen Moltmann.* Minneapolis: Fortress Press, 2001.

Barr, James. "'Abba, Father' and the Familiarity of Jesus' Speech," *Theology* 91 (May 1988): 173-179.

———. "Abba Isn't 'Daddy'," *The Journal of Theological Studies* 39 no. 1 (April 1988): 28-47.

———. *Old and New in Interpretation, A Study of the Two Testaments.* London: SCM Press, Ltd, 1966.

Barth, Karl. "A Thank You and a Bow: Kierkegaard's Reveille." *Christian Journal of Theology.* Translated by H. Martin Rumscheidt, 11 (January, 1965): 3-7.

———. *Karl Barth Letters 1961-1968.* Edited by Jürgen Fangmeier and Hinrich Stoevesandt. Translated and edited by Geoffrey W. Bromiley. Grand Rapids, Michigan: Wm. B. Eerdmans Publishing Company, 1981.

———. *Church Dogmatics.* Edited by G. W. Bromiley and T. F. Torrance. Translated by G. T. Thomson and Harold Knight. Volume 1, parts 1 and 2. Edinburgh: T & T. Clark, 1963.

———. *The Theology of Schleiermacher.* Edited by Dietrich Ritschl. Translated by Geoffrey W. Bromiley. Grand Rapids: Wm. B. Eerdmans, 1982

Bernstein, Richard J. *Beyond Objectivism and Subjectivism: Science, Hermeneutics, and Praxis.* Oxford, England: Basil Blackwell Publisher, Ltd., 1983.

Betz, H. D. "The Concept of Apocalyptic in the Theology of the Pannenberg Group." *Journal for Theology and the Church,* 6 (1969): 192-207.

Bleicher, Josef, *Contemporary Hermeneutics: Hermeneutics As Method, Philosophy, and Critique.* Boston: Routledge & Kegan Paul, 1980.

Bloesch, Donald G. "The Primacy of Scripture," *The Authoritative Word, Essays on the Nature of Scripture.* Edited by Donald K. McKim. Grand Rapids: Wm. B. Eerdmans, 1983.

Bonino, J. Miguez. *Doing Theology in a Revolutionary Stiuation.* Philadelphia: Fortress Press, 1975).

Borgmann, Albert. *Crossing the Postmodern Divide.* Chicago: University of Chicago Press, 1992.

Braaten, Carl E. and Philip Clayton. *The Theology of Wolfhart Pannenberg.* Minneapolis: Augsburg Publishing House, 1988.

Braaten, Carl E. and Roy A. Harrisville. *The Historical Jesus And The Kergymatic Christ.* New York: Abingdon Press, 1964.

———. *History and Hermeneutics.* Philadelphia: Westminster Press, 1966.

Bruce, F. F. *The Canon of Scripture in Christian Theology.* Downers Grove, Illinois: InterVarsity Press, 1988.

———. *The New Testament Documents: Are They Reliable?* Grand Rapids: Wm. B. Eerdmans, 1959.

Bultmann, Rudolf. *Essays, Philosophical and Theological.* Translated by James C. G. Greig. London: SCM Press, Ltd., 1955.

———. "New Testament and Mythology." 1-47 in *Kerygma and Myth,* ed. Hans Werner Bartsch, trans Reginald H. Fuller. New York: Harper & Row, 1961.

———. *The History of the Synoptic Tradition.* Transalted by John Marsh. Oxford: Blackwell, 1963.

Burnham, Frederic B., ed. *Postmodern Theology, Christian Faith in a Pluralist World.* New York: Harper and Row, Publishers, 1989.

Burrow, Rufus. "James H. Cone: Father of Contemporary Black Theology." *The Asbury Theological Journal* 48, no. 2 (Fall 1993): 59-75.

Butterfield, Herbert. *The Origins of Modern Science.* New York: Macmillan Company, 1959.

Calvin O. Schrag, "Subjectivity and Praxis at The End of Philosophy," 25-32 in *Hermeneutics & Deconstruction.* Edited by Hugh Silverman and Don Ihde. Abany, NY: State University Press of New York Press, 1985.

Caputo, John D., ed. *Deconstruction in A Nutshell, A Conversation with Jacques Derrida.* New York: Fordham University Press, 1997.

Cassirer, Ernst. *Kant's Life and Thought*. Translated by James Haden. New Haven: Yale University Press, 1981.

Cassirer, Heinz, *Grace and Law*. Grand Rapids: Wm. B. Eerdmans Publishing Co., 1988.

Cobb, John B., Jr. *God and the World*. Philadelphia: Westminster Press, 1969.

Cornelison, Robert T. editor. *The Promise of God's Future. Essays on the Thought of* Jürgen *Moltmann*. Special book issue of *The Asbury Theological Journal* 55 no. 1 (Spring 2000).

Collingwood, R. G. *The Idea of History*. New York: Oxford University Press, 1976.

Cone, James H. *For My People. Black Theology and the Black Church*. Maryknoll, New York: Orbis Books, 1984.

———. *God of the Oppressed*. Maryknoll, NY: Orbis Books, 1997.

Conford, Philip. *The Personal World: John MacMurray on Self and Society*. Edinburgh: Floris Books, 1997.

Costello, John E. *John Macmurray: A Biography*. Edinburgh: Floris Books, 2002.

Couch, Mal, ed. *The Fundamentals for the Twenty-First Century*. Grand Rapids: Kregel Publications, 2000.

Creamer, David. G. *Guides for the Journey: John Macmurray, Bernard Lonergan, James Fowler*. University Press of America, 1997.

Cullmann, Oscar. *Christology of the New Testament*. Translated by Shirley C. Guthrie and Charles A. M. Hall. Philadelphia: Westminster Press, 1963.

———. *Salvation in History*. Translated by Sidney G. Sowers. London: SCM Press, Ltd., 1967.

D'Angelo, Mary Rose. "Abba and 'Father': Imperial Theology and the Jesus Traditions." *Journal of Biblical Literature* 11 no .4 (Winter 1992): 618.

Daly, Mary. *Beyond God the Father*. Boston: Beacon Press, 1973.

Dell'Olio, Andrew. "Why Not God the Mother?" *Faith and Philosophy* 15 no. 2 (April 1998): 193-209.

Derrida, "Structure, Sign, and Play in the Discourse of the Human Sciences," *The Structuralist Controversy*. Edited by Richard Macksey and Eugenio Donato. Baltimore: Johns Hopkins University Press, 1970.

Derrida, *Aporias*. Translated by Thomas Dutoit. Stanford, California: Stanford University Press, 1993.

Descartes, Rene. *Essential Works of Descartes*. Translated by Lowell Blair with an intro. by Daniel J. Bronstein. New York: Bantam Books, 1966.

Dornisch, Loretta. *Faith and Philosophy in the Writings of Paul Ricoeur*. Lampeter, Dyfed, Wales: Edwin Mellen Press, Ltd, 1990.

Downing, F. Gerald. *Has Christianity a Revelation?* London: SCM Press, Ltd., 1964.

Ebeling, Gerhard. *Word and Faith*. Translated by R. G. Smith. London: Collins, 1961.

Fain, Haskell. *Between Philosophy and History*. Princeton: Princeton University Press, 1970.

Ferm, Deane William. *Third World Liberation Theologies, An Introductory Survey.* Maryknoll, New York: Orbis Books, 1986.

Fish, Stanley. *Is There a Text in This Class? The Authority of Interpretative Communities.* Cambridge: Harvard University Press, 1980.

Frankfort, Henri, Mrs. H. A. Frankfort, John A. Wilson, and Thorkild Jacobsen, *Before Philosophy.* Baltimore, MD: Penguin Books, 1964.

Funk, Robert W. Roy W. Hoover, and the Jesus Seminary, eds. *The Five Gospels, The Search For The Authentic Words of Jesus.* San Francisco, CA: HarperSanFrancisco, 1997)

Funk, Robert W., ed. *Schleiermacher as Contemporary.* New York: Herder and Herder, 1970.

Gadamer, Hans-Georg. *Truth and Method.* Translated by Garrett Barden and John Cumming. New York: Seabury Press, 1975.

Gardavsky, Vitezslav. *God is Not Yet Dead.* Translated by Vivenne Menkes. Baltimore: Penguin, 1973.

Gardiner, Patrick, ed. *Theories of History.* New York: The Free Press, 1959.

Gaussen, Louis. *The Canon of Holy Scriptures.* Boston: American Tract Society, 1862; reprinted Grand Rapids, 1980.

Gay, Peter, ed. *The Enlightenment, A Comprehensive Anthology.* New York: Simon and Schuster, 1973.

Gill, Jerry. *The Possibility of Religious Knowledge.* Grand Rapids: Wm. B. Eerdmans, 1971.

———. *The Tacit Mode, Michael Polanyi's Postmodern Philosophy.* Albany: State University of New York Press, 2000.

Gilson, Etienne. *God and Philosophy.* New Haven: Yale University Press, 1941.

Green, Joel B. and Max Turner, eds. *Jesus of Nazareth, Lord and Christ, Essays on the Historical Jesus and New Testament Christology.* Grand Rapids: Wm. B. Eerdmans, 1994.

Grenz, Stanley J. "Concerns of a Pietist with a Ph. D." *The Wesleyan Theological Journal* 37 no. 2 (Fall, 2002): 58-76.

———. *Theology for the Community of God.* Nashville: Broadman and Holman Publishers, 1994.

Grenz, Stanley J and Roger E. Olson, *20th Century Theology, God and the World in a Transitional Age.* Downers Grove, Illinois: InterVarsity Press, 1992.

Griffin, David R. *A Process Christology.* Philadelphia: Wesminster Press, 1973.

Gundry, Stanley N. and Alan F. Johnson, eds. *Tensions in Contemporary Theology.* Grand Rapids, Michigan: Baker Book House, 1976.

Guthrie, Donald. *New Testament Introduction.* London: The Tyndale Press, 1970.

Gutiérrez, Gustavo. *A Theology of Liberation.* Translated by Caridad Inda and John Eagleson. Maryknoll, N.Y.: Orbis Books, 1973.

———. *The Density of the Present, Selected Writings.* Maryknoll, NY: Orbix Books, 1999.

Hahn, Stephen. *On Derrida.* Belmont, California: Wadsworth, 2002.

Hartshorne, Charles. *A Natural Theology for our Time.* La Salle, Illinois: Open

Court, 1967.

Hartshorne, Charles. *Divine Relativity*. New Haven: Connecticut: Yale University Press, 1948.

Hauerwas, Stanley. *A Community of Character*. Notre Dame, Indiana: University of Notre Dame Press, 1981.

———. *Sanctify Them in The Truth*. Nashville: Abingdon Press, 1998.

———. *The Peaceable Kingdom*. Notre Dame, Indiana: University of Notre Dame Press, 1983.

Hawking, Stephen. *A Brief History of Time*. London: Bantam Books, 1988.

Hegel, *Science of Logic*. Translated by W. H. Johnston and L. G. Struthers, with an introductory preface by Vicount Haldane. London: George Allen and Urwin Ltd., 1929.

———. *Reason in History*. Translated by Robert S. Hartman. New York: The Bobbs-Merrill Co., Inc., 1953.

Heick, Otto W. *A History of Christian Thought*. 2 volumes. Philadelphia: Fortress Press, 1965.

Heidegger, Martin. *Being and Time*. Translated by John Macquarrie and Edward Robinson. London: SCM Press Ltd., 1962.

Heisenberg, Werner. *Physics and Philosophy: The Revolution in Modern Science*. London: George Allen and Unwin, 1959.

Henry, Carl F. H., ed. *Christian Faith and Modern Theology*. New York: Channel Press ,1964.

———. *The Remaking of the Modern Mind*. Grand Rapids: Wm. B. Eerdmans Publishing Company, 1946.

History of Herodotus. Translated by George Rawlinson. London: J. M. Dent and Sons, Ltd., 1924.

Hodges, H. A. *Wilhelm Dilthey: An Introduction*. London: Routledge and Kegan Paul, 1952.

Hordern, William. *New Directions in Theology Today*. Philadelphia: Westminster Press, 1966.

Hughes, Philip Edgcumbe, ed. *Creative Minds in Contemporary Theology*. Grand Rapids: Wm. B. Eerdmans Publishing Co., 1969.

Hume, David. *An Inquiry Concerning Human Understanding*. Indianapolis, Indiana: Bobbs-Merrill Company, Inc., 1955.

Ihde, Don. *Hermeneutic Phenomenology, The Philosophy of Paul Ricoeur*. Evanston: Northwestern University Press, 1971.

Jacob, Edmond. *Theology of the Old Testament*. Translated by Arthur W. Heathcote and Philip T. Allcock. New York: Harper and Row Publishers, 1958.

Jungel, Eberhard. *The Doctrine of the Trinity*. Translated by Horton Harris. Grand Rapids: Wm. B. Eerdmans, 1976.

Kähler, Martin.*The So-called Historical Jesus and the Historic, Biblical Christ*. Translated with an introduction by Carl Braaten. Philadelphia: Fortress Press, 1964.

Kant, *Prolegomena to Any Future Metaphysics*. New York: The Bobbs-Merrill Co., Inc., 1950.

———. *Critique of Pure Reason*. Translated by Normal Kemp Smith. London: Macmillan and Co., Ltd. 1929.

———. *Fundamental Principles of the Metaphysic of Ethics*. Translated by Otto Manthey-Zorn. New York: D. Appleton-Century Co, 1938.

———. *Religion within the Limits of Reason Alone*. Translated with an introduction and notes by Theodore M. Greene, and Hoyt H. Hudson. Chicago: The Open Court Publishing Company, 1934.

Kearney, Richard, ed. *Twentieth-Century Continental Philosophy*. New York: Routledge, 1994.

Kierkegaard, Søren. *A Concluding Unscientific Postscript*. Translated by David F. Swenson and Walter Lowrie. Princeton: Princeton University Press, 1941.

———. *Philosophical Fragments*. Translated by David F. Swenson with an introduction and Howard V. Hong with a new introduction and commentary by Niels Thulstrup. Princeton: Princeton University Press, 1962.

Kimel, Alvin F., Jr. *Speaking the Christian God*. Grand Rapids: Wm. B. Eerdmans, 1992.

Knight, Henry H., III, *A Future of Truth*. Nashville: Abingdon Press, 1997.

Kuhn, Thomas S. *The Structure of Scientific Revolutions*. University of Chicago Press, 1974.

Langford, "Michael Polanyi and the Task of Theology," *Journal of Religion* 46 (1.1) January 1966, 45-55.

Lauer, Quentin. *Phenomenology: Its Genesis and Prospect*. New York: Harper & Row, 1965.

Lessing's Theological Writings. Translated with an introductory essay by Henry Chadwick. London: Adam and Charles Black, 1956.

Lindbeck, George A. *The Nature of Doctrine, Religion and Theology in a Postliberal Age* (Philadelphia: Westminster Press, 1984).

Lindsell, Harold. *The Battle for the Bible*. Grand Rapids: Zondervan Publishing House, 1976.

Lyotard, Jean-Francois. *The Postmodern Condition: A Report on Knowledge*, Translated by Geoff Bennington and Brian Massumi. Minneapolis: University of Minneapolis University, 1984.

Machen, J. Gresham. *Christianity and Liberalism*. Grand Rapids: Wm. B. Eerdmans, 1923.

MacIntyre, Alasdair. *After Virtue, A Study in Moral Theory*. Notre Dame, IN: University of Notre Dame Press, 1984.

Mackintosh, H. R. *Types of Modern Theology*. London: Collins, 1937.

Macmurray, John. *The Self as Agent*. London: Faber, 1995.

———. *Persons in Relation*. London: Faber, 1995.

Marshall, I. Howard. *Biblical Inspiration*. Grand Rapids: Wm. B. Eerdmans Publishing Co., 1982.

May, Gerhard. *Creation Ex Nihilo, The Doctrine of "Creation out of Nothing" in Early*

Christian Thought. Edinburgh: T. & T. Clark, 1994.

McIntyre, John. *The Christian Doctrine of History.* Edinburgh: Oliver and Boyd, 1957.

McIntyre, John. *The Shape of Christology.* Philadelphia: Westminster Press, 1966.

McKim, Donald K., ed. *The Authoritative Word, Essays on the Nature of Scripture.* Grand Rapids: Wm. B. Eerdmans, 1983

Metzger, Bruce M. *The Canon of the New Testament, Its Origin, Development, and Significance.* Oxford: Clarendon Press, 1997.

Miller, Timothy. *Following In His Steps.* Knoxville: The University of Tennessee Press, 1987.

Mitchell, R. G. *Einstein and Christ, A New Approach to the Defence of the Christian Religion.* Edinburgh: Scottish Academic Press, 1987.

———. *Coming of God: Christian Eschatology.* Translated Margaret Kohl. London: SCM Press, 1996.

Moltmann, Jürgen. *Creating a Just Future: The Politcs of Peace and the Ethics of Creation in a Threatened World.* Translated by J. Bowden. Philadelphia: Trinity Press International, 1989.

———. *Experiences in Theology. Ways and Forms of Christian Theology.* Translated by Margaret Kohl. Minneapolis: Fortress Press, 2000.

———. *God in Creation.* Translated by Margaret Kohl. San Francisco: Harper and Row, 1985.

———. *History and the Triune God. Contributions to Trinitarian Theology.* Translated by John Bowden. New York: Crossroad, 1992.

———. "Response to the Essays," *The Asbury Theological Journal* 55.1 (Spring 2000): 131.

———. *The Church in the Power of the Spirit: A Contribution to Messianic Ecclesiology.* Translated by Margaret Kohl. London: SCM Press, 1977.

———. *The Crucified God. The Cross as the Foudnation and Criticism of Christian Theology.* Translated by R. A. Wilson and J. Bowden. London: SCM Press, 1974.

———. *The Spirit of Life.* Translated by Margaret Kohl. Minneapolis: Fortress Press, 1992.

———. *The Trinity and the Kingdom* of God. Translated by Margaret Kohl. New York: Harper & Row, Publishers, 1981.

———. *The Way of Jesus Christ.* Translated by Margaret Kohl. New York: HarperCollins, Publishers, 1990.

———. *Theology of Hope.* Translated by James W. Leitch. New York: Harper & Row, 1965.

Newman Carey C., ed. *Jesus & The Restoration of Israel, A Critical Assessment of N. T. Wright's Jesus and The Victory of God.* Downers Grove, Illinois: InterVarsity Press, 1999.

Newton, Judith. "History As Usual?: Feminism and the "New Historicism,'" *Cultural Critique* 9 (1988).

Niebuhr, R. R. *Schleiermacher on Christ and Religion.* New York: Charles Scribner's

Sons, 1964.

Nietzsche, *The Portable Nietzsche*. Translated by W. Kaufmann. New York: Viking Press, 1968 (1954).

North, Robert. "Pannenberg's Historicizing Exegesis," *The Heythrop Journal* 12 no .4 (October 1971), 393;

North, Robert. "Pannenberg's Historicizing Exegesis," *The Heythrop Journal* 2 no. 4: 377-400.

Olson, Roger E. "Is Moltmann An Evangelical's Ally?" *Christianity Today.* January 11, 1993), p. 32.

Pannenberg, Wolfhart. *Basic Questions in Theology*. Translated by G. H. Kehm. London: SCM Press, Ltd., 1971.

———. *Faith and Reality*. Translated by John Maxwell. Philadelphia: Westminster Press, 1977.

———. "Feminine Language About God." *The Asbury Theological Journal* 48 no. 2 (Fall 1993): 27-29.

———. "Hermeneutics and Universal History." Translated by Paul J. Achtemeier. pp. 122-152 in *History and Hermeneutic*. Edited by Robert W. Funk. New York: Harper & Row, Publishers, 1967).

———. *Jesus—God and Man*. Translated by Lewis L. Wilkins and Duane A. Priebe. Philadelphia: Westminster Press, 1968.

———. *Metaphysics and The Idea of God*. Translated by Philip Clayton. Grand Rapids: Wm. B. Eerdmans, 1990.

———., ed. *Revelation as History*. Translated by David Granskou and Edward Quinn. London: Sheed and Ward, 1969.

———. *Systematic Theology*. Translated by. Geoffrey W. Bromiley. 3 volumes. Grand Rapids: Wm. B. Eerdmans, 1988-1993.

———. "The Revelation of God in Jesus of Nazareth," *Theology As History*. Edited by James M. Robinson and John B. Cobb, Jr. New York: Harper and Row, 1967), pp. 101-103.

———. *Theology and the Kingdom of God*. Edited by Richard John Neuhaus. Philadelphia: Westminster Press, 1969.

———. "Theta Phi Panel Discussion with Wolfhart Pannenberg," The Asbury Theological Journal 46 no. 2 (Fall 1991): 37-41.

Placher, William C. "Hans Frei And The Meaning of Biblical Narrative." *Christian Century* 106 (May 24-31, 1989): 556-559.

Plekon, Michael. "Kierkegaard at the End: His 'Last' Sermon, Eschatology and the Attack on the Church." *Faith and Philosophy* 17 no. 1 (January 2000): 68-86.

Polanyi, Michael. "From Copernicus to Einstein," *Encounter* (September 1955), 54-63.

———. *Personal Knowledge*. University of Chicago Press, 1958.

———. *The Study of Man*. Chicago: University of Chicago Press, 1959.

Polkinhorne, John. *Faith, Science, and Understanding*. New Haven, Connecticut: Yale Nota Bene, 2001.

————. *The Quantum World.* London: Longman, 1984.

Ramm, Bernard. *Protestant Biblical Interpretation.* Grand Rapids: Baker Book House, 1970.

Ricoeur, Paul. *Essays on Biblical Interpretation.* Edited with an introduction by Lewis S. Mudge. Philadelphia: Fortress Press, 1980.

————. *Interpretation Theory: Discourse and the Surplus of Meaning.* Fort Worth: Texax: Christianity University Press, 1976.

————. *Oneself As Another.* Translated by Kathleen Blamey. Chicago: University of Chicago Press, 1992.

————. *Freud and Philosophy: An Essay on Interpretation.* Translated by Denis Savage. New Haven: Yale University Press, 1970.

————. *The Conflict of Interpretation.* Evanston: Northwestern University, 1974.

————. *The Symbolism of Evil.* Translated by Emerson Buchanan. Boston: Beacon Press, 1967.

Ricoeur, Paul and André Lacocque. *Thinking Biblically: Exegetical and Hermeneutical Studies* (Chicago: University of Chicago Press, 1998).

Roberts, David D. *Nothing but History: Reconstruction and Extremity After Metaphysics.* Berkeley: University of California Press, 1995.

Robinson, James and John B. Cobb, Jr., eds. *The New Hermeneutic.* New York: Harper and Row, Publishers, 1964.

Rorty, Richard. *Philosophy and the Mirror of Nature.* Princeton: Princeton University Press, 1979.

Ryn, Claes G. "Defining Historicism," *Humanitas* 11 no. 2 (1998): 86-101.

Sanks, T. Howland and Brian H. Smith, "Liberation Ecclesiology: Praxis, Theory, Praxis," *Theological Studies*, 38.1 (March 1977): 1-6.

Schleiermacher, Friedrich. *Hermeneutik.* Edited by Heinz Kimmerle. Heidelberg: Carl Winter, Universitätsverlag, 1959.

Schneiders, Sandra M. *Women and the Word: The Gender of God in the New Testament and the Spirituality of Women.* New York: Paulist, 1986.

————. *The Revelatory Text.* Second edition. Collegeville, MN: The Liturgical Press, 1999.

Schweitzer, Albert. *The Quest of the Historical Jesus.* New York: The Macmillan Company, 1954.

Segundo, Juan Luis. *The Liberation of Theology.* Translated by John Durry Maryknoll, New York: Orbis Books, 1976.

Shadowitz, A. *Special Relativity.* Philadelphia: W. B. Saunders Company, 1968.

Silverman, Hugh J. (ed). *Derrida and Deconstruction.* New York: Routledge, 1989.

————. *Textualities, Between Hermeneutics and Deconstruction.* New York: Routledge, 1994.

Smart, James. *The Divided Mind of Modern Theology.* Philadelphia: The Westminster Press, 1967.

Sobrino, Jon and Ignacio Ellacuría, eds. *Systematic Theology, Perspectives from Liberation Theology.* Maryknoll, NY: Orbis Books, 1996.

Stern, Fritz, ed. *The Varieties of History: From Voltaire to the Present.* Cleveland: World, Meridian, 1956.

The Apostolic Fathers with Justin Martyr and Irenaeus. American edition,. Edited by A. Cleveland Coxe. Grand Rapids: Wm. B. Eerdmans, 1981, reprint.

Thorsen, Donald A. D. *The Wesleyan Quadrilateral.* Grand Rapids: Zondervan Publishing House, 1990.

Tillich, Paul. *A History of Christian Thought.* Edited by Carl Braaten. New York: Harper, 1972.

Torrance, Thomas, ed. *The Relevance of Michael Polanyi's Thought for Christian Faith.* Eugene, OR: Wipf and Stock Publishers, 1998.

Troeltsch, Ernst. "Historiography," *Encyclopedia of Religion and Ethics,* ed. James Hastings (1914), 6:718.

———. "Historische und dogmatische Methode in der Theologie," *Gesammelte Schriften.* Tübingen: J. C. B. Mohr, 1913), 2:731-738.

———. *Die Bedeutung der Geschichtlichkeit Jesu für den Glauben.* Tübingen: J.C.B. Mohr, 1911.

Van Hoozer, Kevin. *Biblical Narrative in the Philosophy of Paul Ricoeur.* Cambridge: Cambridge University Press, 1990.

Von Rad, Gerhard. *The Problem of the Hexateuch.* Translated by E. Dickens. New York: McGraw Hill, 1966.

Warfield, B. B. *The Inspiration and Authority of the Bible.* Edited by Samuel G. Craig. Philadelphia: The Presbyterian and Reformed Publishing Company, 1948.

Weinberg, Steven. *The First Three Minutes: A Modern View of the Origin of the Universe.* New York: Basic Books, 1977.

Whitehead, A. N. *Process and Reality.* New York: The Free Press, 1929.

———. *Religion in the Making.* New York: The Macmillan Co., 1927.

Wiley, H. Orton. *Christian Theology.* 3 volumes. Kansas City, Missouri: Beacon Hill Press, 1964.

Wilson-Kastner, Patricia. *Faith, Feminism, and the Christ.* Philadelphia: Fortress Press, 1983.

Wood, Laurence W. *The Meaning of Pentecost in Early Methodism, Rediscovering John Fletcher As John Wesley's Vindicator and Designated Successor.* Lanham, MD: Scarecrow Press, 2002.

Wright, N. T. *Jesus and the Victory of God.* Minneapolis: Fortress Press, 1996

———. *The Resurrection of the Son of God.* Minneapolis: Fortress Press, 2003.

Yoder, John. *The Politics of Jesus.* Grand Rapids: Wm. B. Eerdmans, 1972.

Index

A

Abraham, William 123, 137, 171, 226–229, 234–7
absolute viii, 1–2, 4–6, 21, 23, 31, 61, 67–68, 77, 85–86, 96, 99–101, 115, 132,
    136, 138, 144, 147, 159, 184, 197, 202, 204 208, 214–216, 225, 238
absolute certainty 1, 2, 5, 67
Achtemeier, Elizabeth R. 188, 196
Althaus, Paul 13, 25
American process thought 212–6
analogical thinking viii
apologetics viii, 30, 49, 159, 161, 235
Aquinas, Thomas 7, 70
Athanasius 232–3, 241

B

Bailey, Kenneth E. 52
Barr, James 19–20, 26, 88, 195
Bible
    crisis of the Scriptural principle 27
    inerrancy ix, 12, 23–24, 29, 30, 55, 160
    inspiration ix, xii, 7–9, 11, 12, 27–30, 33, 35–36, 43–45,
    52, 54–56, 108, 177, 229–231, 235–236, 240
    Story or History? 19
Barth, Karl xii, 4–6, 9–15, 22–24, 31–34, 36, 43, 61, 123, 126, 129, 148, 159,
    161, 181, 197–202, 204, 208–209, 213, 218–222, 227, 242
    Bible as a witness to the Word of God 9–13
    critique of liberal theology, 4-6
    defined the modern concept of revelation 5–6
    direct self-revelation 9, 14–16, 21, 56, 200
    Pannenberg's critique of Barth 13–14
    Jesus Christ the only revelation 6
Bernstein, Richard J. x, xiii, 78, 87, 151
Biblical inspiration 7, 27, 29, 35–36, 43–45, 52, 56, 108

Black liberation hermeneutics 180–184
Bloesch, Donald E. 29
Boethius 206, 209
Borg, Marcus J. 47, 49, 58
Bultmann 9–10, 13, 24, 31–34, 36–41, 46–47, 57, 98, 113–6, 117–121, 125–126, 129–131, 134, 136, 153, 161

C
Calvin 106, 151
canonical heritage xii, 123, 226–7, 229, 236–9
Cappadocian Fathers xii, 31, 74, 146, 204
Cartesian 61, 68
Cassirer, Heinz 238-40
Christ of faith xi, 38–39, 114, 118, 131, 134–135, 225
Cobb, John B. xi, 26, 34, 56, 58, 123, 126, 212–4
Collingwood, R. G. 74, 76, 99–102, 104
Cone, James H. 180–184, 194
Council of Nicea 232–4
critical philosophy viii, 3, 81–84, 108, 155, 161, 199
Cullmann, Oscar 25, 27, 36–48, 52–54, 57, 151, 231

D
Daly, Mary 184, 194
    patriarchal ideology 184
deconstructionism 129, 140–143
Dell'Olio, Andrew 188–9, 196
Derrida, Jacques 140–143, 150–151
Descartes vii, xi, 1–3, 21, 64–70, 79, 111, 132–3, 138
    foundationalism vii, 54, 86, 92–93, 214–6
Dewey, John 80
dialectic 10, 143, 193, 199, 217,
Dibelius, Martin 37
Dilthey, Wilhelm 91, 110–115, 120, 123–4, 129, 131

E
Early Church Fathers x, xii, 39, 70–72, 74, 145, 156 229
Ebeling, Gerhard 58, 115–118, 121, 126, 137
empty tomb 45, 99, 101–102, 115–7, 154, 237
enlightenment viii, ix, xi, 2–3, 5, 8–9, 12, 22, 27, 29, 33–34, 37, 43–44, 49, 54, 85, 107–108, 130, 143, 148, 161, 182, 198–9, 208, 228, 236
epistemology ix, xi, 2, 41, 46, 78, 80–81, 83–84, 86, 95, 99, 101–102, 108, 110–111, 113, 123, 129, 131–5, 147, 159, 164, 214, 225, 226, 228, 236
eschatology 7, 16, 18–19, 21, 46,–48, 50–51, 98, 122, 125–7 ,146, 177, 200–201, 218

eschaton 16, 19, 21, 44, 217–8
evangelical vii–ix, xii, 29–30, 54–55, 135–6, 160, 164–5, 212, 219, 223, 228
ex nihilo 118, 147, 209, 212–3, 223
existentialist 13, 25, 31, 33–34, 37–38, 48, 113, 114–8, 121, 131 132–3, 136, 144,
    159, 201, 223, 236–7

F
Fain, Haskell 102, 104
faith and history xi, 2, 31, 47, 100, 235–6
feminist liberation theology 180–82, 184–93
Feske, Millicent 182
Feuerbach 34, 139, 180, 200, 214
Fish, Stanley 140, 150
Form criticism 36–40, 46–49, 52
Frei, Hans 153–70, 166
Freud 34, 130, 148, 151, 173–4, 187, 193
Fuchs, Ernst 116–8, 121, 126, 137
fundamentalism viii, 27–30
    Biblical literalism 27–29

G
Gadamer 80, 102, 121, 123–4, 127, 129, 148, 151
Gospel of Thomas 53
Grenz, Stanley J. 30, 55, 222
Gutiérrez, Gustavo 177–8, 193

H
Harnack, Adolf 4
Hartshorne, Charles 213–5, 223
Hauerwas, Stanley 159–171
Hegel 6, 14–15, 22, 61, 91, 125, 132, 154, 198–9, 208, 217, 221
Heidegger, Martin 70–71, 113–17, 130–4, 141, 144, 148,
Heilsgeschichte 18, 21, 31
Hermann, Wilhelm 4
hermeneutics viii, xi, xiii, 67–69, 80–81, 105–123, 126, 129, 131–4, 140, 142,
    144, 148, 151, 153, 157, 173–4, 179–180, 183–4, 225, 228
    critical hermeneutics 108–122
    phenomenological hermeneutics 129–152
    pre-critical hermeneutics 105–108
historical criticism 4, 8–10, 20, 23, 27, 31–32, 43–46, 52, 97, 158, 201, 252
historical method 27, 32–33, 35–36, 43–44, 46–48, 51–52, 54, 92, 95–97, 112,
    120
historicism 49, 91–92, 95, 103

history as reality 217–8
Hooker, Richard 64, 130–1, 137
Hume, David 66–67, 95
Husserl, Edmund 64, 130–131, 137

I

intellectualism viii, 199
Irenaeus 145, 223, 229–31, 235, 240,
irrefutable knowledge vii, viii, 1, 2, 30–31, 92, 101, 132–3, 136, 139, 143–4

J

Jacob, Edmond 25
James, William 80
Jesus of history xi, 27, 38–39, 47–48, 114–8, 131, 134–5, 225
Julian of Norwich 192
Jungel, Eberhard 218

K

Kähler, Martin 4, 22
Kant, Immanuel viii, 2–3, 21–22, 63–69, 82–83, 108, 110–112, 132–3, 138,
    144, 155–6, 161, 198–202, 208, 215, 221, 238–9
Kierkegaard 100, 104, 235–6, 237, 241–2
Kuhn, Thomas 78, 83, 87, 143

L

Latin American liberation theology 174–9
Lessing, Ephraim 2, 22, 182, 198, 235–6, 241
liberalism 3–4, 28–29, 55, 86, 114, 155–7, 162, 197–8, 201
Lindbeck, George 155–8, 164, 169–170
Luther, Martin 7, 30, 106, 231
Lyotard, Jean-Francois 54, 60, 85–86, 89

M

Macarius 188
Machen, J. Gresham 29, 55
Macmurray, John 61, 62–64, 74
    primacy of the practical 64
Marheineke, Philipp 6
Marx 130, 173–4, 176–7, 179
Mascall, E. L. 74
McIntyre, Alasdair 68
McIntyre, John 23, 72
metanarrative 53, 85

method
    cognitivist-propositional 155–7
    cultural-linguistic method 155–7
    experiential-expressive 155–7
    multidimensional concept of experience 200–203
Metzger, Bruce 230–231, 235, 240–241
modern thought vii– xi, 1, 2, 5, 61, 63, 79, 85–86, 113, 133–4, 138, 142, 199, 202
Moltmann xi, 53, 130, 179–223
    experience as multi-dimensional, 200–203
    Joachim of Fiore, 198
    perichoretic unity of the Trinity 203–205
    relational categories of the Trinitarian Persons 205–210
    Trinitarianism as panentheism 213

N

narrative ix, xii, 20–21, 26, 37, 53, 64–65, 67–68, 85, 91, 137–8, 147, 149, 153–69, 202
new hermeneutic 58, 116, 118, 123, 126
Nicea 232–3
Nicene Creed 146, 203, 232, 234
Nietzsche 65, 67–71, 75, 130, 173, 174
    nihilism viii, x, 136, 142, 144

O

objectivism viii, x–xiii, 49, 87, 91–92, 129, 151, 225, 237
Ockenga, Harold J. 29, 55, 160
Olson, Roger 210, 212, 222–4
orthodoxy vii, ix, 5, 8, 10, 12, 28, 30–33, 106, 155–6, 161, 198, 201, 229, 235

P

panentheism 209–210, 212–3, 216, 220
Pannenberg, Wolfhart xi, xiii, 7, 9, 14–16, 19–48, 52, 54–56, 58, 66, 75, 84–85, 89, 91–104, 119–123, 126–7, 130, 137–8, 151, 154, 158, 161, 170, 180, 190–192, 196, 205, 210, 217, 219, 221–2, 224
    critique of historicism, 91–92
    historical method, 92–102
    historicity of Jesus' resurrection, 98–102
    indirect self-revelation, 14-20
    reality as history, 93–96
    universal history, 91–104
Parmenides 94

Pietism 30, 55, 106, 108, 123, 155, 160–161, 163–4, 197–9
Plato 87, 94, 105, 123, 215
pneumatology 199, 201, 203–204, 219, 235
Polanyi, Michael viii, xiii, 81–85, 88–89, 95, 155
Polkinghorne, John 87, 215–6, 224,
post-critical vii–ix, xi–xii, 27, 30–31, 61, 77, 81, 83–84, 85, 105, 130, 134, 158,
     225, 239
post-critical evangelical vii, ix, xii, 30
post-foundationalism vii, 54, 86, 92–93, 214–6
postliberal 153, 156–8, 164, 222
postmodern vii, ix–xii, xiii, 30, 55, 60, 62, 64, 77–78, 83, 85–86, 89, 113, 129–
     130, 142, 147, 150–151, 173, 194, 213–5, 220
premodern vii, ix, x, xi, 1, 5, 70–72, 79, 133, 139–140
probabilities 3, 5, 30, 100, 119–120, 160

R
reader-response 140–141, 185, 237–8
realistic narrative 153–5
reason vii–viii, 1–3, 12, 14, 19, 22, 30, 35, 43, 53, 62, 65, 66–84, 92, 96–97,
     101, 106–107, 110–11, 113, 123, 132, 138–9, 142–4, 148, 159–61, 163, 208,
     214, 215, 216, 219, 221, 227–8, 232, 237–240
     autonomous reason vii, 3, 138
     universal rational criteria ix, xi
relational ontology 61, 69, 74
resurrection 2, 3, 13, 16–17, 19–21, 26, 28, 30, 32–33, 38–45, 51–52, 58–59,
     69, 95, 97–103, 119, 122, 135, 137, 145, 147, 153–4, 158, 169, 181–4, 216,
     219, 235, 237–8
revelation of God viii–xii, 1–2, 3, 5–26, 30–31, 33–36, 39, 43–45, 56, 59, 61,
     71–72, 84, 91, 93, 96–97, 103, 105, 107, 122, 135, 137, 138, 139, 143, 144,
     146, 156, 159, 161, 165, 169, 180–181, 183, 187–188, 190, 192, 197, 199–,
     200, 205–206, 210, 212, 214, 216–217, 220–221, 226, 231, 236, 245
     Bultmann's view of self-revelation as the human self 31
     direct vs. indirect self-revelation 14-15
     God revealed as "I Am Who I Am" 7, 71–72
     God revealed as Three Persons 203–206
     Jesus as the only self-revelation 6
     no natural proof of revelation 12
     progressive revelation 15, 216–219
     revelation as *self*-revelation 5–6
     revelation "from above" rather than "from below" 200
     source of the modern notion of selfhood 206–209
     Word of God 5, 8–9

Ricoeur, Paul xi, 64–72, 75, 123, 129–140, 143–5, 147–51, 154 169, 173–4,
    178, 193, 225, 228, 240.
    "To believe again" 129, 225, 228
    hermeneutic phenomenology 129–34, 148–52, 193
    second naivete, 130, 228
    surplus of meaning 140–141, 144–8
Riesenfeld, H. 39
Roberts, David D. 87, 92, 102–103, 147, 151
Rorty, Richard xiii, 78–81, 83, 87–88, 92, 143, 151

S
salvation history xii, 5, 20, 31–36, 39–40, 48, 53–54, 91, 97, 119, 136, 145–7,
    159, 183, 188, 205, 211, 219, 223, 231
Sartre, Jean-Paul 72, 73
Schleiermacher, Friedrich 108–115, 120, 123–4, 129, 143, 155, 161, 197–199,
    201, 221, 227
Schneiders, Sandra M. 184–5, 194–5,
Second-Temple Judaism 50
secular viii, 25, 86, 142, 197, 199, 219–20
Segundo, Juan Luis 177–9, 193
sola scriptura 34, 107–108, 227
subject-object distinction viii, 1, 61, 65, 79–80, 132–3, 237
symbolic viii, x, 50, 106, 115, 118, 135

T
third quest 46–48, 52
Tillich, Paul 7, 23, 25, 28, 55, 123–4, 129, 161, 170, 212, 221–2
Torrance, Thomas 81, 84, 87–88
Trinity vii, xii, 3, 6, 9, 30–31, 42, 44, 50, 61, 74, 135, 146–7, 160, 182–3,
    185–190, 196–8, 200–201, 203–213, 217–24, 238
Troeltsch, Ernst 3–4, 22, 47, 91–92
truth vii, ix–xii, 1–3, 5, 10, 12, 21, 23, 28, 33, 35, 38, 42–44, 54–55, 62, 64–67,
    75, 77–78, 80–81, 83–86, 91, 93–97, 102, 105, 122, 130, 132–4, 136,
    138–44, 147–8, 157, 160–2, 165–8, 170–1, 190–1, 198–9, 201, 211, 214–6,
    225–31, 235, 239

V
Vanhoozer, Kevin 135
virgin birth 28, 31, 43, 160

W
Warfield, B. B. ix, xii, 29, 55
Wesley, John 7–8, 23, 30, 55, 106–108, 123, 146, 161, 163–4, 168,

Wesley (Con't)
　170–171, 182, 227 240–241
Whitehead, A. N. xi, 212–15, 223–4
Wiley, H. Orton 8, 23, 56
Wilson-Kastner, Patricia 187–9, 191–2, 195–6
Word of God 5, 7–15, 31–35, 43, 118–8, 126, 129, 145, 161, 164, 177, 183, 199, 230, 240
Wright, N. T. iii, 20, 26–27, 45–54, 58–59, 103, 169

Z
Zinzendorf, Count 188

About the Author

Laurence W. Wood received the B. A. degree from Asbury College (1963), the M. Div. degree from Asbury Theological Seminary (1966), and the Th. M. degree from Christian Theological Seminary (1970). He also studied at Butler University and Indiana University. He received the Ph. D. degree from Edinburgh (Scotland) in 1972. He has taught at Roberts Wesleyan College (Rochester, New York), Houghton College (Houghton, New York), and has been the Frank Paul Morris Professor of Systematic Theology at Asbury Theological Seminary since 1976. He was the founding editor of *The Asbury Theological Journal* in 1986. Among other books, Dr. Wood is author of *The Meaning of Pentecost in Early Methodism, Rediscovering John Fletcher As Wesley's Vindicator and Designated Successor* (published by Scarecrow Press in the Wesleyan-Pietist Series). This book won the 2003 Smith-Wynkoop Book of the Year Award presented by the Wesleyan Theological Society. He has also contributed articles to various journals. His essay on "Recent Brain Research and The Mind-Body Dilemma" was selected to be included in *The Best in Theology* (published by *Christianity Today*). Dr. Wood's most recent book is entitled, *God and History, The Dialectical Tension of Faith and History in Modern Thought*. Dr. Wood is an ordained elder in the Kentucky Conference of the United Methodist Church.